Corporate Valuation Modeling

WITHDRAWN
UTSA LIBRARIES

Founded in 1807, John Wiley & Sons is the oldest independent publishing company in the United States. With offices in North America, Europe, Australia and Asia, Wiley is globally committed to developing and marketing print and electronic products and services for our customers' professional and personal knowledge and understanding.

The Wiley Finance series contains books written specifically for finance and investment professionals as well as sophisticated individual investors and their financial advisors. Book topics range from portfolio management to e-commerce, risk management, financial engineering, valuation and financial instrument analysis, as well as much more.

For a list of available titles, please visit our Web site at www.WileyFinance.com.

WITHDRAWN
UTSA LIBRARIES

Library
University of Texas
at San Antonio

Corporate Valuation Modeling

A Step-by-Step Guide

KEITH A. ALLMAN

WILEY

John Wiley & Sons, Inc.

Library
University of Texas
at San Antonio

Copyright © 2010 by Keith A. Allman. All rights reserved.

Published by John Wiley & Sons, Inc., Hoboken, New Jersey.
Published simultaneously in Canada.

No part of this publication may be reproduced, stored in a retrieval system, or transmitted in any form
or by any means, electronic, mechanical, photocopying, recording, scanning, or otherwise, except as
permitted under Section 107 or 108 of the 1976 United States Copyright Act, without either the prior
written permission of the Publisher, or authorization through payment of the appropriate per-copy fee to
the Copyright Clearance Center, Inc., 222 Rosewood Drive, Danvers, MA 01923, (978) 750-8400, fax
(978) 646-8600, or on the web at www.copyright.com. Requests to the Publisher for permission should
be addressed to the Permissions Department, John Wiley & Sons, Inc., 111 River Street, Hoboken, NJ
07030, (201) 748-6011, fax (201) 748-6008, or online at http://www.wiley.com/go/permissions.

Limit of Liability/Disclaimer of Warranty: While the publisher and author have used their best efforts in
preparing this book, they make no representations or warranties with respect to the accuracy or
completeness of the contents of this book and specifically disclaim any implied warranties of
merchantability or fitness for a particular purpose. No warranty may be created or extended by sales
representatives or written sales materials. The advice and strategies contained herein may not be suitable
for your situation. You should consult with a professional where appropriate. Neither the publisher nor
author shall be liable for any loss of profit or any other commercial damages, including but not limited
to special, incidental, consequential, or other damages.

Designations used by companies to distinguish their products are often claimed as trademarks. In all
instances where John Wiley & Sons, Inc., is aware of a claim, the product names appear in initial capital
or all capital letters. Readers, however, should contact the appropriate companies for more complete
information regarding trademarks and registration.

For general information on our other products and services or for technical support, please contact our
Customer Care Department within the United States at (800) 762-2974, outside the United States at
(317) 572-3993 or fax (317) 572-4002.

Wiley also publishes its books in a variety of electronic formats. Some content that appears in print may
not be available in electronic books. For more information about Wiley products, visit our web site at
www.wiley.com.

Library of Congress Cataloging-in-Publication Data:

Allman, Keith A., 1977–
    Corporate valuation modeling : a step-by-step guide / Keith A. Allman.
        p.   cm.
    Includes index.
    ISBN 978-0-470-48179-0 (paper/cd-rom)
    1. Corporations—Valuation.   2. Business enterprises—Valuation.   I. Title.
    HG4028.V3.A474   2010
    332.63'2042—dc22

                                                                    2009027783

Printed in the United States of America.

10 9 8 7 6 5 4 3 2 1

Contents

Preface

Another book about financial modeling? You might be rolling your eyes and muttering under your breath, "Why? Aren't there plenty of books that cover this topic?" Yet, you still chose to look inside and see what this one is about. The motivation behind looking at financial modeling books is most likely related to a desire to learn financial modeling in an easy-to-understand, time-efficient, low-cost manner. However, after poring over a few books with the words *Financial Modeling* in the title, you might be left feeling like you know more about specific skills and topics, but not a working financial model. Perhaps these books have given you an understanding of how the model should work, but you are confused as to how to practically implement the information provided. Ultimately, an easy-to-understand, integrated analysis still eludes you.

There's a vast sea of approaches authors take with financial modeling books. Some try to encompass every concept in finance and provide examples of how to implement each concept in Excel. Those are the cookbooks of finance. Introduce a topic, show an Excel example, and then move on to the next topic. Others take a similar approach, but vary the medium. Rather than use Excel, they offer books on financial modeling entirely in code with languages such as VBA or C++. Although many of these books can be highly informative, they often leave it up to the reader to figure out how to connect the individual concepts.

The answer, some say, is books that focus on specific concepts. Rather than covering all possible finance topics, these books hone in on specific areas such as fixed income or derivatives. The problem with many of these books is they often rely too much on delving into the details of the topic and demonstrating formula derivations, instead of dedicating time to showing how to implement the concept. Or, they discuss the implementation and show some screenshots, but fail to provide clear instructions, open functions, and code, much less a complete working model.

To me, the best type of financial modeling book is one that is dedicated to a specific topic within finance, offers multiple examples of implementation, is written in a clear and easy-to-understand manner, and provides a completely integrated example model. There are a few books that have been written in this fashion on topics such as credit risk, interest rates, options, and structured finance, but I find that few have addressed corporate valuation in this manner.

It seems to me that corporate valuation modeling too often gets lumped together in the *general financial modeling* book category. Since a company encompasses many topics in finance it may seem appropriate to cover all of those topics and then assume that the reader can value the company. Unfortunately, connecting the concepts theoretically and implementing those connections on a computer can be just as hard as understanding the individual concept or computer-based implementation in the first place.

Take depreciation as an example. Some books show how to use Excel's prebuilt depreciation functions to create a depreciation schedule. Others discuss depreciation concepts. Yet, few show readers how to create the depreciation schedule in a way that is automated with the associated asset's creation. Further, the prebuilt depreciation functions in Excel need to be turned off so the asset is not overdepreciated depending on the forecast period of the model. Then, once we get the schedule correct, we have to accumulate the depreciation on the balance sheet, remove it from different sections of certain financial statements, and perhaps add it back when dealing with valuation calculations.

This book attempts to address many of these shortfalls by providing a comprehensive, integrated approach to modeling a corporate entity with the primary goal of determining a firm's value. Theory is introduced to guide the reader along the valuation process and connect each concept with the prior and future concepts. Along the way, clear, step-by-step instructions are provided that cover every cell of the included example model. No sections are hidden, password protected, or incomplete.

Beyond concept and implementation issues, after teaching courses on corporate valuation modeling hundreds of times, I have also come to realize that an added layer of complexity is the preexisting skill level of readers. Some are very new to finance and Excel, others new to just finance, others new to just Excel, and some are seasoned in both, but wanting to learn more. While the text itself addresses the finance topics and shows an integrated implementation, the Excel skills can be a challenge for some and a bore for others who already know them. For this reason, there is a Toolbox at the end of each chapter that provides additional information on the Excel functions and techniques that are used in the chapter. This way, the text is not full of background knowledge that would bore the intermediate Excel users, but the content is still there for the beginning Excel user to learn more.

I hope that this book is a valuable resource for people new to finance, seasoned professionals engaged in analysis, and experienced executives trying to learn what their junior staff is doing all night long. I also continually strive to improve my books, find the best possible methods to teach, and ensure that every reader learns. If you are confused by any section or topic related to this book or my other books, if you think you may have found an error, or if you just want to discuss finance-related topics, please feel free to review the Books and Blog section of my company's web site www.enstructcorp.com or personally e-mail me at keith.allman@enstructcorp.com.

KEITH A. ALLMAN

Acknowledgments

My father always suggested that I focus on math and quantitative subjects. Early on, I rebelled, thinking he couldn't be further off topic from what I would do in my career. Given that this is my third book on financial modeling, I suppose I should state that he was right. My mother was less adamant about the subject, but to not acknowledge her would undermine the value of her support even to this day. While on the family track, I should note two more family members who have influenced this work. The first is my sister, who was my academic rival when we were children. That energy fomented the fervor with which I have approached all subjects of interest to this day. The second is my grandfather, who lives and breathes the stock market. I am convinced our conversations subconsciously caused my gravitation toward finance. As for more direct acknowledgments, Susan Jane Brett reviewed the book in detail and offered critical comments that led to revisions and clarifications. Her thoroughness is very much appreciated. Also, all of my corporate valuation class participants over the past three years have contributed to this book through the study of their learning methodologies, the development of the curriculum for their courses, and the critical thought caused by their questions. Finally, I would like to thank all of the staff at John Wiley & Sons who work on my books, especially Bill Falloon, Meg Freeborn, and Mary Daniello.

K.A.A.

CHAPTER 1

Introduction

Corporate valuation modeling consistently proves challenging because it requires a thorough understanding of two bodies of thought that demand disparate skill sets: finance and technology. On the finance side, we must understand fundamental topics such as *time value of money*, *growth rates*, *debt calculations*, and other subjects that blend accounting, economics, and mathematics. In particular, accounting is a subject that corporate valuation analysts must be well versed in because generally accepted accounting principles (GAAP) or international financial reporting standards (IFRS) need to be followed to make sure analyses are consistent. On the technology side, we must select a program or programming language to utilize and understand the technical functionality of that program well. In many cases, the program is Excel, which requires knowledge of a number of program-specific functions and techniques in order to transfer the financial concepts to an orderly, dynamic analysis. Prior to jumping right to the construction process, we will take a step back and examine the overall process.

OVERVIEW OF THE CORPORATE VALUATION PROCESS

The corporate valuation analysis process itself is quite complex with many moving parts that are intricate to stitch together. Taking a reverse approach, that is, starting with the firm value and tracing back its calculations and components, is a good method of gaining an overview of this process.

Projecting Cash Flow

Figure 1.1 provides a graphical overview of the discounted cash flow valuation process. First, we should establish that we will take a discounted cash flow approach to determining corporate value. Many other methods exist, such as relative valuation and adjusted present value, but the most popular detailed analysis is to *discount expected future cash flows*.

Discounting expected cash flows is a method used in many areas of finance. Bond pricing, securities analysis, and project valuation all use discounted cash flow techniques. Any discounted cash flow technique has two general components: future

1

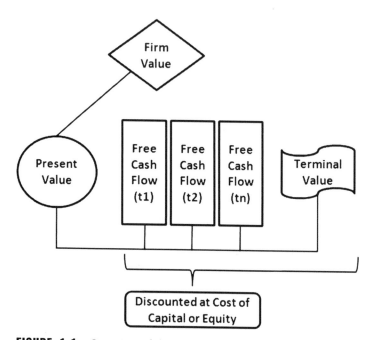

FIGURE 1.1   Overview of the corporate valuation process.

expected cash flows and a rate or rates to discount those cash flows to bring them to the present value. The sum of all present-valued cash flows is the *value*. So the path we first go down is making sure we do the best possible job of estimating future cash flow and calculating discount rates.

Starting with the future cash flows, we have to think about what constitutes cash flow. Is it gross profit, or net income, or earnings before interest and taxes (EBIT)? While those are standard metrics for cash flow, they do not wholly represent cash that can be freely distributed to parties of the firm. We must be able to distinguish between real cash and non-cash items that flow through financial statements and ensure that the company can meet its capital expenditure requirements and fund working capital needs.

Each of the items that lead us to our cash flow can be broken apart into detail. Specific capital expenditures or debt financing plans can be modeled. For instance, we may anticipate debt financing and be the lead bank in a syndicated funding or be part of a bilateral arrangement. In such cases we may be concerned with the priority of cash flows. This level of detail can lead us to more accurate projections of cash flow.

The next challenge with cash flow is the duration of cash flow projection. In discounted cash flow modeling, we typically distinguish between a *forecast period* valuation and a *terminal* valuation. This means that we forecast specific cash flows only for a certain amount of time depending on the purpose of our valuation. Continuing with the debt example, if we plan to issue five-year debt, we may project

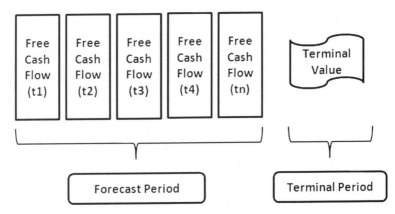

FIGURE 1.2 The forecast period is typically in alignment with a unique period of time for the company. This can be due to a startup period, distress, buyout, new funding, or new projects. The terminal value is the assessment of value after the forecast period.

out five years of a company's cash flow. If we ignore time beyond the five periods, then we make the assumption that the firm is worth nothing after that time period; it essentially vanishes. This is unlikely, because at bare minimum a firm has assets that can be disposed of and the proceeds returned to debt and equity holders. It is even more likely that the firm would continue operations.

Whether we assume the firm is liquidated after the forecast period or that it continues into perpetuity, we need to do more work to make a terminal value assumption. This could require altering assumptions to a long-term perspective and in general applying a different methodology than just cash flow forecasting. Figure 1.2 depicts forecast and terminal value periods.

Discounting Cash Flow

Once we are confident in our cash flow and terminal value, we must determine the proper discount rates to apply to the values in order to get the present-day valuation. If we are looking at the firm from a comprehensive viewpoint, we need to examine what both an equity holder and a debt holder would demand for the firm's risk, respectively known as the *cost of equity* and the *cost of debt*. Picking apart those calculations leads us to further detail.

The cost of equity can be determined using the *capital asset pricing model* (CAPM), which quantifies the rate of return for an equity investor based on a risk-free return, a market-based return, and a quantification of nondiversifiable risk. These factors materialize in the form of the *risk-free rate*, the *market risk premium*, and *beta*. Multiplying beta by the market risk premium and then adding the risk-free rate gets us to the cost of equity for one period. Although this is a good start, we may have different assumptions throughout time for each of these items.

The cost of debt also contributes to our eventual discount rate for the cash flows. The credit quality of the firm and current market conditions determine the spread over the risk-free rate that the company must pay for its debt. Because interest is tax deductible in most cases, the firm's *after-tax* cost of debt is more relevant, meaning we need to also estimate the tax rate to get an accurate assumption.

Overall, both rates may change over the forecast period and can have completely different assumptions for the terminal value period. Further complicating matters is that we do not take a simple average of the two values, but weight each rate by the amounts of debt and equity. Whereas in theory these should be market values, book values are sometimes used as proxies in projections. In cases of expected capital structure changes, the weights can change over time and significantly affect the discount rates, which ultimately affect the valuation.

CONCEPTUAL ROADMAP

Our heads may be spinning in a whirlwind of financial concepts right now. The immediate way to bring order to this chaos is to open our medium of operation, Excel, and start entering information. But without a carefully laid-out plan, this can be disastrous. To prevent such disaster, we will lay out a conceptual roadmap that will guide the corporate valuation process and its materialization in Excel. This conceptual roadmap is shown in Figure 1.3.

The first destination on this map is dates and timing, which provide the framework for our analysis. Once we know what timeframes we are working with, we need to fill in the required information for each period. Because dates and timing is the first concept, it does bring along with it some administrative qualities, such as setting up our assumptions in an intelligible manner and creating an auxiliary sheet to handle administrative items.

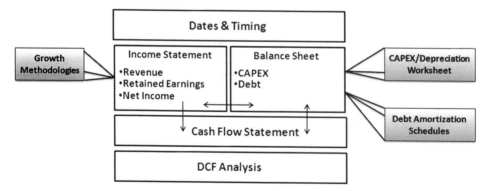

FIGURE 1.3 Building a corporate valuation model should be done using a conceptual approach.

We can then move to the next few locations on our map, which are the financial statements. It's usually easiest to begin with the *income statement*. On that statement our biggest concern is most likely revenue growth, because many assumptions are predicated on this projection. We should therefore focus on understanding growth projection methodologies. Inextricably linked to the income statement is the *balance sheet*. Capital expenditures, depreciation, and debt are key items to the balance sheet, which require further analysis. Once both statements are established, we need to understand their linkages and create functionality that allows the sheets to work harmoniously in projections.

After building in the key calculations of cash flow, we need to make sure that we did so in a precise manner and in a way that is representative of the firm's value. The cash flow statement is established to reconcile cash and validate the model's calculations. Other tests are also built in to focus on important parts of corporate cash flow. Eventually we need to summarize this cash flow in a way that represents the value of the firm, otherwise known as *free cash flow*. The free cash flow is calculated for each period of the forecast period, a terminal value determined, and all values discounted back to the present value at appropriate discount rates.

While our core valuation ends there, we might want to analyze the system we have set up in more detail and build in efficiencies for working with our analysis. An output summary can reorganize information in formats that people are used to, charts can be created to graphically represent data, and automation can be built to allow sensitivity analyses en masse.

TECHNICAL ROADMAP

While the concepts behind corporate valuation may start to make sense, actually transforming these concepts into a model adds the final layer of challenge. Depending on one's background, utilizing Excel for the transformation of corporate valuation concepts to a corporate valuation model is much more challenging than understanding the concepts themselves. Quite frequently people suffer from what I have termed *sheet 1 syndrome*. This condition occurs when someone is intimidated by the vastness of the financial modeling process and stares at the first sheet of a new, blank Excel workbook, wasting time and fretting about what to do first. We will quickly develop a technical roadmap to prevent such an unpleasant condition. Overall, our technical progress should take the following steps in order:

1. Brainstorm and sketch
2. Data collection
3. Assumption verification and aggregation
4. Structural construction
5. Internal validation
6. Output reporting
7. Interpretation

Brainstorm and Sketch

While this seems as if we are going back to elementary school, it is worth taking 30 minutes to an hour to think about the problem that requires modeling. You should employ techniques that are optimized for how you work through problems. For example, I am a very visual problem solver and like to draw out each sheet as a box, connect lines to boxes that represent links in the future Excel model, and write out notes that indicate special functionality that might be required. I once started a model while at a job late at night without taking this step. On the second day of working through the model, I realized I had forgotten a core component and then spent an entire half-day linking up the inserted component. I wasted hours verifying that the links were correct, and probably would not have had to do so if I had inserted the concept in a logical order.

Data Collection

In this book, all of the necessary data is provided, which is unrealistic in our day-to-day jobs. Most financial analysts spend a significant amount of time searching for the best data to use for their analyses. This is done by searching through financial statements, industry reports, consultant studies, and market databases, and engaging in ongoing client communication.

Assumption Verification and Aggregation

Once our data has been collected it is rarely in a format that is ready for use. Financial data may be in values that we do not want to use for our analysis. For instance, we most likely would want a revenue growth rate assumption for our company. We could look historically at revenue amounts and then try different methods of calculating the growth rate. Once we settle on a growth rate methodology, we might want to verify that this is in line with management's plans or that there are non-historical factors that might affect the assumption. We should be rigorous in our approach and do this for as many assumptions, in as much detail, as possible.

Structural Construction

Constructing the framework for calculation is the focus of much of this book. We will definitely cover topics such as assumption verification and aggregation, outputs, and so on, but the core problem people have is binding all of this together in a cohesive model. I believe that the structure of the model is the easy part of the analysis process, once it is understood. After you gain fluidity in the model construction process, the actual framework for the model should occupy about 20% of your time. Determining what goes into the model and understanding the correct analyses to make should occupy the remaining 80%.

Internal Validation

Unfortunately, many people are so anxious to get a result that the moment they come up with a figure they stop. There are many more steps to a proper modeling analysis. As a model is being built it should be constantly tested for validity. Concepts such as assets equaling liabilities plus shareholder's equity or cash from the cash flow statement equaling the cash from the balance sheet should be tested.

Output Reporting

In my first position in a quantitative analytics group there came a time when I finally was responsible for my own analysis. When I turned the analysis in, I handed over nearly a hundred pages of cash flow scenarios with a summary sheet on top. My manager took the packet of information, ripped off the summary sheet, and threw the rest in the trash bin. The point of explaining this is that you should understand what data your audience wants. In that case, I was presenting results to a manager who wanted only a top-level understanding of the data. If I had presented the data to a risk manager or another quantitative analyst, they might have wanted the cash flow scenarios. The best models and modelers can get overlooked due purely to output presentation (sad, but true in the field of finance).

Interpretation

Finally, you must understand the model that you have built. Especially if you must present the analysis to others, you must be well versed in the resulting changes in the model given changes in the assumptions. This means that you should test the model with reasonable extremes. Take growth down to 0% in one scenario. What happens to the firm's value? Then take growth up to 100% each period. Does the firm's value increase? Try out many combinations of assumptions, such as increasing capital expenditures and adding a debt layer to pay for it. Can the company afford the expected debt payments each period? Similar to output reporting, people lose faith in a model that returns unexplainable results.

A FEW BEST PRACTICES REGARDING FINANCIAL MODELING

Over the years of financial modeling development, I have discovered a number of best practices. Conforming to the following allows other users easier interpretation and prevents errors:

1. *Use consistent formulas for rows or columns.* Whether it is to be dragged across columns or up and down rows, the formula should be the same. Differences usually occur during certain time periods, which suggests the need for functions that give our formulas optionality.

2. *Never combine a hard-coded assumption with a formula.* If you find yourself inserting numbers into a formula, you should consider making that number a formal assumption in the appropriate section.
3. *Hard-coded values should be formatted using blue bold font.* Formulas are typically kept in black-colored font. The origins of these formatting conventions are unclear, but they are market practice and allow users to quickly identify assumptions and formulas.
4. *Corporate models frequently organize time going across columns, whereas asset-based and project finance models occasionally organize time going up and down rows.* This convention is due to the 256-column constraint of Excel 2003 and earlier. Although Excel 2007 has plenty of columns, I have found that many financial modelers still adhere to these conventions.

HOW THIS BOOK WORKS

This book is designed in a manner similar to the corporate valuation courses I teach in person. Both rely on theory and practical exercises to transform the concepts into a dynamic, usable model. Just as my courses work through individual *modules* of corporate valuation that culminate in a complete firm valuation, this book has readers work through similar modules, chapter after chapter. Each section begins with a discussion of theory and then moves on to a Model Builder exercise where the theory is transferred to an application in Excel. Eventually, as all theory concepts are read and Model Builder exercises completed, the reader should have an operational model that is identical to the one included on the CD-ROM that is packaged with this book.

While theory and implementation are two critical elements, one of the biggest challenges of teaching financial modeling is the different skill levels of readers. In my classes, I am able to teach to various levels of difficulty and explain functionality as needed. In print, this is clearly not possible, but I have tried to address the issue of varying skill levels by creating sections at the end of each chapter called *toolboxes*. These sections explain Excel functions and techniques that are used throughout the chapter. Readers who are beginners will find it valuable to go through every Toolbox. Intermediate readers can selectively choose which Toolbox sections to read, and advanced readers can skip them altogether. Figure 1.4 depicts the book's approach.

Excel 2003 and Earlier versus Excel 2007

At the current time, many users have switched to Excel 2007; but many, if not more, are still using Excel 2003. While the powerful differences between the two versions of Excel are related to memory accessibility and usage, there are major shifts in the menus. When technical books provide instruction for only one version, and the user has a different version, the alterations to the menus can cause confusion. For

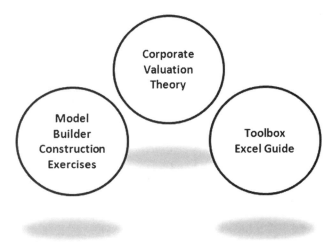

FIGURE 1.4 Each chapter will follow a similar pattern, starting with corporate valuation theory, then model implementation, followed by a Toolbox to assist with Excel functions and techniques.

this reason, I will provide instruction for both versions of Excel wherever there are instructions that could be significantly different between the two versions.

Differences between Excel versions will not be an issue when this book discusses Visual Basic Applications (VBA) in Chapter 11, since the Visual Basic Editor (VBE) and the VBA code have largely gone unchanged. The only caveat is that users who are using Excel 1997 or earlier may encounter problems since there were many updates to VBA after that version.

A Few Words about Semantics

Learning about financial modeling can be tricky in written form since words translate into *commands*, which can be very specific for computer programs. In this text we are using Excel as the modeling program, which is primarily operated by *menus*, *worksheets*, and *cells* within the worksheets. For the menus in Excel 2003, I will often use the word *select*, which would be synonymous with left-clicking the stated menu. There could be multiple options, where once you left-click you might have to move the cursor down and over to find the correct sub-selection. For instance, if you wanted to open the Add-Ins dialogue box you would have to select **Tools**, then move the cursor down to **Add-Ins** and select or left-click again. The process is slightly different for Excel 2007, where there is a *ribbon system*. In the ribbon system you still must select or left-click on a tab, but instead of having a drop-down of sub-selections there are graphical icons that must be selected. These graphical icons are grouped into subsets, such as the Font subset, within the Home tab.

The process of using workbooks and cells is relatively similar between Excel 2003 and Excel 2007. The key is that there are four main operations we will perform on a cell:

1. Enter a *value*. When the Model Builder exercises ask for a value to be entered, this will be a number, date, or Boolean (TRUE or FALSE) value. These are values that will be referenced for some type of calculation purpose.
2. Enter a *label*. A label is text in a cell to help the model operator understand values and formulas in relative proximity. Note that I use the word as a verb as well. For example, I may say "label cell A1, **Project Basic Cash Flow.**" This means that the text "Project Basic Cash Flow" should be entered into cell A1.
3. *Name* a cell or range of cells. Not to be confused with labeling, naming is a specific technique that converts the reference of a cell or range to a user-defined name. This process is detailed in the Toolbox section of this chapter.
4. Enter a *formula*. The core reason we are using Excel is for calculation purposes. A formula is initiated in Excel with the "=" sign. When I say to enter a formula, I will provide the cell it should be entered in and the exact formula that should be entered. Often I have copied this formula from the Excel model itself to ensure that the text corresponds to the example model provided on the CD-ROM.

MODEL BUILDER 1.1: INITIAL SETTINGS AND ASSUMPTIONS SHEET SETUP

In our first Model Builder, we should take a moment to understand how this section differs from other parts of the book. Each Model Builder is an instructional section that should be completed with the use of a computer running Excel. It should be followed step-by-step using the instructions. Each Model Builder assumes that the previous Model Builder was read and implemented. The eventual result of the Model Builder sections is the Corporate_Basic.xls model provided on the CD-ROM. If at any point you find yourself lost, you should open the Corporate_Basic.xls file to see how the relevant section should be completed.

This first Model Builder is to make sure that our versions of Excel are all set to identical settings and to start constructing the model on the Assumptions sheet. Depending on how you installed Microsoft Excel or Office, you might need the installation disc to enable all of these settings.

1. We will be using a few functions and tools that require the Analysis Tool Pak, Analysis Tool Pak VBA, and Solver Add-Ins to be installed. To do this:
   - *For Excel 2007:* Select the **Office** button, select **Excel Options**, select **Add-Ins**, and then select the **Go** button, which is to the right of Manage, and a box that should default to Excel Add-Ins. This will bring up the same box as in

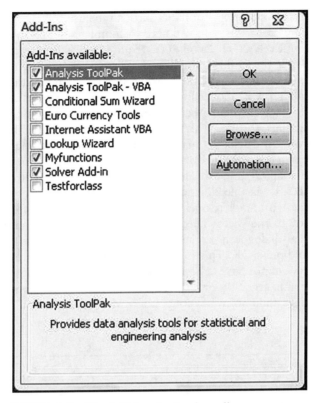

FIGURE 1.5 The Add-In selection box allows users to install pre-created or user-created add-ins.

Figure 1.5. Check the boxes for Analysis Tool Pak, Analysis Tool Pak VBA, and Solver. Select **OK**. If the Add-Ins are not installed, it may prompt you with a few messages stating that Excel will need to install them. Depending on how Excel was initially installed, you might need the installation disc to complete the install.

- *For Excel 2003 and earlier:* Select **Tools**, select **Add-Ins**, and check the boxes for Analysis Tool Pak, Analysis Tool Pak VBA, and Solver. Typically the Analysis Tool Pak and the Analysis Tool Pak VBA are the first two Add-Ins on the Add-Ins list. Solver is usually at the bottom. Select **OK**. If the Add-Ins are not installed, it may prompt you with a few messages stating that Excel will need to install them. Depending on how Excel was initially installed, you might need the installation disc to complete the install. Figure 1.5 depicts the Add-In selection box.

2. The next setting we should set is the ability to run macros. While the core model does not require the use of any macros, Chapter 11 will add significant

automation and functionality through the use of VBA. If you would like to take advantage of this, you will need to complete the following steps.

- *For Excel 2007:* Excel 2007 requires a bit more setup to work with macros. Select the **Office** button, and select **Excel Options**. On the default tab, the Popular tab, check the third checkbox down, entitled "Show the Developer tab in the Ribbon." Press **OK**. Once the Developer tab is visible, select it and then select **Macro Security**. In Excel 2007, you have four options for Macro settings, three of which are similar to Excel 2003. The only exception is that you can disable all macros except ones with a digital signature. Since hardly anyone has taken Microsoft up on their security measures and people rarely use digital signatures for Excel files, we will ignore that option. We can safely set it to disable all macros with notification. The notification will occur when the workbook is opened and will be a button with Options . . . in it at the top of the sheet. Select this button. A new dialogue box will open. Within that dialogue box, under Macros and Active-X, select **Enable This Content** and press **OK**. This dialogue box is shown in Figure 1.6. In Excel 2007, you should not have to restart Excel for this to take effect.

- For Excel 2003 or earlier: Select **Tools**, select **Macros**, select **Security**. You have the choice of either Low, Medium, or High. Low will allow macros

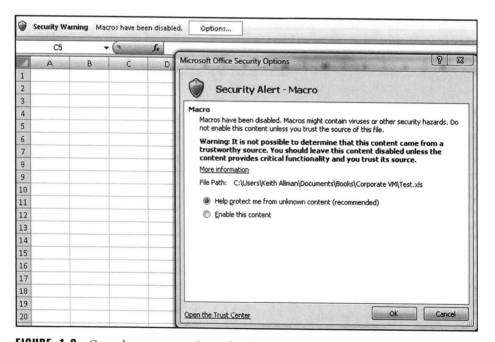

FIGURE 1.6 Once the macro security setting is set to Disable All Macros with Notification, the following Options . . . button appears when workbooks with macros are opened.

without prompting, medium will prompt you to enable or disable macros within a workbook when it is opened, and high disables macros in a workbook. The main concern is that viruses can be built into macros, which can cause significant damage or security concerns. The Corporate_Basic.xls model contains no viruses and can be safely opened with macros enabled. You might want to set your computer to medium security so that you enable only trusted workbooks. For the changes to take effect you must shut down Excel and reopen it. When prompted to enable macros for the Corporate_Basic.xls file, select **Enable**.

3. Once the Add-Ins are installed and the macro security is set, we can actually start constructing our model. The next step is to notice the default setting of the worksheets. There should be three blank sheets named Sheet1, Sheet2, and Sheet3. Change the name of Sheet1 to **Assumptions**.

4. Next we will create a label for the entire project. On the Assumptions sheet in cell A1, enter the text **Project Basic Cash Flow**. Format this text bold blue. The reasoning behind the formatting is grounded in a financial modeling convention, where all variables that are inputs entered as values (otherwise known as *hard coded*) are formatted bold blue. Values returned from formulas are typically left in standard black-font format.

5. Name cell A1 **inputs_ProjName**. Naming cells is distinctly different from entering text as the previous step instructed. For basics on naming cells, refer to the Toolbox section of this chapter for a thorough primer on naming cells and ranges. Cell A1 should look like Figure 1.7.

6. The final step of this brief Model Builder is to save the file—a simple yet commonly forgotten step. As a suggestion, you might want to just add your initials to the end of **Corporate_Basic.xls** (Corporate_Basic_KA.xls, in my case). Most Excel 2003 or earlier users are familiar with the steps to saving, but Excel 2007 users should be careful as there are many new options. In Excel 2007, under Save As, if you select **Excel Workbook** it will save it as the default file for Excel. This is usually set to a macro-free .xlsx file. This means that if you created any code in the file, it will automatically be stripped out and lost. If you want to save a workbook with code (which will be the case if you implement the VBA for the Corporate_Basic model), then you should save it as an Excel Macro-Enabled

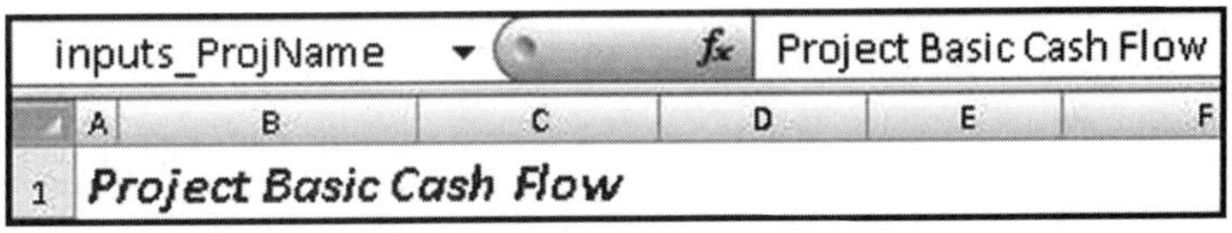

FIGURE 1.7 In cell A1, on the Assumptions sheet, we create a label for the cell by entering text. Notice the cell is also named, as seen by the name inputs_ProjName in the Name Box.

Workbook. Both of these formats are .xlsx and are not compatible with earlier versions of Excel unless the user downloads a special file from Microsoft. If you or another user anticipate using this file with lower versions of Excel, you should save the file as an Excel 97–2003 Workbook. This format is .xls and will not automatically remove macros. The possible file formats for Excel 2007 are shown in Figure 1.8.

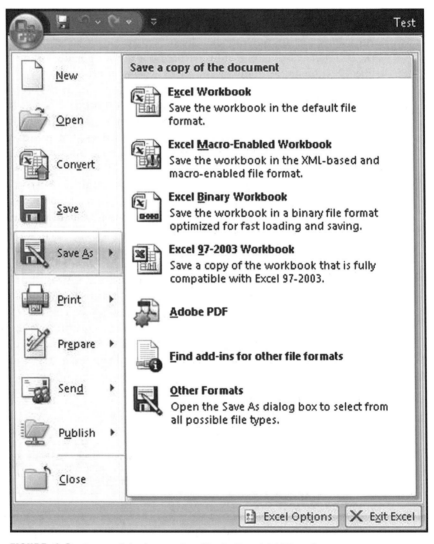

FIGURE 1.8 Be careful when saving files in Excel 2007 as there are many more options.

TOOLBOX: NAMING CELLS

A very common technique used throughout financial modeling is to name a cell or range of cells. To name a cell or a range of cells is to provide an alternative name other than the standard row/column name, such as *cell A1*. Naming cells has a number of advantages:

1. *Named cells are easier to work with in formulas since we can name them with meaning.* For instance, rather than using the range B3 to refer to the current fiscal year date of a model, we could name cell B3 **FY_Current**. When working with formulas, the name would be used rather than *B3*, and the formula would be easier to understand.
2. *Named cells automatically take on absolute references in formulas.* When cells are referenced in formulas, their default setting is set to relative references. This means that if we referenced cell B3 in a formula and dragged the formula cell across one column, the new formula would reference cell C3. This can be prevented by locking down the cell, as described in Chapter 5's Toolbox, or by using a name. A named range is automatically locked down. We can still use the row/column reference, but would have to enter this in by hand since named cells will automatically display the name when referenced.
3. *Named cells allow us to reference values for data validation lists on sheets other than the sheet where the list is being created.* If this is not clear, you should read about data validation lists in Chapter 2's Toolbox section.
4. *Named cells allow the user to find inputs and references faster.* When we push cell F5, we are provided with the Go To dialogue box. This allows us to jump to sections in a model very quickly. When we use named ranges, we can move between them very quickly.
5. *Named cells make in-and-out processes easier when we start using Visual Basic Applications (VBA).* We will come back to this in Chapter 11 when we implement basic VBA code.

Cells can be named very quickly using the *Name Box* in both Excel 2003 and 2007. The Name Box is located near the upper-left corner of any Excel sheet. Figure 1.9 shows the location of this box.

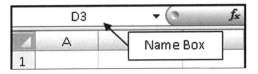

FIGURE 1.9 The Name Box is an area that allows a user to quickly create a name for a cell or range of cells.

There are a couple of rules regarding naming:

1. *Names cannot have spaces.* If you want to use a name with spaces, use underscores. For instance, if you wanted a cell that was named Reserve Account, you would have to name it **Reserve_Account**.
2. *In Excel 2003 and earlier, names cannot begin with a number.* Excel 2007 will allow this; however, when the spreadsheet is saved in Excel 2003 or earlier, a prompt will be generated that informs a user that the names will have the number values removed. This can cause problems if the numbers were the only differentiation between names in the workbook.

Finally, the most common source of error in naming is when the names need to be changed or deleted. Many users try to change names by selecting the cell or cells that are named and typing over the name in the Name Box. While this will generate a new name, it will not get rid of the existing name. The same is true when a user selects a named range, highlights the name in the Name Box, and presses **delete**. In Excel 2003, names should be deleted or references edited under the Insert menu, Names submenu, Define option. This selection brings up the Name dialogue box, which allows a user to delete or edit the name reference. In Excel 2007, users can go to the Formulas tab and select the **Name Manager** button. This selection brings up a similar dialogue box as Excel 2003's Name dialogue box; however, there is additional functionality. In particular, users can edit the name of a range directly through this dialogue box.

CHAPTER 2

Dates and Timing

Consider a world without time and how that would impact a financial analysis. It would greatly limit the methodologies we could use to value a company and simultaneously limit the value that could be derived for the firm. At the most extreme level, all we would have would be the current financial statements. Determining the best investment would be a relative analysis involving the highest multiple of earnings with consideration to a strong corporate structure at that given moment. Issues of revenue potential, future cost factors, operating expenditure plans, and financing strategies would not exist. In fact, most of us would be out of jobs since we get paid to project and manage the uncertainties caused by time.

A slightly more advanced level of analysis would give credit to the fact that items on the balance sheet can grow in value either by their operating potential or just by inflation. This still ignores many components of a fully operational firm. The more complex analysis that comes out of completely integrating all factors of time is a discounted cash flow methodology where we make projections of many facets of the firm's structure and operations.

Within the complex framework of a discounted cash flow analysis, multiple time-related issues arise. Andy Warhol once said, "They say time changes things, but you actually have to change them yourself." I rarely quote celebrities, but this epitomizes the issues we deal with in regard to time and discounted cash flow modeling. On one hand, we have to manage concepts that will naturally change over time, such as straight-line depreciation of an asset; on the other hand, we have the ability to change assumptions that affect how the concept changes over time. In the case of depreciation, we can change the useful life of assets that determine the depreciation amounts. These changing time-based variables are true for many of the topics in corporate valuation modeling.

THE NEED FOR A FLEXIBLE SYSTEM

Not only do dates and timing affect multiple parts of an analysis, but they also change frequently. Every day that passes can have a new effect on the analysis. For instance, our model could use the current stock price and shares outstanding to calculate the market value of equity. The stock price changes continuously throughout trading,

Monthly									
	9/1/2009	10/1/2009	11/1/2009	12/1/2009	1/1/2010	2/1/2010	3/1/2010	4/1/2010	5/1/2010
Revenue	529	532	535	538	542	545	548	551	555

Quarterly									
	9/1/2009	12/1/2009	3/1/2010	6/1/2010	9/1/2010	12/1/2010	3/1/2011	6/1/2011	9/1/2011
Revenue	1596	1625	1654	1684	1704	1725	1745	1766	1788

Semi-Annual									
	9/1/2009	3/1/2010	9/1/2010	3/1/2011	9/1/2011	3/1/2012	9/1/2012	3/1/2013	9/1/2013
Revenue	3220	3338	3429	3512	3596	3683	3772	3862	3955

Annual									
	9/1/2009	9/1/2010	9/1/2011	9/1/2012	9/1/2013	9/1/2014	9/1/2015	9/1/2016	9/1/2017
Revenue	6558	6941	7280	7634	8005	8394	8796	9219	9661

FIGURE 2.1 Revenue is shown on a monthly, quarterly, semi-annual, and annual basis. Typically, models will have only one timing set for a scenario. This can be made flexible for fast customization.

while the shares outstanding can also change depending on corporate actions on any given day. As we push the analysis date further into the future, values of the many components of the company change: the rates from which variable-rate interest is indexed, debt amortization, asset depreciation, intangible amortization, capital expenditure plans, and so on. Therefore our modeling will require flexibility as to how we enter dates and set up timing.

Further complicating matters is the division of time into aggregated units. While we could attempt to model out a company on a daily basis or even more granularly on a real-time basis, the amount of data would be overwhelming. In order to rationalize the amount of data and to make the data discrete, we often group data into monthly, quarterly, semi-annual, or annual amounts. Setting such periodicity allows us to see trends and align important events that affect the company. For example, if most of the debt of a company is paying on a quarterly basis, it may be worth projecting the company's cash flows on a quarterly basis to see how well the company can cover the periodic debt service. Figure 2.1 shows some of the common possibilities for organizing timing in a corporate model.

THE FORECAST PERIOD

Another issue that we will run into is the limit of our ability to forecast certain items. Corporate valuation using a discounted cash flow methodology is particularly challenging because we are trying to project cash flows that can have multiple uncertain factors. We are trying to capture many capricious elements such as management's ability to adjust to changing economic and competitive conditions, market changes for unit volumes and prices, and variable capital structures and costs of financing.

This is markedly different from other financial analyses, such as project finance or asset-based financings where contracts exist, which define assumptions that allow an analyst to have a clearer path to determining periodic cash flows.

Due to the increasing uncertainty of forecasted variables over time, we limit our detailed analysis to a forecast period. This forecast period is characterized by periods of frequently changing variables. For instance, if we were to take a look at an Internet company during the late 1990s, we would have expected a very high growth rate, with an eventual reduction of growth to a stable level. This period of high growth would be the forecast period. Converse to a high-growth scenario can be one of distress. An example of this is U.S. automakers, such as General Motors and Chrysler. At the end of 2008, they requested government support to stay solvent and were asked by Congress to provide projected financial statements. In their case, they would have had a forecast period that included a contraction of growth, lower price points, and perhaps increased costs until they could return to a stabilized level. The forecast period would focus on using assumptions that caused contracted growth, prices would be lower in each of the periods, and costs would be ramped up.

Forecast periods also can be determined by planned events. For instance, if a company knew it would have an aggressive capital expenditure plan, then the forecast period would be focused on the periods of capital expenditure. But this forecast period for the same company can vary by perspective. For example, the bank financing the capital expenditure would focus on the term of the debt used for the financing as the forecast period. The forecast period is a limited amount of time that analyzes unusual, short-term situations for a firm.

THE TERMINAL PERIOD

If we used only a forecast period in a valuation, we would be attributing value to the company for only those years. While this could be true for some companies, many companies believe they will be in existence *in perpetuity*—otherwise known as a *going concern*. For this reason, we must estimate a value for the company in perpetuity. This is done by changing assumptions for the short-term forecast period to a long-term expectation and applying a perpetuity-based formula. Typical changes would include switching the growth rate to a stable expectation, using maintenance capital expenditure assumptions rather than specific plans, altering the short-term working capital expectations, and so on. Figure 2.2 is a graphical representation of the difference between the forecast and terminal periods. We will look at the details of calculating a terminal value in Chapter 9, but for now we should understand that there will be a distinction between the forecast period and the terminal value.

HISTORICAL TIME PERIODS

Whereas the forecast and terminal periods will be the focus of analysis, the basis for these items is often rooted in historical data. It is convenient to store this data

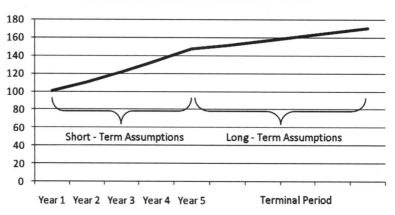

FIGURE 2.2   In the forecast period, short-term assumptions are used, whereas in the terminal period we will switch variables to long-term, stable assumptions.

in the financial model since we may use it for multiple reasons. Historical income statement data can give us important information such as revenue growth rates, whereas balance sheet data can show us historical capital structure ratios. Often, historical, audited annual financial statements going back at least three to five years are used for these purposes.

Where multiple years of data is useful to calibrate performance assumptions, a thorough analysis looks at *trends* within a year, particularly since many companies experience cyclicality due to the nature of their business or industry. For instance, agribusinesses have revenues and costs that correspond to the harvest season of the crops that they grow and sell. For this reason, we would want to examine historical data and perhaps structure our forecast period to a level of detail that captures the cycle. Adjusting the analysis for cyclicality can help ensure that there are no periods of stressed cash flow that causes liabilities to go unpaid.

Beyond normal operational trends, we should also be concerned by performance trends caused by unusual market or idiosyncratic forces. What if the industry or region is experiencing a negative trend in performance? How has a change in management affected the company's performance? To help flush out these details, we may look at the last 12 months (LTM) of a company's performance in detail. Although it is common to use the LTM, do not feel trapped by convention. If management changed, or if there was a severe industry dislocation further back, it might make sense to adjust a detailed historical analysis to coincide with such events.

Besides using historical data to assist in calibrating the assumptions for our model, we will also use the most recent audited financial statements as a basis for our projections. If, for instance, we believe that the first year's growth of a company's forecast period is 8%, then we could take the last audited revenue figure and grow

	A	B	C	D	E	F	G
1	**Income Statement**						
2					Projected ---->		
3				**12/31/2007**	**12/31/2008**	**12/31/2009**	**12/31/2010**
4							
5		Sales units		**100.00**	105.00	110.25	115.76
6		Sales Price		**2.00**	2.10	2.21	2.32
7		Sales Revenue		200.00	220.50	243.10	268.02
8		Cost Units		**0.50**	0.53	0.56	0.60
9		Cost of goods sold		**70.00**	70.62	64.49	71.76

FIGURE 2.3 The information from 12/31/2007 is hard coded, historical information, whereas data to the right is based on percentage expectations.

it by 8%. The process of using historical information for calibration and as a basis for projection is demonstrated by Figure 2.3.

EVENT TIMING

Thus far we have discussed time on a macro level; however, date and timing issues also permeate throughout specific events within the forecast period. Such events could include debt issuance, capital expenditure, intangible acquisition, and so on. For each of these events there are specific dates and timing that initiate or terminate sub-events. For instance, assume a company anticipates purchasing a warehouse one year from the beginning of an analysis. During the first projection year there would be no capital expenditure related to this event. However, on the expected purchase date gross fixed assets would increase and either cash decreases or some other liability financing takes place. One period from the purchase of the warehouse, a depreciation calculation of some type would take place. The depreciation would continue every period until the asset is fully depreciated. At that point, the asset and its accumulated depreciation is kept on the books until it is removed by disposal. Figure 2.4 is a conceptual depiction of the event timing for a single capital expenditure. In Chapter 5 we will examine this concept further, but it is important now to realize that we must build in functionality to monitor and alter outcomes based on these sub-events.

Event:	Nothing	Capex	Depreciation	Depreciation	Depreciation	Depreciation	Nothing
Timing:	Period 1	Period 2	Period 3	Period 4	Period 5	Period 6	Period 7

FIGURE 2.4 Many items such as capital expenditures have specific sub-events that require the timing to be monitored.

MODEL BUILDER 2.1: DATES AND TIMING ON THE ASSUMPTIONS SHEET

1. This first Model Builder for dates and timing will focus on the assumptions sheet. Go to the Assumptions sheet and enter the text **Dates, Timing, & Global Assumptions** in cell B3. This will be a label for the relevant date and timing variables.

2. In cell B8, enter the text, **Last Historical FY**. FY stands for *Fiscal Year*. In cell D8, enter a proxy date of **12/31/2007**. This will be the latest date that we have audited financial information from. For instance, the balance sheet that we will use in our analysis will be as of 12/31/2007. Also, name cell D8 **inputs_LastFY**.

3. In cell B9, enter the text, **Current FY**. In cell D9, enter a proxy date of **12/31/2008**. This will be the first projection period that we will work with. Also, name cell D9 **inputs_CurrentFY**.

4. In cell B10, enter the text, **Periodicity**. We will very shortly create our first data validation list to toggle between input data. In this case, we will create a data validation list to switch the model between various periodicities. Data validation lists are explained in detail in this chapter's Toolbox; however, we should take a moment to discuss the management of these lists. The actual values for the lists will be stored on a separate sheet that will be hidden once we complete the model. Let's create this sheet right now by changing the name of Sheet2 to **Hidden**.

5. Go to the Hidden sheet and enter the text **Hidden** in cell A1. Still on the Hidden sheet, enter the following text in the corresponding cells:

   A3: **lst_Periodicity**
   A4: **Annual**
   A5: **Semi-Annual**
   A6: **Quarterly**
   A7: **Monthly**

6. Name the range A4:A7 **lst_Periodicity**. Note that cell A3 is merely a label for the list that we have named below. Such a system, where the name of a named range is easily viewable, helps in the development and adaptation of the model.

7. In the following cells on the Hidden sheet enter the corresponding values:

   B4: **12**
   B5: **6**
   B6: **3**
   B7: **1**

8. Do not worry if you are looking at the complete model and a cell seems to be missing on the Hidden sheet. There is some functionality that we have left off the Hidden sheet, in cell B8, that we will come back to later.

9. Go back to the Assumptions sheet. In cell D10, create a data validation list using the named range **lst_Periodicity**. If creating data validation lists is unclear or new to you, refer to this chapter's Toolbox at this point. Name cell D10 **inputs_Periodicity** and select **Annual** from the list as the starting value.

10. In cell B11, enter the text **Months Projected**. In cell D11, enter a proxy value of **60**. This section will allow the user to adjust the forecast period duration. We will see later that this will also help us identify the terminal period. Name cell D11 **inputs_MoProj**. With this done, we have finished the core dates and timing for the Assumptions sheet. We will now take the inputs on the Assumptions sheet and put them into action on a new sheet.

MODEL BUILDER 2.2: INTRODUCING THE VECTORS SHEET

1. Change the name of Sheet3 to **Vectors**. You may want to move the sheet to the left so it is placed between the Assumptions and the Hidden sheets. On the Vectors sheet, in cell A1, enter the text **Vectors**.

2. In cell D10, enter the following formula:

=inputs_LastFY

This cell references the last historical date that we entered on the Assumptions sheet.

3. In cell E10, enter the following formula:

=inputs_CurrentFY

This cell references the current date that we entered on the Assumptions sheet. Notice that this is a rare instance where we violated the precept of keeping the same formula for each continuous row or column. In this case, we should never have to adjust these two dates since the historical date is there for a reference and column E will always contain the current date of the analysis.

4. Prior to completing the next logical cell, cell E11, we need to go back to the Hidden sheet to add some functionality. On the Hidden sheet in cell B8, enter the following formula:

=OFFSET(Hidden!$B$3,MATCH(inputs_Periodicity,lst_Periodicity,0),0)

This is a classic OFFSET MATCH combination of functions. The technique is described in the Toolbox section of this chapter if you are unfamiliar with either function or the pairing of the two functions together. In this case, we are offsetting the top of the list of period values on the Hidden sheet by matching the periodicity label that a user selects from the data validation list on the Assumptions sheet. For example, when a user selects Annual for the periodicity on the

Assumptions sheet, then this cell will return a 12; when a user selects Monthly, this cell will return a 1. Still on the Vectors sheet, name cell B8 **ctrl_Periodicity**. We will need this cell momentarily since its value is the number of months between periods based on the selected periodicity from the Assumptions sheet.

5. The next cell we will work on is going to contain a much more complex formula than we have seen thus far. If any of the functions that are used are unclear or new to you, go to the Toolbox section of this chapter, where they are explained in detail. Otherwise, back on the Vectors sheet, enter the following formula in cell F10:

   =IF(E10="","",IF(EDATE(inputs_CurrentFY,inputs_MoProj+12)>(EDATE (E10,ctrl_Periodicity)),EDATE(E10,ctrl_Periodicity),""))

   Let's break up this formula section by section. The formula begins with an IF function to test whether the prior cell was blank. Double quotes ("") are a way to check whether a cell is blank. There are other functions, but this is simple enough. The formula checks the prior cell in time to the left to see whether it is blank. If it is, then for presentation reasons, we should not have a value show up in the cell to the right. However, if there is a value in the prior cell, we may want a value in the next cell. This value is determined by first testing to see whether we are within the forecast period. The test is accomplished by checking the date of the terminal period and making sure that it is greater than the prior period's date increased by the number of months between periods. If this test returns a TRUE, then the current date is the prior period's date increased by the number of months between periods using the EDATE function. If it is FALSE, then the cell is kept blank using double quotes. If you are unfamiliar with the IF and/or EDATE functions, refer to the Toolbox section of this chapter for additional explanation. Otherwise, copy and paste this formula over the range F10:Z10.

   Astute readers will notice that on the Assumptions page we indicated a 60-month projection period, yet a date that is 72 months from the last historical fiscal year appeared. This is because that final period is the terminal value period. Often a confusing concept, we need to have a period to enter many of our terminal value assumptions. In reality, this is not a true period such as the ones in the forecast period range, but it is necessary so we can set assumptions for the terminal value.

6. For visualization and referencing purposes, we might want to have labels indicating whether we are in the forecast period or the terminal period. To do this, enter the following formula in cell D9:

   =IF(D10=inputs_CurrentFY,"Projected —->",IF(EDATE(inputs_CurrentFY, inputs_MoProj)=D10,"TV Year",""))

   This formula uses IF functions to test the dates in row 10 for the corresponding column in row 9. If the date in row 10 is the current fiscal year, then a label that indicates the start of the projection is returned. If the date in row 10 is equal to the current fiscal year increased by the number of months in the projection period, then a terminal period label is returned. Otherwise the cell is kept blank by entering double quotes. Copy and paste this formula over the range D9:Z9.

SUMMARY OF DATES AND TIMING

We are now done with the core dates and timing functionality. Some of the functionality that we have implemented is incomplete at this point. While it is interesting to see the dates change by using a drop-down list and hide or disappear depending on our forecast period, our goal is valuation. If we try to maintain a conceptually based flow, once we have the shell of our model created from dates and timing, we should begin to fill it in. One of the most influential factors of a firm's valuation is the earnings ability of the company. For this reason we will implement revenue generation and the income statement in Chapter 3.

TOOLBOX

This Toolbox will cover a number of Excel tools that allow us to control user entry, anticipate variable assumptions, and automate lookups. These include:

- Data validation lists
- OFFSET function
- MATCH function
- OFFSET MATCH combination
- VLOOKUP function
- EDATE function
- EOMONTH function
- IF function

Data Validation Lists

Good financial modelers work like computer programmers by reducing error before it can enter the system they are creating. One method is to limit a model user's possible entries. This can be achieved in a few ways, each having its own advantages and disadvantages. The first one we will explore is creating a data validation list.

When a data validation list is specified to a cell, it provides a selection of possible entries in a list format when the cell is selected. The list is based on a list that exists in a different range in the workbook. Figure 2.5 shows the results of creating a data validation list in cell D3, using data from B2:B5.

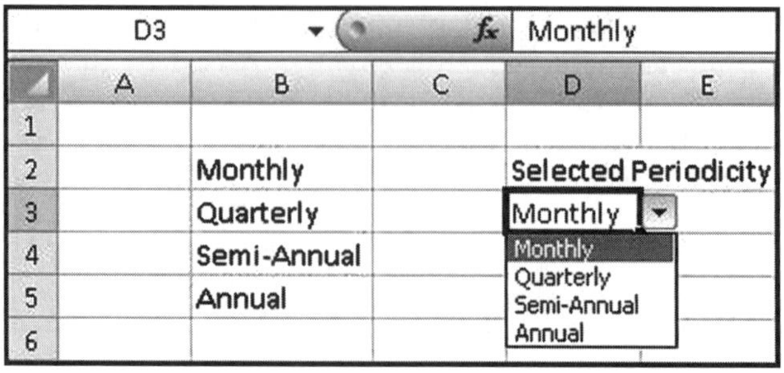

FIGURE 2.5 Data validation lists allow a user to select a value from a list of possible values that the model builder creates.

To create such a list in Excel 2003, go to the Data menu and select **Validation**. From the Validation dialogue box under the Allow label, select **List**. Under the Source label, put the cursor in the box and then select a range on the sheet and then press **OK**. An identical process can be done in Excel 2007 by going to the Data tab and pressing the **Data Validation** button. The Validation dialogue box should look identical to Figure 2.6.

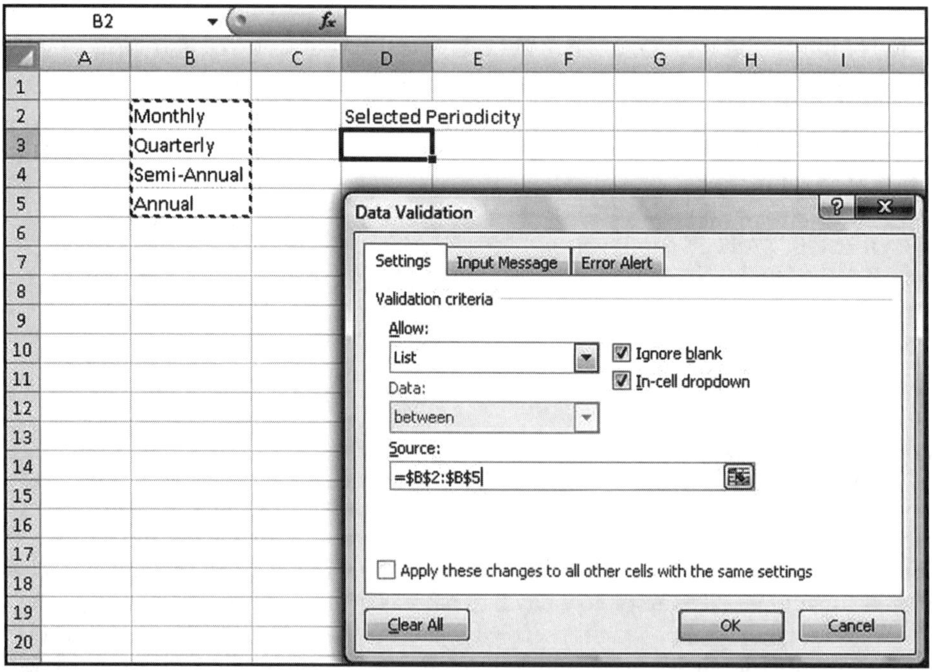

FIGURE 2.6 The Data Validation dialogue box allows a user to designate the cell where the list will be created and the reference for the items that will be contained on the list.

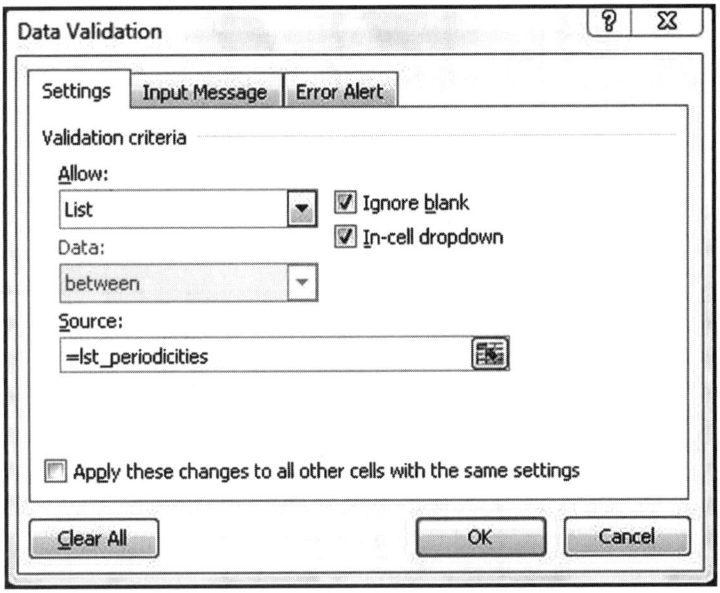

FIGURE 2.7 Named ranges must be used in the Data Validation dialogue box if the user wants to store lists on separate sheets from the cell containing the data validation list.

A very important nuance of using data validation lists is that if the source list remains unnamed, then the source list must be on the same sheet as the cell that the validation list is being created in. Try to create a data validation list on Sheet1 using a source list from Sheet2. In neither Excel 2003 nor 2007 will you be able to select a different sheet for the source list. This can be easily overcome by naming the source list and then using the named range as the source. Make sure to still use an equal sign; otherwise, the name that was entered in the source list will appear in the cell! See Figure 2.7 for an example of using a named range in the source field of the Validation dialogue box.

OFFSET

Financial modelers are consistently tasked with manipulating data throughout their models. Much of this is nonmathematical, but rather more administrative. The OFFSET function is a reference function, which is incredibly useful for moving and referencing data within a model. The function requires the following parameters:

> =OFFSET(reference cell, number of rows from reference cell to move up or down, number of columns from reference cell to move left or right)

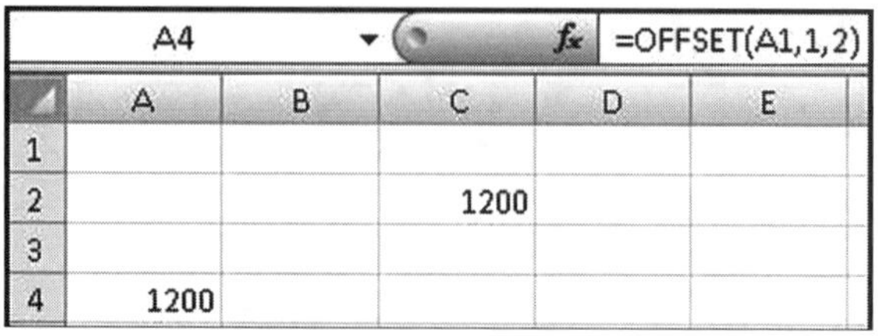

A4				f_x	=OFFSET(A1,1,2)
	A	B	C	D	E
1					
2			1200		
3					
4	1200				

FIGURE 2.8 The OFFSET function is a reference function to return values based on numerical parameters.

Figure 2.8 is an example with OFFSET returning a value by referencing cell A1 and offsetting it by 1 row and 2 columns. This reference returns the value from cell C2, which is 1200. When positive numbers are used for the rows, then OFFSET moves down from the reference location, while negative numbers will move up from the reference location. Similarly, when positive numbers are used for the columns, then OFFSET moves right from the reference location while negative numbers will move left from the reference location.

OFFSET is better used with arrays or lists of data. In Figure 2.9, there are revenue figures organized horizontally in row 4. In order to rearrange that data vertically, the OFFSET function is used with the assistance of a series of numbers that correspond to the reference location.

One of the more confusing aspects of using the OFFSET function is where to set the reference location cell. OFFSET is best used by starting the reference

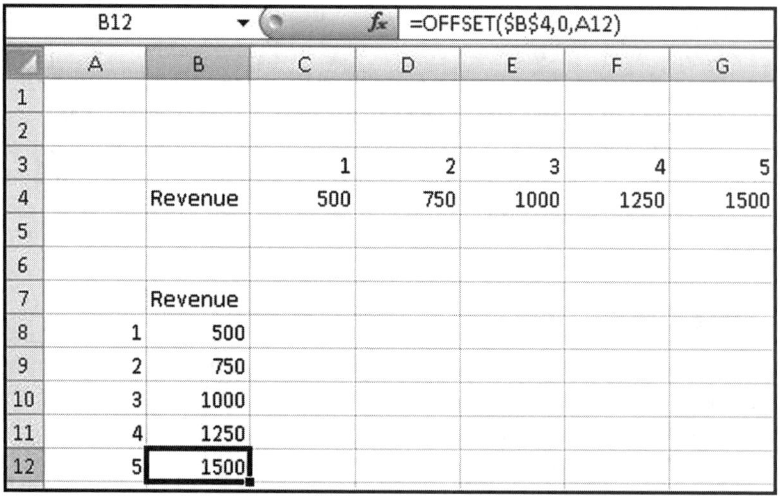

B12				f_x	=OFFSET($B$4,0,A12)		
	A	B	C	D	E	F	G
1							
2							
3			1	2	3	4	5
4		Revenue	500	750	1000	1250	1500
5							
6							
7		Revenue					
8	1	500					
9	2	750					
10	3	1000					
11	4	1250					
12	5	1500					

FIGURE 2.9 The OFFSET function is valuable to reference data in different directions and orders.

	A	B	C	D	E	F	G	H	I
1									
2		Single-Dimension Array			Two-Dimensional Array				
3									
4									
5		500	Use these			97.71%	78.73%	78.32%	18.95%
6		1250	cells to set			58.67%	10.38%	40.04%	43.05%
7		1750	the reference			25.81%	18.46%	55.46%	64.77%
8		2300	location cell.			83.82%	17.11%	69.09%	51.13%
9		3600				81.18%	66.90%	49.56%	57.29%

FIGURE 2.10 The starting reference point can be confusing for users new to the OFFSET function. When using OFFSET to reference single-dimension lists, start at the top. For two-dimensional sets of data, start at the corner.

location at the top of a single-dimension array or at the upper-leftmost corner of a two-dimensional array. Although we could use OFFSET anywhere on the sheet to reference the data in a single- or two-dimensional array, the most efficient locations are the ones closest to the data described earlier. See Figure 2.10 for a graphical representation of the best places to set the reference location.

One final aspect of the OFFSET function to notice is that it accepts numbers for the number of rows and columns to move from the reference location. To prepare for how we will use this function with another function, think about the inconvenience it would cause if we always had to provide the OFFSET function with numbers. Conveniently, the next function in this chapter's Toolbox is a function that converts more understandable inputs into numbers that OFFSET can accept.

MATCH

On its own, the MATCH function is incredibly easy. It returns the ordinal value of a lookup value compared to a list of values. The entry parameters for the MATCH function are:

=MATCH(value to be looked up, range of cells that could contain the value being looked up, type of match)

Since this function's parameters may need to be reread a few times, it is probably best explained by looking at an example. In Figure 2.11 we have a list that contains the possible periodicities that a model could be set to: Monthly, Quarterly, Semi-Annual, and Annual. If a user provided the periodicity that she was looking for, the MATCH function would return the ordinal number from the list. So, if the user typed **Quarterly** in a separate cell and designated that cell as the lookup value and the list of periodicities as the list of values, then the MATCH function would return a 2.

The MATCH function itself requires three parameters: the lookup value, the lookup array, and the type of match. The first parameter is the value that the user

	E3	▾		f_x	=MATCH(E2,B2:B5,0)	
	A	B	C		D	E
1						
2		Monthly			User Selected Periodicity:	Quarterly
3		Quarterly			MATCH Function Return:	2
4		Semi-Annual				
5		Annual				

FIGURE 2.11 The MATCH function returns a 2 because Quarterly is the lookup value and the second item on the lookup array.

is trying to look up. This can be text, dates, or a number. The second parameter is the lookup array or the list of values. The final parameter that the MATCH function requires is the number 0, 1, or –1. This parameter designates the type of match that takes place. When working with text or exact values that can be found on a list, the 0 should be used since this parameter signifies an exact match. When a lookup is being attempted with a number that can fit within a range of numbers, the 1 or –1 should be used. A –1 indicates that the ordinal position of the smallest value that is greater than the lookup value will be returned. A 1 indicates that the ordinal position of the largest value that is greater than the lookup value will be returned. These last two options for match type are very useful when presented with buckets or stratifications of data that require values to be looked up against.

OFFSET MATCH Combination

We will definitely find utility for the OFFSET and MATCH functions on their own, but the real power of these two functions is when they are combined to find values or reference cells. Recall that the OFFSET function accepts numbers for the number of rows and columns to move away from a reference cell. It would be cumbersome to always have to provide OFFSET numbers as entries. Conveniently, we learned that the MATCH function returns numbers based on ordinal position. Let's take a look at an example of the OFFSET MATCH combination, first in a decomposed form and then combined.

In our example we are going to try to return the number of months between periods, depending on the periodicity that the user selects. For instance, if the user selects **Monthly**, the return should be 1 month between periods. If the user selects **Annual**, the return should be 12, and so on. To set this up, we need a list of the possible periodicities and the corresponding number of months between periods. Figure 2.12 shows this initial setup.

In a separate cell, we could create the functionality by just using the OFFSET function. If we offset cell C1 by 1 row and 0 columns, a 1 would be returned. If we offset cell C1 by 2 rows and 0 columns, a 3 would be returned, and so on. So, we could build in functionality where the user provides a number for the periodicity and

	A	B	C
1			
2		Monthly	1
3		Quarterly	3
4		Semi-Annual	6
5		Annual	12

FIGURE 2.12 To demonstrate the utility of OFFSET MATCH, we will use a periodicity-related example.

the OFFSET function returns the number of months between periods. Figure 2.13 depicts this addition.

Now many readers will say to themselves, in the current state this seems entirely useless and makes the process more complicated. If a user had to remember the order number of the periodicity, he might just as well enter the number of months between periods. The only advantage this setup currently has is it restricts users to four possible periodicities, rather than allowing the user to create custom periodicities that the model builder did not anticipate. However, we can make the process much more intuitive by introducing the MATCH function into the process.

Rather than having the user enter a number to return the number of months between periods, it would be better to allow him to enter something with more context, such as a description of the periodicity. We can alter the previous example by writing in the name of the periodicity that we want in cell E3. In cell F3, we could use the MATCH function by using cell E3 as the lookup value and the list of periodicities in range B2:B5 (note that this range was named **lst_periodicities** earlier) to return the ordinal location of the desired periodicity. Keep in mind that a 0 match type was used to designate an exact match. This will return a number from 1 to 4

E5			f_x	=OFFSET(C1,E3,0)			
	A	B	C	D	E	F	G	H
1								
2		Monthly	1		Selected Periodicity			
3		Quarterly	3		4			
4		Semi-Annual	6		Number of Months Between Periods			
5		Annual	12		12			

FIGURE 2.13 While not complete, we can see in this example that OFFSET uses a number to offset the top of the list and return the correct number of months between periods.

	F3			f_x	=MATCH(E3,lst_periodicities,0)		
	A	B	C	D	E	F	G	H
1								
2		Monthly	1		Selected Periodicity			
3		Quarterly	3		Annual	4		
4		Semi-Annual	6		Number of Months Between Periods			
5		Annual	12		12			

FIGURE 2.14 The final addition is to use the MATCH function to derive the number that is used by the OFFSET function. Combined with a data validation list, the user can now select a periodicity based on name and have the number of months between periods easily returned.

depending on the desired periodicity and the order of the list. The altered example is shown in Figure 2.14.

Now we can connect the row reference for the OFFSET function to the return from the MATCH function in cell F3. Look in the formula bar in Figure 2.15 to see this quick change.

We can clean up this process in two ways:

1. It is precarious to have users type in the name of the periodicity that they want since if they make a misspelling or use different semantics the MATCH function could break down. To prevent such error, we should implement a data validation list in cell E3 that is based on the periodicity list from range B2:B5.
2. We do not need an additional cell for the MATCH function. We could replace the row reference in the OFFSET function that is currently set to cell F3 with the entire MATCH function that is in cell F3.

Figure 2.16 shows the completion of both of these efficiencies.

A number of discussion points are raised by this technique. The first is, why not just use the VLOOKUP function, which provides similar functionality, but with one function? While VLOOKUP is a powerful function, the major disadvantage is that the data must be contained in a continuous block or table of data. With OFFSET

	E5			f_x	=OFFSET(C1,F3,0)		
	A	B	C	D	E	F	G	H
1								
2		Monthly	1		Selected Periodicity			
3		Quarterly	3		Annual	4		
4		Semi-Annual	6		Number of Months Between Periods			
5		Annual	12		12			

FIGURE 2.15 The OFFSET function is connected to the MATCH function's return.

	E5			f_x	=OFFSET(C1,MATCH(E3,lst_periodicities,0),0)			
	A	B	C	D	E	F	G	H
1								
2		Monthly	1		Selected Periodicity			
3		Quarterly	3		Annual			
4		Semi-Annual	6		Number of Months Between Periods			
5		Annual	12		12			

FIGURE 2.16   We can clean up the two separate cells by combining the functions.

MATCH, we can create our lists anywhere and set the OFFSET in a completely different cell and/or sheet location. Additionally, VLOOKUP works only as its name implies: vertically. This means that if we wanted to implement a dual lookup, where we are looking up both vertically and horizontally, we would run into trouble. The OFFSET function can accept another MATCH function for a column lookup to pinpoint data in two-dimensional data sets. The final limitation is that VLOOKUP is limited in its ability to work with imperfect matches, such as trying to match 3.8 against the list 3,4,5. VLOOKUP would return 3. The MATCH function can handle more types of imperfect matches than VLOOKUP.

VLOOKUP

Although the VLOOKUP function was not used in this chapter, it is frequently used by financial modelers, and therefore should be explained. The *V* in VLOOKUP stands for *vertical*. Pairing the words together we have a function that will return a value by looking at information in a vertical list. The entry parameters for VLOOKUP are:

=VLOOKUP(value to be looked up, continuous range of all values with the vertical list in the leftmost column, the column number from the lookup column where the return value is located, a TRUE or FALSE to determine the match type)

As with many preliminary explanations in this book, a first read-through can be confusing. It's best to show VLOOKUP within the context of an example. Let's use an example similar to the one from the OFFSET MATCH combination. Figure 2.17 shows the setup.

In this example, we have the list of periodicity names in range C3:C6 and the corresponding number of months between dates in range D3:D6. While it cannot be seen from the figure, there is a data validation list in cell F4. The VLOOKUP function is entered in cell F6. The first parameter (the value to be looked up) is the user-selected periodicity name (cell F4). The range that is required for the VLOOKUP is C3:D6, which is the second parameter entered. Next, the function needs to know which

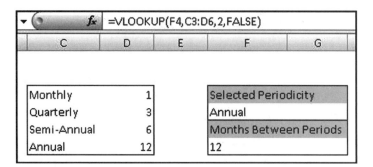

FIGURE 2.17 The VLOOKUP function is an alternative to the OFFSET MATCH combination; however, it is less flexible and more cumbersome to use with complex lookups.

column to provide the results from the range that was just specified. In this case it is column 2, which is hard coded in the formula. Finally, similar to the MATCH function, we need to specify whether our lookup value will be exactly matched to the list of possible values or approximately matched. In this case, we want an exact match, since the word *Annual* can be found exactly as it is spelled in the range C3:C6. Exact matches are designated by entering FALSE as the last parameter in the function. Many users new to VLOOKUP get odd results because they are trying to implement an exact MATCH, but leave the last parameter blank. If this parameter is omitted, the default setting is TRUE, which can return incorrect results.

EDATE

Realizing the importance of date functionality, Excel developers created the EDATE function. This function takes a starting date and a numerical entry for months, and returns a date based on those two parameters. For instance, if the starting date were October 1, 2009, and the numerical entry were 3, the date returned would be January 1, 2010. The function accepts parameters in the following way:

=EDATE(start date, number of months from start date)

Figure 2.18 shows two uses of the EDATE function. The first one uses a positive number to return a date in the future, whereas the implementation below that example uses a negative number to return a date in the past. Notice that there were no hard-coded values within the EDATE function. This is an important habit to get into to maintain flexible modeling. We can also begin to see that the number that is referenced for the number of months from the start date can be dynamic itself. That number can be changed by other functionality, which would in turn change the EDATE return.

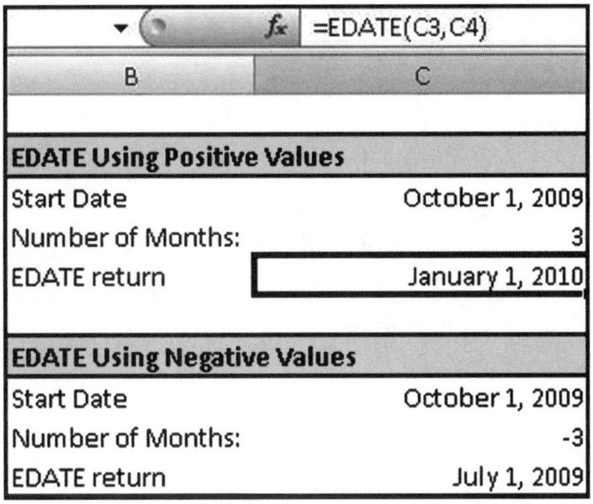

FIGURE 2.18 The EDATE function can accept positive or negative values to return a date in the future or past.

There are three important points to keep in mind when using the EDATE function:

1. *The parameters entered are very specific.* The date must be in serial format if it is directly entered into the formula. This means that if you try to put **10/1/2009** directly in the formula, Excel will think you are trying to divide 10 by 1 by 2009. Also make sure that the value entered to move from the start date is in months. This cannot be changed, but it can be manipulated to work in quarterly, semi-annual, or annual periodicities, as shown earlier.
2. *In order for EDATE to work, the Analysis Tool Pak add-in must be installed.* Otherwise, a #NAME? error will be returned, which will populate through any references. If you get an advanced model with multiple #NAME? errors, a good troubleshooting technique is to install the Analysis Tool Pak add-in.
3. *EDATE returns a date exactly the number of months from the start date.* This means that there is no differentiation between 30- and 31-day months. For example, if the start date is on the 15th and a 1 is used as the number of months from the start date, the return date will fall on the 15th regardless of the starting month's number of days.

For those creating models with settlement in mind or other date functionality, there is a function similar to EDATE that we will look at next.

▾	fx	=EOMONTH(C3,C4)
B		C
EOMONTH Using Positive Values		
Start Date		October 15, 2009
Number of Months:		3
EOMONTH return		January 31, 2010

FIGURE 2.19 EOMONTH always returns the last day of the month.

EOMONTH

The EOMONTH function is virtually identical to the EDATE function, with the difference being the day of month that gets returned. EOMONTH returns the last day of the month that is the specified number of months from the start date. The entry parameters are the same as EDATE:

EOMONTH(start date, number of months from start date)

To really show the difference, let's use 10/15/2009 as a start date and enter a 3 as the number of months from the start date. In Figure 2.19, we can see that instead of returning 1/15/2010 as EDATE would, EOMONTH returns 1/31/2010.

IF

Many readers are used to IF functions, but we should formally cover them in case there is any confusion. An IF function has one of two possible returns based on a conditional test. In normal-speak, that means we will devise some sort of test and depending on the outcome of that test return a value. The value could differ if the outcome of the test differs. We have quite a bit of flexibility in creating the test, but it must be a *conditional* test—a test that returns either a TRUE or FALSE depending on a conditional operator. What is a conditional operator? There are many. The conditional operators seen in Figure 2.20 are the most common ones in Excel.

To use a conditional operator, you can put it between two values, such as 3 < 5. In this case, the translation of that statement is "three is less than five." Now, imagine that we want to test that statement. We can write:

=IF(3 < 5

Although this formula is incomplete, we are telling Excel that we want to test the condition 3 < 5. In this case it is TRUE. If the statement is TRUE, then we might

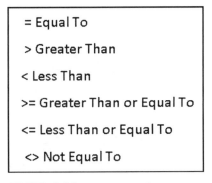

= Equal To

> Greater Than

< Less Than

>= Greater Than or Equal To

<= Less Than or Equal To

<> Not Equal To

FIGURE 2.20 Conditional operators help build conditional tests.

want a value to be entered in the cell where this formula resides. If the statement is FALSE, then we might want a different value entered in the cell. We could write:

=IF(3 < 5,"OK","ERROR")

Now the cell would have a text VALUE of "OK" since the statement is TRUE. IF functions return the first value that is after the conditional test if the conditional test is TRUE and the second value if the conditional test is FALSE.

Keep in mind that IF functions are very flexible. The conditional tests can compare values, dates, and text. They can also be formulas compared to each other. Similarly, the values that are returned can be numbers, text, dates, or formulas that calculate numbers, text, or dates.

We can also use IF functions in an intermediate fashion by *nesting* them. This means that we can test more than just one condition. This is done by writing an IF function and then writing another IF function if the first IF function is FALSE. For example:

=IF(A1>B1,"OK",IF(A1>A2,"OK","ERROR"))

This formula tests the value in cell A1 and returns "OK" if it is greater than the value in cell B1. If that statement is FALSE, then cell A1 is compared to cell A2, and "OK" is returned if that statement is TRUE. If all of the conditional tests are FALSE, then "ERROR" is returned. You can nest up to eight IF functions.

CHAPTER 3

Revenue, Costs, and the Income Statement

The firm's ability to generate revenue beyond costs is one of the most important components to a valuation. This excess revenue creates value to debt holders in the form of interest payments, or to equity holders in the form of dividends, or kept internally, which also yields return for equity holders in the form of capital appreciation. If a company has a decline of revenue or has none, then it must pay costs with other sources. Typically, some type of short-term facility, long-term loan, or equity infusion would be required to meet these costs. If there is a continued lack of revenue generation, then the liabilities of a firm can grow beyond the assets and the company could technically be classified as defaulted. Given the critical nature of generating revenue beyond costs, a significant amount of time should be spent analyzing the revenue and cost assumptions that go into a model and the methodologies employed for projections.

Once a growth analysis is complete, it's equally important to have a practical implementation of the various revenue and cost assumptions in the model. This is done by creating a flexible scenario selector system and adhering to standard accounting methods through the creation of an *income statement*. Whereas the revenues, costs, and income statement will provide key insights to the earnings of the firm, we will find that they are inextricably linked, both conceptually and technically, to the capital structure of the firm. For this reason, we will cover a majority of the earnings concepts in this chapter, but revisit them later in the text after going through the capital structure and balance sheet.

REVENUE

We should start with one of the most basic goals of a firm, generating revenue. *Revenue* is any inflow or expected inflow of funds based on the sale of a product or the performance of a service by a company. We should examine revenue through an accounting lens. When an item is sold or a service completed, a receivable is generated, which can be paid immediately with cash or left as a receivable and paid over a short period of time. It's important to note that revenue should be

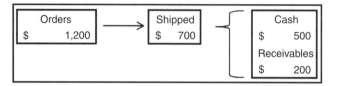

FIGURE 3.1 Even though $1,200 worth of goods were ordered and considered sold, the only revenue that we should recognize is the $700 that was actually shipped. After the other $500 is shipped, then it can be recognized.

recognized only when a product is shipped or a service is completed. Our modeling should use figures based only on these conditions so that our numbers will tie to the company's income statement and balance sheet. Otherwise, we may create an aggressive assumption, which people who are trying to manipulate the books of a firm will attempt on purpose. Figure 3.1 shows the difference between orders and revenue. We would count only $700 in revenue in this example.

Here is a word of caution on the split of revenue from cash and accounts receivable. In some businesses, accounts receivable can make up a disproportionate part of revenue. For instance, a consumer goods company might sell items such as appliances and electronics to customers, and give them the option to pay in cash or through financing. If most of the revenue comes through financing, then the accounts receivable might need to be analyzed in more detail, particularly with concern to nonpaying receivables. We will discuss this further in Chapter 4, when we go through accounts receivable on the balance sheet.

Revenue is also important because many other variables are based on periodic revenue values. For example, for a manufacturing firm that sells chocolate bars, revenue is derived from the sale of the chocolate bars. However, for each chocolate bar sold there are associated costs. If our revenue assumption is inaccurate for any reason, then the cost assumption will also be wrong. Since many items in the model may use revenue or a component of revenue to derive a value, we should spend time making sure our revenue assumption is as accurate as possible.

Estimating Revenue Based on Historical Data

The past may not be the best indicator of future performance, but it does provide data points that we can use to establish a *base case* valuation. In Chapter 2 we discussed the idea of obtaining historical financial information of a company, possibly on an annual basis or the past 12 months, to look for cyclicality. We could store this data in the model that we are creating, or we could maintain a separate source. It really doesn't matter where this data is stored; what matters are the assumptions we derive from this data.

There are multiple techniques for deriving assumptions from historical financial data. In regard to revenue, we are primarily concerned with projecting the expected growth rates. In practice, on Wall Street, there is a range of sophistication employed to derive revenue growth rates. From simple arithmetic averages to complex autoregressive integrated moving averages (ARIMA), growth rates are derived so they can be used for projections. The upcoming Model Builder is slightly different from the previous ones, as we will not be working on the core model. Instead, it focuses on three possible techniques at estimating revenue growth in a separate workbook. The results of the analyses can then be used for modeling.

MODEL BUILDER 3.1: THREE METHODS FOR ESTIMATING REVENUE BASED ON HISTORICAL DATA

This Model Builder will walk readers through the process of estimating growth rates using a variety of methods. The incomplete workbook is named GrowthRates.xls, while the complete workbook is named GrowthRates_Complete.xls. Both are provided on the CD-ROM. The incomplete workbook is provided so readers do not have to enter in the raw data by hand and can focus on the analysis. Just as with the core model, if there is any confusion with the instructions, refer to the complete version for guidance.

1. Open the Excel workbook GrowthRates.xls from the CD-ROM. Look over the sheet to see what data is provided. You should see four separate sections with years and corresponding revenue amounts for each year. An excerpt of the workbook is depicted in Figure 3.2.
2. Our first task will be to determine the annual growth rates for each year. This is a simple process involving a mathematical function. In cell D7, enter the following formula:

$$=(C7-C6)/C6$$

1) Arithmetic Average	
Year	**Revenue**
2002	150
2003	178
2004	210
2005	247
2006	275
2007	295
2008	310

FIGURE 3.2 The years and associated revenues are provided for each of the four sections of this exercise.

1) Arithmetic Average		
Year	**Revenue**	**Growth Rate**
2002	150	
2003	178	18.67%
2004	210	17.98%
2005	247	17.62%
2006	275	11.34%
2007	295	7.27%
2008	310	5.08%

FIGURE 3.3 The first step is to calculate the growth rates between years.

Copy this formula over the range D7:D12. This is a basic growth-rate formula that takes the new amount, subtracts the old amount, and divides that result by the old amount. An easy mnemonic is *New Minus Old Over Old*. Figure 3.3 shows this completed.

3. In cell D13, enter the following formula:

=AVERAGE(D7:D12)

The AVERAGE function takes the arithmetic average of the newly created growth rates. For more information on the AVERAGE function, jump to the Toolbox at the end of this chapter.

4. For Excel 2007 users there is a new function called AVERAGEIF that can also provide additional functionality for this analysis. Create a label by entering the text **Include** in cell E5.

5. Enter the following letters in the corresponding cells:

E7: N
E8: N
E9: N
E10: Y
E11: Y
E12: Y

The N's stand for "No, do not include in the analysis," and the Y's stand for "Yes, include in the analysis."

6. In cell E13, enter the following formula:

=AVERAGEIF(E7:E12,"Y",D7:D12)

1) Arithmetic Average			
Year	Revenue	Growth Rate	Include
2002	150		
2003	178	18.67%	N
2004	210	17.98%	N
2005	247	17.62%	N
2006	275	11.34%	Y
2007	295	7.27%	Y
2008	310	5.08%	Y
Arithmetic Avg:		12.99%	7.90%

FIGURE 3.4 The arithmetic mean section is complete using the AVERAGE function. Additional functionality with the AVERAGEIF function is also implemented.

Users of the SUMIF function will recognize AVERAGEIF's strong similarity. The function examines the range E7:E12 to see which ones have a value of "Y" and calculates only the average on the values in range D7:D12, where the column E criterion has been met. This functionality is useful if there are many data points that we are examining and we want to be able to quickly switch the values of a range that we are examining. Otherwise, we would have to redo the AVERAGE function and possibly reorganize the numbers each time we wanted to make a change. For more help on AVERAGEIF, see the Toolbox at the end of this chapter. Also refer to Figure 3.4 for the complete arithmetic average section.

7. Now keep in mind a very important point. Many disagree with using the arithmetic mean for analyzing growth rates. I also disagree with such a use, but am showing the arithmetic mean because it is still used by a number of professionals. I also want to establish an example for a *back test*. Let's test the arithmetic mean by starting with the 2002 revenue and growing that revenue number by the arithmetic mean each period. In cell J5, create a label for this test by entering the text **Back Test**. In cell J7, enter the following formula:

=C6*(1+$D$13)

We need to grow this new value by the same mean, so enter the following formula in cell J8:

=J7*(1+$D$13)

Copy and paste this formula over the range J8:J12. As shown in Figure 3.5, cell J12 should have a value of 312, which is greater than the last historical value

1) Arithmetic Average				
Year	Revenue	Growth Rate	Include	Back Test
2002	150			
2003	178	18.67%	N	169
2004	210	17.98%	N	192
2005	247	17.62%	N	216
2006	275	11.34%	Y	245
2007	295	7.27%	Y	276
2008	310	5.08%	Y	312
Arithmetic Avg:		12.99%	7.90%	

Notice larger revenue than historically shown for the final year. ←

FIGURE 3.5 When back tested, the arithmetic mean produces more revenue than we have seen in history and does not account for trending.

recorded. The arithmetic mean here is slightly aggressive. Another concern is that the growth rate appears to be tapering off. The arithmetic mean of all the time periods does not account for this.

8. To help solve some of the problems caused by using the arithmetic mean with growth rates, most professionals use the *geometric* mean instead. The geometric mean is introduced to finance professionals as the *compounded annual growth rate* (CAGR). This can be confusing because it is implemented in various ways. The simplest way to implement CAGR is by solving for the rate, which grows our starting value to the ending value. This can be implemented by entering the following formula into cell D24:

=(C23/C17)^(1/6)-1

This formula takes the latest value in time, divides it by the earliest value, and takes that result to the 6th root. We subtract 1 from this entire value to get only the percentage increase each period. Notice that this results in a value that is less than the arithmetic average. We can then implement a similar back test as we did with the arithmetic average. Use the same formulas in range J7:J12, except replace the arithmetic average with the CAGR derived from this example. Do this in range J18:J23. The last back-test figure (cell J18) should be the same as the last year's revenue in the historical data set. Figure 3.6 shows the completed section.

9. Although the previous CAGR is better than the arithmetic average, it misses the intermediate data. We are examining only two data points with the previous CAGR method, the beginning and the end. This implies that there is a smooth growth over time. We should be concerned that the revenue changes are not smooth and occur in some type of pattern or with a trend. In the case of the example data, there is a trend toward reduced growth. We can employ another

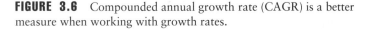

2) Compounded Annual Growth Rate (CAGR) - No Intermediate Data			
Year	Revenue	Growth Rate	Back Test
2002	150		
2003	178	18.67%	169
2004	210	17.98%	191
2005	247	17.62%	216
2006	275	11.34%	243
2007	295	7.27%	275
2008	310	5.08%	310
CAGR		12.86%	

FIGURE 3.6   Compounded annual growth rate (CAGR) is a better measure when working with growth rates.

CAGR technique, the geometric mean, which takes these intermediate figures into account. This can be done by entering the following formula in cell D35:

=(D29*D30*D31*D32*D33*D34)^(1/6)

This formula returns the geometric mean, which is the *n*th root of the product of *n* values. This calculation can be simplified by using the PRODUCT function, which multiplies an array of values by each other:

=PRODUCT(D29:D34)^(1/6)

10. We could make the equation even simpler by using the GEOMEAN function built into Excel. The GEOMEAN function takes the following entry parameters:

=GEOMEAN(**values to geometrically averaged**)

If either the PRODUCT or GEOMEAN functions are new to you or require further clarification, jump to the Toolbox at the end of this chapter. Otherwise, let's practice using the GEOMEAN function by entering the following formula in cell G35:

=GEOMEAN(D29:D34)

Notice that by including the intermediate values the growth rate decreases even more. Figure 3.7 shows the completed section. This is due to the decrease of the growth rate over time. While the geometric mean is a good technique to employ, there are times when it is not ideal. For instance, change the revenue amount in cell C31 from 247 to 205. The two geometric mean calculations

3) Compounded Annual Growth Rate (CAGR) - Intermediate Data		
Year	Revenue	Growth Rate
2002	150	
2003	178	18.67%
2004	210	17.98%
2005	247	17.62%
2006	275	11.34%
2007	295	7.27%
2008	310	5.08%
CAGR Math		11.63%

CAGR Formula   11.63%

FIGURE 3.7   The geometric mean takes into account each data point over time.

should return #NUM! errors. This is because our switch in revenue numbers causes one of the growth rates to be negative. The geometric mean calculation and the GEOMEAN function cannot work with negative numbers, although companies can experience negative growth.

11. To expand on our techniques and work with even distressed historical data, we can use *regression* as a tool of measuring growth. Many people shudder at the thought of recalling how to complete a full regression by hand. Thankfully, Excel has many prebuilt regression functions that make running a regression fast and accurate. We will work with one of the many regression features Excel offers, but if you would like to learn more detailed regression functions you can jump to the Toolbox at the end of this chapter.

Returning to our revenue-growth example in the context of a regression, we should define a few terms. The specific technique we will be focusing on is a *least squares* regression. The heart of performing this regression is the relationship between one variable and one or more other variables. Specifically, a least squares regression seeks to analyze the dependence of a *dependent* variable on one or more *independent* variables. A simple example of a least squares regression is testing the dependence of income on education level. We could try to substantiate through statistics whether the amount someone earns is dependent on her level of education by sampling the population and gathering information on many people's education level and associated income. We could get fancier with this analysis and add in more independent variables such as age groups, geographic location, subjects studied, and so forth.

Let's get back to our revenue-growth example. What are the dependent and independent variables? The dependent variable is *revenue* and the independent variable is *time*. Just think of the question we are seeking to answer: "How does revenue depend on time?" It would be odd the other way around: "How does time depend on revenue?"

Revenue vs. Time

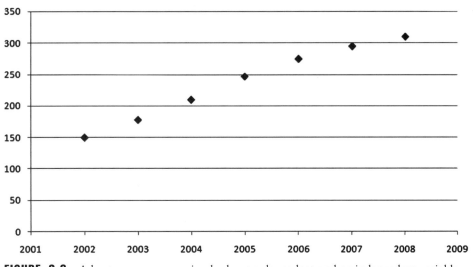

FIGURE 3.8 A least squares regression looks at a dependent and an independent variable.

The best way to visualize this problem is to create a scatter plot of revenue and time, such as Figure 3.8.

A relationship between these two variables can be established by trying to create a line that best fits the data on the scatter plot. The ideal line is one that minimizes the distance between the line and the data points. In Figure 3.9, a trend line has been added that best fits the data set.

How do we create such a trend line? In theory, it is the classic formula:

$$y = mx + b$$

In this equation, m is the correlation coefficient between these two variables and b is the intercept constant. If we plug in an independent data point, we should get a dependent data point that is in line with the established historical relationship. The optimal parameters for this equation are solved through regression. They are the ones that produce the least amount of error, otherwise visualized as the distance between data points and the trend line.

12. We will use the SLOPE function in Excel to save time for our example. The SLOPE function runs a least squares regression and returns the slope. This is a measure of the relationship between the two variables, but not a test for dependency. For growth rates versus time, the dependency is implied, so we can use the slope to understand the relationship. Enter the following formula in cell C46:

=SLOPE(C39:C45,B39:B45)

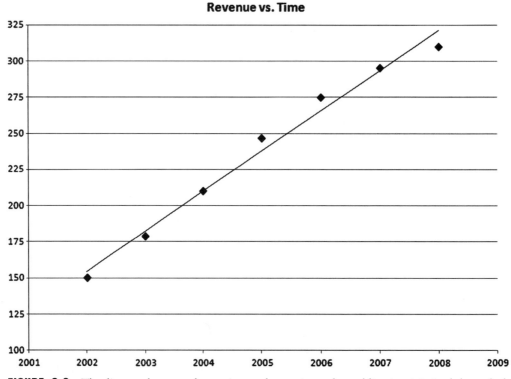

FIGURE 3.9 The distance between data points and an estimated trend line is minimized through the regression methodology.

With the regression function in Excel the first entry parameter is always the dependent value. When you begin typing the SLOPE function, the automatic parameter guide will prompt "known_y's" (see Figure 3.10).

In regression, dependent variables are always referenced on the *y*-axis, whereas independent variables are referenced on the *x*-axis.

To really understand this formula, think about time as our independent variable. In our example, for every unit increase in time we would expect a 27.82 increase in revenue. Therefore, the result of our SLOPE function is *not* the growth rate.

13. We should convert the slope from revenue units to a growth rate. To get the expected growth rate from the slope, we could take the expected increase amount and divide it by the average revenue. In cell D35, enter the following formula:

=C46/AVERAGE(C39:C45)

The result of this division is 11.70%, which is comparable to the previous CAGR figure.

◢	B	C	D
37	**4) Regression**		
38	**Year**	**Revenue**	**Growth Rate**
39	2002	150	
40	2003	178	18.67%
41	2004	210	17.98%
42	2005	247	17.62%
43	2006	275	11.34%
44	2007	295	7.27%
45	2008	310	5.08%
46	=SLOPE(C39:C45,B39:B45)		

FIGURE 3.10 The automatic parameter guide will always ask for the *y*-axis variables before the *x*-axis variables.

The methods described in this Model Builder provide insight in determining a base-case figure. Keep in mind there are many other factors that may affect the expected revenue growth rate for a company. We may want to examine specific historical periods if we think they are more relevant than the entire history, we may want to use different time periods for stages of the analysis if we think there will be fundamental changes, or we may have insight into the company's future plans and adjust the growth factor accordingly.

Our method in this Model Builder is purely quantitative, but never underestimate the impact of *qualitative* issues on growth. For example, years back I worked on an Australian pub transaction. Pub revenue was robust, primarily from gambling machines installed in the locations. Two laws were proposed that could affect the pubs: The first was a smoking ban within pubs; the second was a gambling ban. My analysis given these situations included scenarios that estimated the drop in revenue due to a large smoking client base and/or a loss of gambling revenue. In this case, there would be no way to look at historical data and get an accurate growth rate if either or both of the laws were enacted.

Components versus Consolidation

The previous example of pub revenue brings up an interesting point regarding components of revenue. Given the importance of revenue, we might want to take a detailed look at what drives the overall revenue figure. While it's perfectly acceptable to use a consolidated number, where all the revenue components are rolled up into one figure each period, building a model using specific revenue drivers allows

Consolidated vs. Components

Revenue Expectation Each Period from Chocolate Bar Company

	2009	2010	2011	2012	2013	2014
Consolidated						
Sales $	$ 100.00	$ 106.99	$ 114.53	$ 122.64	$ 131.39	$ 140.83
Sales Growth		6.99%	7.04%	7.09%	7.13%	7.18%
Components						
Dark Chocolate Bars ($ per unit)	$ 4.00	$ 4.20	$ 4.41	$ 4.63	$ 4.86	$ 5.11
Growth		5.00%	5.00%	5.00%	5.00%	5.00%
Milk Chocolate Bars ($ per unit)	$ 3.50	$ 3.61	$ 3.71	$ 3.82	$ 3.94	$ 4.06
Growth		3.00%	3.00%	3.00%	3.00%	3.00%
Almond Chocolate Bars ($ per unit)	$ 4.00	$ 4.24	$ 4.49	$ 4.76	$ 5.05	$ 5.35
Growth		6.00%	6.00%	6.00%	6.00%	6.00%
Dark Chocolate Bars (units)	12	12	12	13	13	13
Growth		2.00%	2.00%	2.00%	2.00%	2.00%
Milk Chocolate Bars (units)	8	8	8	8	8	8
Growth		1.00%	1.00%	1.00%	1.00%	1.00%
Almond Chocolate Bars (units)	6	6	6	7	7	7
Growth		4.00%	4.00%	4.00%	4.00%	4.00%
Sales $	$ 100.00	$ 106.99	$ 114.53	$ 122.64	$ 131.39	$ 140.83

FIGURE 3.11   Revenue can be estimated using a simple consolidated approach or a more detailed components methodology.

a model user more flexibility in creating analysis scenarios. We could then try to identify the most relevant and influential drivers and stress those to see the effects on revenue and, ultimately, valuation. For example, in our modeling of pubs we can take a detailed look at revenue by breaking it down into gambling machines, drink, food, and other revenue (such as special events). If we knew of specific revenue estimates for each gambling machine and the number of machines, we could break down the analysis even further into units and revenue per unit.

The same could be done for our chocolate bar company. We could get as specific as identifying individual items sold, the price per item, and the units expected to sell. Ultimately, a components breakdown takes more time, but can be more flexible and valuable in estimating revenue. See Figure 3.11 for a graphical depiction of the difference between using a consolidated and a components methodology.

Fixed, Variable, and Semi-Variable

When using a components methodology, you should keep in mind whether the revenue is fixed, variable, or semi-variable. Fixed revenue is revenue that has a specific dollar amount per period, whereas variable revenue is an amount of revenue that is predicated on another variable, such as units sold. Semi-variable revenue is more difficult to grasp since historical averages may not reflect that semi-variable nature. Specifically, semi-variable revenue has both a fixed and a variable component. An example of semi-variable revenue would be the case of a financial trainer getting paid a training rate of $1,000 for a class of 20 students and $200 more for each additional student. The $1,000 is fixed revenue, whereas the additional revenue is based on each additional student beyond 20.

COSTS

Thus far we have concerned ourselves with only the positive side of the company, revenue. Equally important are the *costs* associated with generating the revenue. Companies run into trouble when their cost structure is too high and sometimes exceeds their revenue. The key to modeling costs is to understand the drivers and relationships behind the costs. This can be simple or very complicated depending on the level of detail and the type of product or company under analysis. For instance, in our chocolate bar company example we could analyze the historical cost of producing each type of chocolate bar. This way we could create a cost percentage for the amount of revenue generated by each chocolate bar type. In Figure 3.12, a standard assumption set is created for the costs of our chocolate bars. The top section is labeled "Consolidated," where percentages of revenue have been estimated. These estimates could be derived from a historical study of cost versus revenue or alternative expectations regarding chocolate bar costs.

We could go further into this analysis by breaking down the ingredients in the chocolate bar and the costs associated with purchasing each of these separately. This would be a pertinent process for food analysts, given the volatility in some food product prices. Figure 3.12 also shows components methodology, where ingredient costs per unit have been projected. We can now assume that certain costs for each chocolate bar may grow at different rates than the revenue growth and/or different rates than each other ingredient. Incidentally, careful readers will notice that the cost percentage of revenue is the same in both the consolidated and the components approach. This was done to show how the two methods can connect, but in practice these two methodologies often lead to different figures since the consolidated approach is less detailed and uses figures with generic assumptions.

Whether we choose a consolidated or a components approach, we can use statistical techniques that we have just learned to help estimate the numbers to use in the projection. We should also briefly discuss a more powerful alternative. In this case, we may be concerned that cacao beans or sugar might have volatile prices. When dealing with items that exhibit volatility, simulation can help manage risk. A simulation in this case could be run in two ways:

1. The quick-and-dirty way would be to simulate price paths for each food product and use a path given a certain confidence level from the distribution of price paths.

	2009	2010	2011	2012	2013	2014
Consolidated						
Cost as % of Revenue						
Dark Chocolate Bar Costs	30.00%	28.92%	27.88%	26.89%	25.93%	24.97%
Milk Chocolate Bar Costs	29.57%	29.03%	28.60%	28.13%	27.62%	27.14%
Almond Chocolate Bar Costs	27.13%	25.96%	24.86%	23.79%	22.75%	21.78%
Components						
Per Unit Costs						
Dark Chocolate Bars						
Cacao Beans	0.80	0.81	0.82	0.82	0.83	0.84
Sugar	0.05	0.05	0.05	0.05	0.06	0.06
Vanilla	0.20	0.20	0.21	0.21	0.22	0.22
Lecithin	0.15	0.15	0.15	0.15	0.16	0.16
Milk Chocolate Bars						
Cacao Beans	0.60	0.61	0.61	0.62	0.62	0.63
Sugar	0.06	0.06	0.06	0.06	0.07	0.07
Vanilla	0.18	0.18	0.18	0.19	0.19	0.19
Lecithin	0.10	0.10	0.10	0.10	0.10	0.11
Milk	0.10	0.10	0.10	0.10	0.10	0.11
Almond Chocolate Bars						
Cacao Beans	0.55	0.56	0.56	0.57	0.57	0.58
Sugar	0.06	0.06	0.06	0.06	0.07	0.07
Vanilla	0.18	0.18	0.18	0.19	0.19	0.19
Lecithin	0.10	0.10	0.10	0.10	0.10	0.11
Milk	0.10	0.10	0.10	0.10	0.10	0.11
Almonds	0.10	0.10	0.11	0.11	0.11	0.12
Unit Sales						
Dark Chocolate Bars	12	12	12	13	13	13
Milk Chocolate Bars	8	8	8	8	8	8
Almond Chocolate Bars	6	6	6	7	7	7
Dark Chocolate Bar Costs	14.40	14.58	14.76	16.18	16.38	16.59
Milk Chocolate Bar Costs	8.28	8.38	8.49	8.60	8.71	8.82
Almond Chocolate Bar Costs	6.51	6.60	6.70	7.93	8.04	8.16

FIGURE 3.12   Costs also can be estimated using a consolidated method or a more detailed components methodology.

2. A better, more correct method would be to create a distribution of firm values based on simulated price paths and use a firm value for the scenario that is associated with a specific confidence level.

The details of a simulation are a book in itself and beyond the scope of this one; however, the key is to understand that some costs will be directly associated with revenue, whereas others might be so volatile that an alternative analysis might be necessary.

Costs directly related to the production of products or services, such as chocolate bar ingredients, are known as *operating* costs. Beyond operating costs are *non-operating* and *irregular* expenses. These expenses could include financing costs such as interest and dividends, or other extraordinary costs such as lawsuit settlements, natural disaster, infrastructure, or, in international situations, expropriation. We will introduce and work with these items in the upcoming income statement section and in Model Builder 3.2; we will go into more detail on them in Chapter 4.

ORGANIZING REVENUE AND COST ASSUMPTIONS FOR SCENARIO ANALYSIS

Rarely are financial analysts asked to produce one expectation for revenues and costs. Many factors can affect both of these topics and managers want to know the results when projections are worse than expected, or better than expected, or perhaps in specific cases such as the legal scenarios surrounding Australian pubs discussed earlier. For this reason, we should implement our revenue and cost assumptions in a dynamic method that allows us to enter in expected cases quickly and vary the results of our analysis.

We will implement two methods to manage our assumptions, a basic one involving just Excel functions and formulas, and an advanced one in Chapter 11, when we learn more about VBA. The basic one is common to many financial models and is known as a *current* or *live scenario* system. This system works by populating the current or "live" scenario with data stored in other sections of the model. Figure 3.13 is a graphical depiction of the process.

In Figure 3.13, the dotted lines represent the interaction between the Assumptions sheet and two parts of the Vectors sheet. The user selects a scenario from a list of scenarios. A formula on the Vectors sheet in the current/live scenario section will reference this selection in a way to pull the correct data from the scenario data that

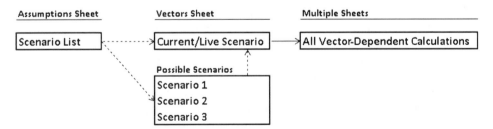

FIGURE 3.13 The user selects a scenario from the Assumptions sheet, which instructs the current/live scenario formula to load up the values from the possible scenarios' data. All calculations are based on the current/live scenario.

is stored underneath the current/live scenario section. All calculations are then based on the data that is in the current/live scenario section. When a user toggles through the scenarios on the Assumptions sheet, the current/live scenario data changes, which then changes linked calculations and ultimately the valuation.

MODEL BUILDER 3.2: INSTALLING AN EXCEL-BASED SCENARIO SELECTOR SYSTEM

1. The data for the possible scenarios will be stored on the Vectors sheet. Go to the Vectors sheet and enter the following text labels in the corresponding cells:

   B3: Scenarios
   B4: Base Case
   B5: Upside Case
   B6: Downside Case
   B9: Live Scenario

   Name cell B4 **vectors_Case1**, cell B5 **vectors_Case2**, and cell B6 **vectors_Case3**. Also, name range B4:B6 **lst_Scenarios**.
2. We will focus only on revenue and cost assumptions so far, which will be captured when we create the income statement. For this reason, we will enter only assumptions pertinent to the income statement. On the Vectors sheet, enter the following text labels in the corresponding cells:

   B11: Income Statement Items
   B12: Sales Unit Growth
   B13: Sales Price Growth
   B14: Cost Unit Growth
   B15: SGA (% of Revenue)
   B16: Op Ex (% of Revenue)
   B17: Non-Op Ex (% of Revenue)

   Just to be clear, rows 12, 13, 14 will contain percentages that represent the growth each period of sales units, prices, and costs. Keep in mind that other rows use the statement "(% of Revenue)," which means that the percentage entered will be applied to the revenue dollar amount for the period. Those are not growth rates. The value of the item that uses "(% of Revenue)" will grow by the sales growth rates though, and should primarily capture items that vary with revenue. Fixed or semi-variable items are poorly captured by this method and may require separate rows for adjustment.

   The next acronym in this section is *SGA*, which stands for *selling, general and administrative costs*. This category encompasses items such as salary, office costs, and other expenses related to the sale of a product or service, such as advertising. All other operating costs that keep the firm's day-to-day operations intact are captured by the Op Ex (Operating Expenditure) row. Expenses incurred that are not part of the core operation of the firm are included in the Non-Op Ex (Non-Operating Expenditure) row. Keep in mind that the Non-Operating Expenditure row does not include concepts such as depreciation, amortization, interest, and dividends. As we encounter those items in later chapters we will explain the theory and implementation.

3. The live scenario section will not have any hard-coded numbers entered as assumptions. Instead the live scenario section will draw its data from scenario data stored below it. For this reason, we should set up areas for the possible scenario data. The labels should reference the Live Scenario labels so we do not have to change each one by hand. Enter the following formulas in the corresponding cells. Note that in the following directions there are multiple cells on the sheet that refer to the same cell from the live scenario section. If any of this is unclear, go to the completed Vectors sheet from the complete model:

B40: =vectors_Case1
B71: =vectors_Case2
B102: =vectors_Case3
B42, B73, B104: =B11
B43, B74, B105: =B12
B44, B75, B106: =B13
B45, B76, B107: =B14
B46, B77, B108: =B15
B47, B78, B109: =B16
B48, B79, B110: =B17

4. For readability of the column periods, we should also reference the dates for each possible scenario. Enter the following formulas in the corresponding cells. Similar to the previous step, there will be multiple cells referencing the same cell in the live scenario section:

D40, D71, D102: =D9
E40, E71, E102: =E9
F40, F71, F102: =F9
G40, G71, G102: =G9
H40, H71, H102: =H9
I40, I71, I102: =I9
J40, J71, J102: =J9
D41, D72, D103: =D10
E41, E72, E103: =E10
F41, F72, F103: =F10
G41, G72, G103: =G10
H41, H72, H103: = H10
I41, I72, I103: =I10
J41, J72, J103: =J10

	A	B	C	D	E	F	G	H	I	J
40		Base Case			Projected ---->					TV Year
41				12/31/2007	12/31/2008	12/31/2009	12/31/2010	12/31/2011	12/31/2012	12/31/2013
42		Income Statement Items								
43		Sales Unit Growth			5.0%	5.0%	5.0%	5.0%	5.0%	2.0%
44		Sales Price Growth			5.0%	5.0%	5.0%	5.0%	5.0%	2.0%
45		Cost Unit Growth			6.0%	6.0%	6.0%	6.0%	6.0%	6.0%
46		SGA (% of revenue)			14.0%	14.0%	14.0%	14.0%	14.0%	14.0%
47		Op Ex (% of revenue)			6.0%	6.0%	6.0%	6.0%	6.0%	6.0%
48		Non-Op Ex (% of revenue)			1.8%	1.8%	1.8%	1.8%	1.8%	1.8%

FIGURE 3.14 This is a partial example of the possible scenarios, which are stored on the Vectors sheet below the live scenario section.

5. We should put assumptions in for the income statement items of the possible scenarios. While the user will ultimately define these numbers based on separate analyses, you should copy the figures in from the complete model on the CD-ROM. The base case section of the Vectors sheet on your model should look like Figure 3.14.

6. Before we can complete the live scenario section on the Vectors sheet, we need to add functionality so the user can switch between scenarios on the Assumptions sheet. Go to the Assumptions sheet and enter the following labels in the corresponding cells:

   B30: **Scenario Controls**
   B31: **Global Scenario Selector**

7. Still on the Assumptions sheet in cell D31, create a data validation list using the lst_Scenarios named range. Name cell D31 **inputs_ScenSelector** and select "Base Case" from the list as the starting value. This section should look like Figure 3.15.

inputs_ScenSelector ▼		*fx*	Base Case
	A	B	C	D
29				
30		Scenario Controls		
31		Global Scenario Selector		Base Case ▼
32				
33				
34				

FIGURE 3.15 The user can select scenarios from the Assumptions sheet using a data validation list.

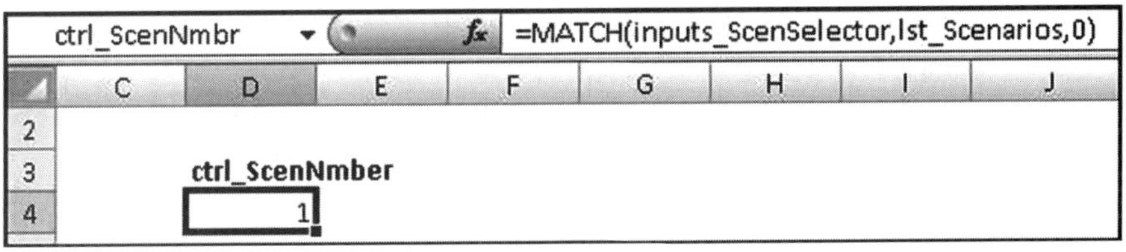

FIGURE 3.16 The text matching is converted to numbers for use in other functions.

8. Next, when most of our model is complete and we are running sensitivities, we may want to adjust the growth rate by a factor for incremental analysis. For this reason, we will create a global growth adjustor that increases or decreases the growth rate by a user-defined percentage. In cell F22, enter the text **DCF Valuation Assumptions**, and in cell I26, enter the text **Global Growth Adjustor**. Also name cell K26 **inputs_GlobalGrowth**. We will wait until Chapter 10 to finish this section since a special tool will be implemented to adjust growth.

9. We need to create one final reference cell on the Hidden sheet. This cell will convert the user-selected scenario from a name to a number. Go to the Hidden sheet and label cell D3 **ctrl_ScenNmber**. Enter the following formula in cell D4:

=MATCH(inputs_ScenSelector,lst_Scenarios,0)

Name cell D4 **ctrl_ScenNmbr**. The MATCH function provides the ordinal number for the scenario that the user selected from the list of possible scenarios. This addition should look like Figure 3.16.

10. We can now jump back to the Vectors page and enter the following formula in cell E12:

=CHOOSE(ctrl_ScenNmbr,E43,E74,E105,E136)*(1+inputs_GlobalGrowth)

Copy this formula over the range E12:J13. The CHOOSE function takes the numeric representation of the scenario and uses it to pull data from the possible scenario data below. For instance, if scenario 1, otherwise known as the "Base Case," is selected, the MATCH function earlier makes the ctrl_ScenNmbr cell a 1, which the CHOOSE function uses as its index number to pull the first set of data. For example, cell E12 will take the data from cell E43. The result from the CHOOSE function is then adjusted by the global growth adjustor created on the Assumptions page. If using the CHOOSE function is new or unclear to you, refer to the Toolbox at the end of this chapter.

As the global growth adjustor pertains only to revenue growth, the other income statement items should not include it. In cell E14, enter the following formula:

=CHOOSE(ctrl_ScenNmbr,E45,E76,E107,E138)

Copy this formula over the range E13:J17. The scenario selector is mainly complete. The user can switch between scenario names on the Assumptions sheet and have the live/current scenario figures change. Soon we will start connecting calculations to the live/current scenario figures. Keep in mind that we will revisit this section in Chapter 11, when we implement additional scenario functionality using VBA.

BRINGING REVENUES AND COSTS TOGETHER: THE INCOME STATEMENT

Understanding the earnings of a company by just analyzing a firm's revenues and costs independently can be challenging. The most common method of organizing revenues and costs is to create an income statement, which is the foundation of the three main financial statements. The income statement, or *profit-and-loss* (P&L) statement as some countries call it, is a report of a company's revenues and costs within a certain timeframe. For an annual statement this time frame is typically a *fiscal* year. As mentioned in Chapter 2, be careful of the fiscal year for a company since it may not line up like a calendar year, where the time period starts in January and ends in December.

Regardless of the fiscal year, most income statements follow a standard pattern, as seen in Figure 3.17. The income statement gives a complete picture of a company's earnings. Items beyond operating revenues and costs, such as interest, depreciation, amortization, taxes, and retained earnings, appear on the income statement. These non-operating items are heavily influenced by the assets, liabilities, and equity of the firm, which is captured by the balance sheet. The balance sheet, the second of the three main financial statements, will be introduced in Chapter 4.

The income statement and the balance sheet are tightly linked and have many dynamic features that we will slowly introduce. In fact, a properly constructed discounted cash flow model will have sheets that represent the income statement and balance sheet with direct reference links between the two. These links will create functionality and maintain the principles of accounting; both the functionality and accounting behind it will be thoroughly discussed as we progress.

MODEL BUILDER 3.3: INTEGRATING THE INCOME STATEMENT

1. Insert a worksheet after the Vectors sheet and name it **Income Statement**.
2. On the Income Statement sheet, enter the text **Income Statement** in cell A1. Also, we will want to retain the timing from the Vectors sheet, so reference the dates and timing cells by entering references to the Vectors sheet. As an example, the

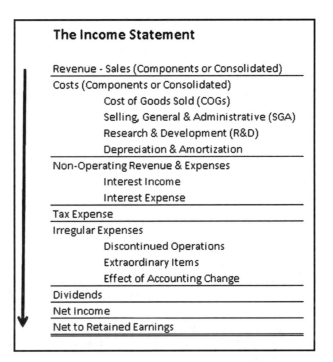

FIGURE 3.17 The income statement is the first of the three financial statements that will help us understand the valuation of a company.

first three cells of this section on the Income Statement sheet should have the following values in the corresponding cells:

D2: =Vectors!D9
E2: =Vectors!E9
F2: =Vectors!F9

This referencing pattern should continue for range G2:Z2. Also, complete a similar referencing pattern for row 3. The first three cells of this section are shown below:

D3: =Vectors!D10
E3: =Vectors!E10
F3: =Vectors!F10

Continue this referencing pattern for range G3:Z3. Refer to Figure 3.18 to make sure you are completing this step correctly.

▲	A	B	C	D	E	F	G	H	I	J
1	*Income Statement*									
2				Projected ---->						TV Year
3				12/31/2007	12/31/2008	12/31/2009	12/31/2010	12/31/2011	12/31/2012	12/31/2013

FIGURE 3.18   The top of the Income Statement sheet is a direct reference to the Vectors sheet.

3. The uppermost concept on the income statement is revenue or sales. Enter the following text in the corresponding cells:

 B5: **Sales Units**
 B6: **Sales Price**
 B7: **Sales Revenue**

4. We will assume we have last period's actual data and will enter it in cells D5 and D6. To tie in with the example model, enter the values **100** in cell D5 and **2.00** in cell D6. When running analyses, these numbers should tie into realized, audited figures from the last period.
5. The values just entered in cells D5 and D6 should be grown over the projection periods by the growth rates from the Vectors sheet. Enter the following formulas in the corresponding cells:

 E5: =D5*(1+Vectors!E12)
 E6: =D6*(1+Vectors!E13)

 Copy and paste these formulas over to column J within their respective rows.
6. Enter the following formula in cell D7:

 =D5*D6

 Copy and paste this formula over range D7:J7. This row represents the amounts of revenue from sales that we would expect to receive over the forecast period.
7. The next two rows on the income statement are where the cost of goods sold is calculated. Enter the text **Cost Units** in cell B8. We will assume the last period's actual data is a value of .5. This should be entered in cell D8. The cost unit is how much each unit cost and is grown by a rate on the Vectors sheet. Enter the following formula in cell E8:

 =D8*(1+Vectors!E14)

 Copy and paste this formula over the range E8:J8.
8. The next row is the actual cost of goods sold. Enter the text **Cost of goods sold** in cell B9. Enter a value of **70** in cell D9 as a historic assumption. As we will

	A	B	C	D	E	F	G	H	I	J
1	**Income Statement**									
2					Projected ---->					TV Year
3				12/31/2007	12/31/2008	12/31/2009	12/31/2010	12/31/2011	12/31/2012	12/31/2013
4										
5		Sales Units		100.00	105.00	110.25	115.76	121.55	127.63	130.18
6		Sales Price		2.00	2.10	2.21	2.32	2.43	2.55	2.60
7		Sales Revenue		200.00	220.50	243.10	268.02	295.49	325.78	338.94
8		Cost Units		0.50	0.53	0.56	0.60	0.63	0.67	0.71
9		Cost of Goods Sold		70.00						
10		**Gross Profit**		130.00						

FIGURE 3.19 The top of the income statement starts with revenue and cost of goods sold to get the gross margin. Note that this will not be complete until we finish the balance sheet.

link the cost of goods sold to our inventory assumption, we cannot complete this section until Chapter 4. In general, though, the cost of goods sold represents the dollar amount of cost to produce the sales revenue.

9. The difference between sales revenue and cost of goods sold is gross profit. Prepare for the gross profit calculation by entering the text **Gross Profit** in cell B10. Enter the following formula in cell D10:

=D7-D9

Copy and paste this formula over the range D10:J10. Thus far, the Income Statement sheet should look like Figure 3.19.

10. After the gross profit, there are more operating expenses to a company, such as selling, general, and administrative costs (SG&A). SG&A can be further broken down into components of sales and non-sales or kept consolidated as in the example model. Salary, rent, administrative costs, advertising costs, and so on are normally captured in the SGA cost line. Enter the text **SG&A expense** in cell B11. Assume the historical period's amount is 27 by entering that value in D11. Here SG&A was calculated as a percentage of revenue. To be consistent with that calculation, enter the following formula in cell E11:

=E7*Vectors!E15

Copy and paste this formula over the range E11:J11.

11. Other operating expenses might also need to be included. For this reason, enter the text **Operating expenses** in cell B12. Enter the value **9.30** for the historical period in cell D12. Then enter the following formula in cell E12:

=E7*Vectors!E16

Copy and paste this formula over the range E12:J12.

12. In cell B13, we will calculate the earnings before interest, taxes, depreciation and amortization (EBITDA). Enter the text **EBITDA** in cell B30. Enter the following formula in D13:

=D10-D11-D12

Copy and paste this formula over the range D13:J13.

13. If you are following along with the complete model on the CD-ROM, you will notice that the next two lines in the income statement are for depreciation and amortization. These are items we will go into more detail with after the balance sheet is introduced and fill in on the income statement later. For now, let's set up some of the functionality for when we return to those topics by entering the text **EBIT** in cell B17. Enter the following formula in cell D17:

=D13-D15-D16

Copy and paste this formula over the range D17:J17. For those unaccustomed to the semantics, *EBIT* stands for *earnings before interest and taxes* (basically EBITDA, less the depreciation and amortization).

14. After the core earnings are determined, there occasionally can be non-operating expenses such as damaged goods, insurance costs, and so on. To incorporate this concept, enter the text **Non-operating expenses** in cell B19. Enter the value **2** in cell D19 for the historical year and then enter the following formula in cell E19:

=E7*Vectors!E17

This formula should be copied and pasted over the range E19:J19.

15. Similar to depreciation and amortization, we are going to skip over the interest income and expense section of the income statement. These amounts will be generated once we work through the balance sheet and then connected to the income statement. Skip down to cell B33 and enter the text **EBT**. This will be where we calculate the EBIT net of interest expense. Enter the following formula in cell D33:

=D17-D19+D25-D32

Copy and paste this formula over the range D33:J33. Note that even though we skipped over concepts, we inserted the addition and subtraction for the future items in this formula. As we complete the income statement in later chapters, this formula will make more sense.

16. We have now added all taxable income and netted tax-shielding expenses. The amount that is left, the earnings before tax (EBT), is what is taxed. We need to set up the Vectors sheet with our tax assumption. As this possibly could be part of scenarios, we will enter the hard-coded percentages under scenario names and

▲	A	B	C	D	E	F	G	H	I	J
61										
62	Tax Rate				30.0%	30.0%	30.0%	30.0%	30.0%	30.0%

FIGURE 3.20 The tax rate figures are stored under each scenario and can be adjusted depending on the scenario selected.

reference them using the CHOOSE function in the live/current scenario section. To do this, go to the Vectors sheet and enter the label **Tax Rate** in cell B31 and then set cells B62, B93, and B124 equal to cell B31.

17. For all of the scenarios each period, assume the tax rate is 30%. This value should be entered in each cell in the following ranges:

E62:J62
E93:J93
E124:J124

Figure 3.20 shows the new addition to the base case section of the Vectors sheet.

18. Enter the following formula in cell E31 on the Vectors sheet:

=CHOOSE(ctrl_ScenNmbr,E62,E93,E124,E155)

Copy and paste this formula over the range E31:J31.

19. With the Vectors sheet done for this section, go back to the Income Statement sheet. Enter the text **Tax Provision** in cell B35. Enter the following formula in cell D35:

=D33*Vectors!E31

Copy and paste this formula over the range D35:J35. This formula multiplies the EBT by the current period's tax rate to determine the tax liability.

20. The major item of the Income Statement, the net income, can now be calculated. Enter the text **Net Income** in cell B36 and then enter the following formula in cell D36:

=D33-D35

Copy and paste this formula over the range D36:J36.

21. Enter the text **Dividends** in cell B38. Assume historical dividends were **5** by entering the value in cell D38. We will assume a growing expectation of dividends. Enter the following values in the corresponding cells:

E38: **5**
F38: **5**
G38: **10**

A	B	C	D	E	F	G	H	I	J
33	**EBT**		85.20						
34									
35	Tax Provision		25.56						
36	**Net Income**		59.64						
37									
38	Dividends		5.00	5.00	5.00	10.00	10.00	10.00	10.00
39	**Net to Retained Earnings**		54.64						

FIGURE 3.21 The bottom of the income statement contains very important items, including the net income and the net to retained earnings.

> H38: **10**
> I38: **10**
> J38: **10**

This is just a proxy value to get information into the income statement, but dividends would tend to be estimated based on performance, historical payouts, and shares outstanding. Keep in mind that dividends usually get locked out if the company is distressed. We will examine this idea later since we can build a switch to lock out dividends if necessary.

22. Enter the text **Net to Retained Earnings** in cell B39. Then enter the following formula in cell D39:

> =D36-D38

Copy and paste this formula over the range D39:J39. Retained earnings are very important since they represent the equity put back into the firm. From a modeling perspective, this line is also very important since it will be directly referenced on the balance sheet. The bottom of the income statement should look like Figure 3.21.

A WORK IN PROGRESS

The income statement is not done yet, but we have made significant progress. Throughout future Model Builders we will add to the Assumptions, Vectors, and Income Statement sheets. Keep in mind that the model is being assembled in a conceptual fashion. We will complete concepts as much as possible until we run into sections where one concept is dependent on another concept. This is the case after finishing a majority of the income statement, which describes the general cash flow of the business. The dependent concept is the capital structure of the firm, which is captured by the balance sheet and the various items that make up assets, liabilities, and equity.

TOOLBOX

AVERAGE

The AVERAGE function is a very easy function to determine the arithmetic average of a set of numbers. The entry parameters are the numbers that are to be averaged:

AVERAGE(value 1, value 2, ... value n)

The mathematical operation performed adds up all of the values of the numbers and divides by the count of items. For example, if we entered the following formula we would get an answer of 6:

=AVERAGE(3,5,10)

The answer returned starts with $3 + 5 + 10$, which is equal to 18. Divide 18 by the count of 3 numbers that were added together, and we get 6.

AVERAGEIF

AVERAGEIF is a useful function if there are conditions to the average that we are creating. The entry parameters require three different pieces of information:

AVERAGEIF(range that contains a condition to be tested, the conditional test, possible values to average)

In this chapter, we used AVERAGEIF when explaining growth-rate methodologies. In Figure 3.22, we can see that range E7:E12 contains values of Y and N. These are just text values depending on the user's preference and entry, and would be the first entry parameter for the AVERAGEIF function. The second entry parameter is a conditional test. In this example we want to average values only if there is a Y in the range E7:E12. The conditional test that should be entered is just the letter we are looking for: "Y." Make sure to use double quotes around the Y; otherwise, Excel will think you are trying to reference a named range or a different function. The last entry parameter is the range of values that can possibly be included in the average (range D7:D12).

Here are three important points to keep in mind when using AVERAGEIF:

1. The range that contains the condition to be tested must have the exact same number of items as the range that contains the possible values to average.
2. Conditional tests done with text must be bounded by double quotes on each side.
3. If you want to use more than one conditional test, there is an AVERAGEIFS function that accepts multiple conditions.

	A	B	C	D	E
1	*Growth Rates*				
2	The following exercise will examine three different me are four sections, but two of the sections are based on t				
3					
4	1) Arithmetic Average				
5		Year	Revenue	Growth Rate	Include
6		2002	150		
7		2003	178	18.67%	N
8		2004	210	17.98%	N
9		2005	247	17.62%	N
10		2006	275	11.34%	Y
11		2007	295	7.27%	Y
12		2008	310	5.08%	Y
13	Arithmetic Avg:			12.99%	7.90%

FIGURE 3.22 The AVERAGEIF function allows users to define conditional tests so only certain values are captured in the arithmetic average.

PRODUCT

The PRODUCT function is a mathematical function that returns the product of values that are entered as an array. The PRODUCT function's entry parameters include:

PRODUCT(value 1, value 2, value n)

For instance, if **=PRODUCT(1,3,2)** were entered, the cell value would be 6 (1 * 3 * 2).

GEOMEAN

Rather than calculating the geometric mean by hand, the GEOMEAN function calculates it for us. The entry parameters for the GEOMEAN function include:

GEOMEAN(value 1, value 2, value n)

The official formula for GEOMEAN is (value 1 * value 2 * value n)^(1/n). In this example, n stands for the eventual number of values to be averaged.

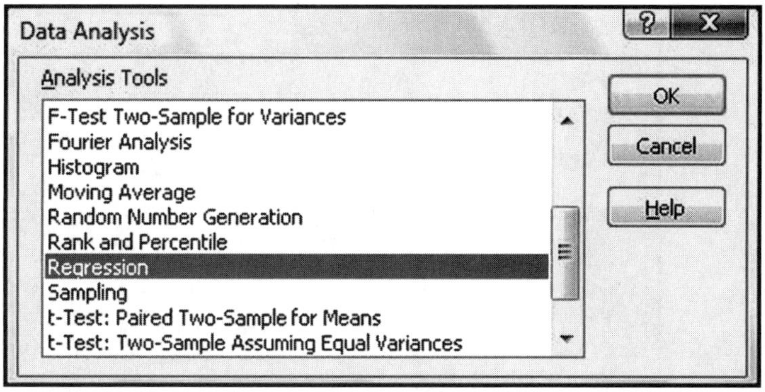

FIGURE 3.23 There are a number of data analysis tools to quickly perform complex analyses on data sets.

Data Analysis—Regression

Excel 2003 and 2007 provide powerful data analysis tools. Many can be recreated using math or prebuilt functions, but Excel's data analysis tools often provide the most complete flexibility and results. To access data analysis tools in Excel 2003, go to the Tools menu and select **Data Analysis**. For Excel 2007, go to the Data menu and select the Data Analysis button from the Analysis grouping. If you did not install the Analysis Tool Pak Add-In, the Data Analysis selections will not appear.

Regardless of your Excel version, after you select data analysis you will be presented with the Data Analysis dialogue box seen in Figure 3.23.

As part of this example we will select the Regression option from the list of possible data analysis techniques. This brings up the Regression data analysis dialogue box as shown in Figure 3.24.

For example purposes we will use a data set with an obvious relationship: the price of oil and Nigerian GDP from the years 2000 to 2005. In this example we assume that Nigerian GDP is dependent on the price of oil. To establish this relationship and understand how we could forecast Nigerian GDP based on the price of oil, we will use Excel's regression tool. Once we have the Regression dialogue box open, we need to determine the dependent variable and the independent variable(s). As we learned from step 12 of Model Builder 3.1, the known y's are the dependent variable data points. The known x's are the independent variables. The regression tool changes the terminology slightly and asks for the "Input Y-Range" for the dependent variable and the "Input X-Range" for the independent variable. Figure 3.25 shows the Regression dialogue box with the entry parameters for the dependent and independent variables.

A very important nuance is the "Labels" box, which in the example is checked. This means that the variable data's first row contains a label and not data. Notice that the range references in the dialogue box encapsulate the labels on the worksheet

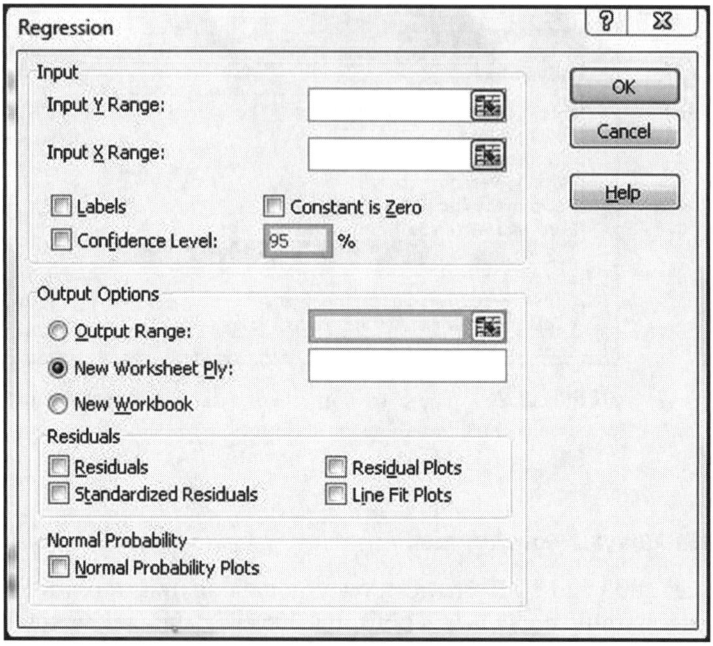

FIGURE 3.24 Regression parameters are entered into a dialogue box to give us the most flexibility with our analysis.

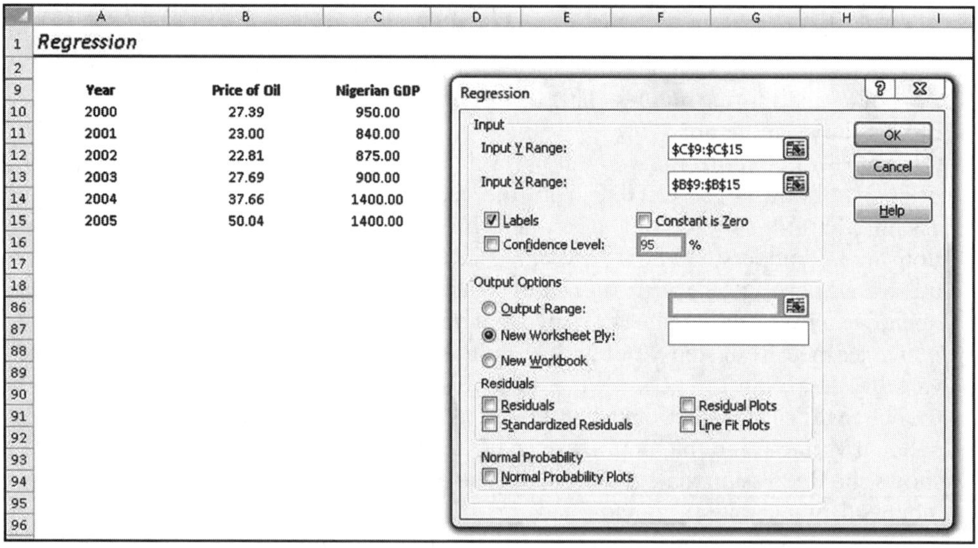

FIGURE 3.25 Entry parameters using the dependent and independent variable data are loaded into the Regression dialogue box.

(both cell B9 and cell C9 are labels, which are referenced in the dialogue box). If we referenced those cells without checking the labels box we would get an error. Even worse, if we merely referenced data cells and left the Labels box checked we would miss data since Excel would think the first row was a label. It is recommended to use labels since the regression outputs are difficult enough to interpret on their own and even harder without labels!

Also notice in Figure 3.25 that there is a section in the Regression dialogue box called "Output Options." In this area, we can choose to have the regression data output as a separate workbook, a worksheet within the current workbook, or on the sheet where the data is contained. The regression output takes 18 rows' and 9 columns' worth of cell space, so if it is kept on the sheet there should be plenty of room. Otherwise, the output could overwrite existing data. In our example, we will export the data to cell E9 on the current worksheet. There is a particularly annoying issue when selecting "Output Range:" as we do in this example. When the option button is selected, the dependent data is automatically highlighted. If a user immediately selects cell E9, the dependent data entry parameter will be overridden to reference cell E9. After selecting the Output Range: option button, make sure to click in the associated field in the dialogue box to avoid this problem. Once the output option is selected, we are ready to run the regression by pressing **OK**. There are many other options for the regression, but we will demonstrate the minimum inputs necessary to get the regression data.

If you have been following along, the output should look similar to Figure 3.26. This figure also highlights the more important sections of the output using bold borders.

	E	F	G	H	I	J	K	L	M	N
9		SUMMARY OUTPUT								
10										
11		*Regression Statistics*								
12		Multiple R	0.92							
13		R Square	0.85							
14		Adjusted R Square	0.81							
15		Standard Error	115.17							
16		Observations	6							
17										
18		ANOVA								
19			*df*	*SS*	*MS*	*F*	*Significance F*			
20		Regression	1	298460.87	298460.87	22.50	0.01			
21		Residual	4	53059.96	13264.99					
22		Total	5	351520.83						
23										
24			*Coefficients*	*Standard Error*	*t Stat*	*P-value*	*Lower 95%*	*Upper 95%*	*Lower 95.0%*	*Upper 95.0%*
25		Intercept	335.73	159.93	2.10	0.10	-108.31	779.78	-108.31	779.78
26		Price of Oil	23.07	4.86	4.74	0.0090	9.57	36.57	9.57	36.57

FIGURE 3.26 The Excel regression tool returns a robust set of results.

	A	B	C	D	E	O
				D10 ▼	f_x	=$G$26*B10+$G$25
3						
4						
5						
6						
7						
8						
9	Year	Price of Oil	Nigerian GDP	Back Test		
10	2000	27.39	950.00	967.60		
11	2001	23.00	840.00	866.32		
12	2002	22.81	875.00	861.94		
13	2003	27.69	900.00	974.52		
14	2004	37.66	1400.00	1204.52		
15	2005	50.04	1400.00	1490.11		

FIGURE 3.27   A back test of our regression output should yield figures that are close to our dependent variable.

The first part of the regression that we want to understand is the relationship between Nigerian GDP and the price of oil. Recall the scatter plot in Model Builder 3.1 and the formula for determining the trend line between the data points: $y = mx + b$. In this case our slope is m, which we can find in the Excel outputs as the Price of Oil Coefficient (23.07). Our intercept is b, which is appropriately labeled Intercept Coefficient (335.73). This means that our formula for the relationship between the Nigerian GDP and the price of oil is $y = 23.07x + 335.73$, with x being the price of oil and y being Nigerian GDP. How can we back-test this to make sure we are doing things correctly? Let's use this formula on the example's historical oil prices and see what Nigerian GDPs would be returned. Figure 3.27 shows the Excel formula referencing the regression output and the results of applying the regression formula.

The results of the back test are close to the historical values, but not exact. Inexact figures from the back test are normal since most regression analyses have error. The standard error of each variable and the regression are also returned by Excel, as seen in Figure 3.26. Standard errors give us an indication of the variation of each of the data sets and the regression as a whole. The main result to notice is that our P value is less than .05, which means our regression is significant. The other critical element is the R square. This tells us how strong of a relationship the two variables have. The R square will be a number between 0 and 1. The higher the R square, the more the variability witnessed by the dependent variable is explained by the independent variable. In our example, 85% of the variability in Nigerian GDP is caused by the variability in oil prices.

Here are three final points to keep in mind when using the regression tool in Excel:

1. Up to 16 independent variables can be loaded as the Input X-Range.
2. The P value is *not* the probability of the variable occurring.
3. The ANOVA information is typically useful only if you are testing more than three variables for explanatory purposes. Otherwise, in a two-variable situation the significance F and the P value for the correlation coefficient will be the same.

LINEST

Rather than have a full set of outputs returned, a shortcut to getting key regression information is using the LINEST function. LINEST stands for *line estimate* and generally returns information necessary for creating and assessing a trend line estimate for a least squares regression. The function accepts the following entry parameters:

LINEST(known y's, known x's, constant, statistics)

Just as before, the known *y*'s are the dependent variables, the known *x*'s are the independent variables, the constant is an optional entry if we have one for the line estimate, and the statistics entry is either a TRUE or FALSE. If the statistic entry is left blank or FALSE, the function will return only the slope and the intercept. If the statistic entry is set to TRUE, then the function returns the slope, intercept, standard error of the variables, standard error of the regression, the R square, the regression F statistic, the residual degrees of freedom, and the residual sum of squares.

Using LINEST is tricky though because it is set up to be used as an array function. An array function can return multiple values using the same formula. To get the LINEST function to work correctly and return the full set of statistics, we need to highlight a two-column-by-five-row area on the sheet. The correct amount of cells along with the previous Toolbox section's data set is depicted in Figure 3.28.

We can then enter the formula by typing in the function, referring to the dependent and independent variables in the correct order, skipping over the constant entry, but remembering to type TRUE for the statistics entry. The complete formula should look like:

=LINEST(C4:C9,B4:B9,,TRUE)

Finally, instead of just pressing **ENTER**, we need to hold down **CTRL** and **SHFT** and then press **ENTER**. This tells Excel that we are entering an array formula. If CTRL-SHFT is not held down while pressing ENTER, then only the upper-leftmost cell, from the cells that were highlighted, will be populated with the first return value: the slope.

	E3	▼	f_x	{=LINEST(C4:C9,B4:B9,,TRUE)}	

	A	B	C	D	E	F
1	*LINEST*					
2						
3	Year	Price of Oil	Nigerian GDP		23.0691	335.7331
4	2000	27.39	950.00		4.863404	159.9328
5	2001	23.00	840.00		0.849056	115.1737
6	2002	22.81	875.00		22.49989	4
7	2003	27.69	900.00		298460.9	53059.96
8	2004	37.66	1400.00			
9	2005	50.04	1400.00			

FIGURE 3.28 The LINEST function can return the main statistics we need from a least squares regression. This must be done in a very specific manner since LINEST is meant to be used as an array function.

Individual Regression Functions (SLOPE, INTERCEPT, RSQ, STEYX)

Sometimes even the LINEST function returns too much information. In the case of our growth rates, we are often concerned with only a few specific statistics. Namely, we would like to know the slope and perhaps a few other measures of confidence in our figures. For many of the important regression statistics there are individual functions that can be used. Each one accepts the same entry parameters:

"Any regression based function"(known y's, known x's)

The following important functions work in the same way and are depicted in Figure 3.29:

SLOPE returns the slope of the regression.
INTERCEPT returns the intercept of the regression.
RSQ returns the R square of the regression.
STEYX returns the standard error of the regression.

FORECAST

A function that often goes overlooked but is actually very powerful is the FORECAST function. This function runs a full least squares regression on historical data, takes a new independent sample, and then provides the forecasted dependent data. The entry parameters for the FORECAST function are as follows:

FORECAST(new independent data, known y's, known x's)

	A	B	C	D	E	F
1	**Individual Regression Functions**					
2						
3	**Year**	**Price of Oil**	**Nigerian GDP**			
4	2000	27.39	950.00		SLOPE	23.0691
5	2001	23.00	840.00		INTERCEPT	335.7331
6	2002	22.81	875.00		RSQ	0.85
7	2003	27.69	900.00		STEYX	115.1737
8	2004	37.66	1400.00			
9	2005	50.04	1400.00			

FIGURE 3.29 Individual functions can be used to return regression results.

For example, we can demonstrate the FORECAST function and prove its calculations using the oil/Nigerian GDP example. In Figure 3.30, an estimate of Nigerian GDP is provided given a $100 price of oil. This is done in two ways: the first using the slope and intercept of the data and then using the equation $y = mx + b$, and the second using the FORECAST function.

Essentially, the FORECAST function returns the estimated dependent value given a new independent data point and a set of historical data that defines the relationship between the two variables.

E11			f_x	=FORECAST(D11,E4:E9,D4:D9)			
	A	B	C	D	E	F	G	H
1	**FORECAST Function**							
2								
3			**Year**	**Price of Oil**	**Nigerian GDP**		**Slope**	23.0691
4			2000	27.39	950.00		**Intercept**	335.7331
5			2001	23.00	840.00			
6			2002	22.81	875.00			
7			2003	27.69	900.00			
8			2004	37.66	1400.00			
9			2005	50.04	1400.00			
10	Using Formula		Test Price	100.00	2642.64			
11	Using FORECAST		Test Price	100.00	2642.64			

FIGURE 3.30 The FORECAST function runs a least squares regression and provides dependent data estimates based on new independent data.

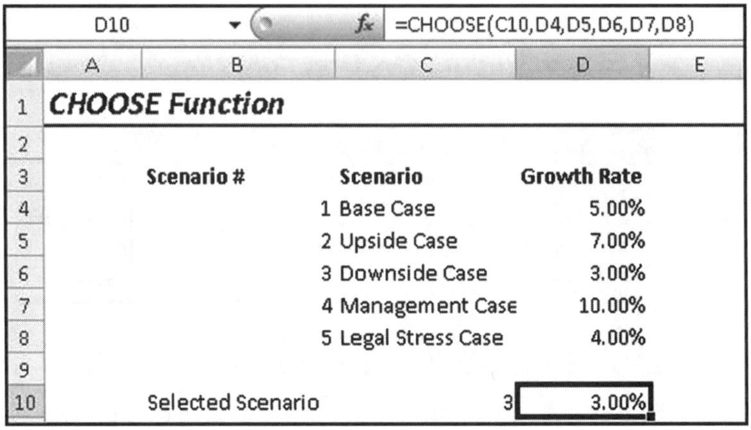

D10 | =CHOOSE(C10,D4,D5,D6,D7,D8)

	A	B	C	D	E
1	**CHOOSE Function**				
2					
3		Scenario #	Scenario	Growth Rate	
4			1 Base Case	5.00%	
5			2 Upside Case	7.00%	
6			3 Downside Case	3.00%	
7			4 Management Case	10.00%	
8			5 Legal Stress Case	4.00%	
9					
10		Selected Scenario	3	3.00%	

FIGURE 3.31 The CHOOSE function is frequently used to manage scenarios.

CHOOSE

The CHOOSE function is often used in corporate valuation models for scenario selection. The entry parameters for the CHOOSE function are as follows:

CHOOSE(index number, choice 1, choice 2, choice 3 . . .)

The way this function works is the user enters or references what is known as the *index number*. This number is the selection from the upcoming choices that will be returned. For instance, if the index number is a 2, then choice 2 will be returned. Figure 3.31 depicts this functionality with an index number of 3 and the third value of five possible values being returned.

Keep in mind that we could further automate this example by using a data validation list so the user selects a scenario, then using a MATCH function to return the scenario number, and then referencing or integrating the MATCH return into the CHOOSE function. This functionality also can be seen in the Toolbox Ch.3.xls file.

Here are some important points to keep in mind when using the CHOOSE function:

- The values must be entered one at a time. You cannot reference a range of possible values such as CHOOSE(1,D15:D19). This would have to be entered:

  CHOOSE(1,D15,D16,D17,D18,D19)

- Alternative scenario systems can be implemented using a reference combination such as OFFSET MATCH. These systems are faster to implement, but are problematic if there are different numbers of rows for scenarios or the data is not in a continuous range.

CHAPTER 4

Capital Structure and Balance Sheet

Even with strong revenue, a firm can experience financial stress and possible bankruptcy if its assets, liabilities, and capital structure are poorly selected or structured. Management has the ability to select or partially control nearly all items that relate to the sources and uses of funds in the firm. On the asset side, the more obvious items are large capital expenditure projects such as building a new warehouse; a more obscure one could be directing in-store advertising toward more cash versus credit sales. As for the liabilities and capital structure, management is responsible for determining how to fund assets. They have the ability to select different types of debt and equity or work with other entities to structure financing to fit the company's needs. All of the financing comes at a cost, which revenue must be able to cover in the long term.

Companies can have innumerable variations of assets, liabilities, and capital structure. There is an expansive spectrum of combinations. On the extremes, a manufacturing firm may have multiple warehouses and machinery and be financed mostly with equity, while a financial services company may have assets consisting of complex financial instruments and equally complex financial products making up its capital structure. To make sense of all of these possibilities, accountants created a financial statement known as the *balance sheet*. This financial statement is an organized account of what the company owns, what the company owes, and how much of the company is owned. It is broken down into standard categories, typically organized from the most liquid items to least liquid.

Each of the items that compose a firm fits into one of the standard categories of the balance sheet, as shown in Figure 4.1. The most critical concept that accountants built into the creation of the balance sheet is the *balance principle*: Assets must always equal liabilities plus equity. Simply put, nothing is free. Whenever an asset is created, funds are used to do so. If there is an imbalance between assets and liabilities plus equity, it means something is unaccounted for and the analyst's view of the company is incomplete.

An unbalanced balance sheet should never occur in past audited financial statements. This is because historical balance sheets reflect a specific moment or snapshot in time. In corporate valuation modeling, we are making predictions about the future, which could create instances of an unbalanced balance sheet. For example, we may assume the company will build a particular plant that is primarily funded

ASSETS		LIABILITIES	
Cash and near cash		Accounts payable	
Marketable securities		ST borrowings	
Accounts receivable		Other current liabilities	
Inventories			
Other current assets			
Current assets		**Current liabilities**	
Gross fixed assets		LT borrowings	
Accumulated depreciation		**Total liabilities**	
Net fixed assets			
		EQUITY	
Intangibles		Minority interest	
Amortization		Total common equity	
Net intangibles		Retained earnings	
		Total equity	
LT investments & receivables			
Total assets		**Total liabilities & equity**	

FIGURE 4.1 Although each company's balance sheet could have a variety of items, most are grouped in standard categories in descending order of liquidity.

by a long-term debt issuance. Multiple assumptions that vary across possible stress scenarios can easily throw off the balance of assets, liabilities, and equity. One example would be an expected decrease in the cost of the building the plant. Holding all other variables constant, we would have a situation where we issued more funds from the loan than necessary. This causes the balance principle to be violated by having liabilities and equity greater than assets. Our model needs to account for and repair any imbalance. We will see that in corporate valuation modeling we will always maintain the cardinal rule of assets equaling liabilities plus equity, but rather than wasting time balancing the balance sheet each period, we will set up our model in such a way that it does so automatically. Figure 4.2 is a graphic of this cardinal rule.

To accomplish our goal of thoroughly understanding the balance sheet and implementing it in a model, we will dedicate two additional chapters beyond this one. Since the balance sheet describes the entire underpinnings of a company, there are sections that we will want to analyze in as much detail as possible. Although this could vary among companies, the most common sections that require in-depth analysis are capital expenditures, depreciation, amortization, and long-term debt. This chapter will provide an overview and framework for the balance sheet; Chapters 5

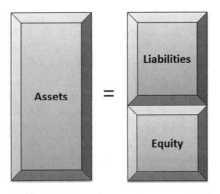

FIGURE 4.2 Assets must always equal liabilities plus equity. Historically, this is easy to see, but in a projection model we must automate the balancing process.

and 6 examine the aforementioned sections in detail. As with all chapters, we will begin with theory and concept discussion, move on to Model Builder instructions, and wrap up with a Toolbox.

WHAT THE COMPANY OWNS

An asset is an item that the company owns. The more tangible items include warehouses, plants, machinery, and equipment. Financial instruments such as cash, receivables, and securities are also classified as assets. Regardless of the type of asset, the focus of analysis for assets is understanding their value. Some assets are easy to value, such as cash or highly liquid securities, while others are problematic, such as illiquid securities or defaulting receivables. To get a better understanding of the nuances involved in analyzing assets, we will go through the primary asset categories, their descriptions, and valuation issues.

Cash and Highly Liquid Securities

One of the most seemingly straightforward but often misunderstood concepts is cash. I typically distinguish between three types of cash in a valuation:

1. *Cash:* the minimum amount necessary to operate the company
2. *Surplus cash:* any cash projected that is above and beyond the minimum amount necessary to operate the company
3. *Marketable securities:* securities that are highly liquid

Be careful when distinguishing between these three. The first item, cash, is the cash necessary for the company to operate. For most nonfinancial institutions this should not be an extraordinary number. Cash projected can be valued at its face value. Rare exceptions include businesses in emerging market countries with highly devaluing currency. These businesses may keep large reserves of foreign currency or may have entered into currency swaps, which will show up on a different part of the balance sheet. Also keep in mind that cash typically earns a small amount of interest, which can be integrated into a valuation model each period.

Surplus cash is merely a concept for projection models. This is technically the "plug" on the asset side. When a model's liabilities plus equity are greater than the assets, the remaining cash can be thought of as surplus. Think about what would cause liabilities and equity to become greater than the assets. A tangible example would be a capital expenditure that actually costs less than what was funded through debt. If the capital expenditure cost $98 million and $100 million of long-term debt was issued, there is $2 million of surplus cash. We will work with this concept in detail when we must set up an automatic balancing of the model.

The third and final cash item is marketable securities. These could be investments in money market accounts, certificates of deposit, or guaranteed investment contracts (GICs). They are typically very secure, short-term investments that are valued at their face amount. Figure 4.3 depicts the three cash items and when they occur.

Accounts Receivable

When an order is shipped or a sale is made in a store, a receivable is generated. That receivable either can be paid instantly with a form of cash or it can be paid over time. Usually businesses try to keep accounts receivable to as short a duration as possible and will offer deals such as *2% 10 net thirty*, meaning that if the customer

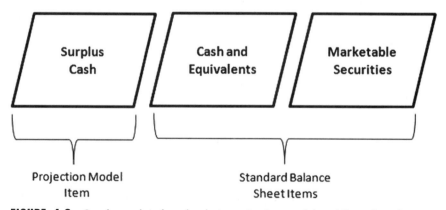

FIGURE 4.3 Surplus cash is found only in projection models, while cash and marketable securities are standard balance sheet items.

pays within 10 days of goods delivery, then a 2% discount will be applied to the receivable; otherwise, the receivable is due in 30 days.

Other forms of discounts can include product-placement discounts or discounts eventually passed on to customers, for which the firm is ultimately responsible. These discounts should be noted in the company's financial statements. For corporate valuation modeling it's important that the figures used to project accounts receivable include these discounts; otherwise, the accounts receivable value could be overstated.

Another valuation problem with accounts receivable relates to doubtful accounts or a bad loan reserve. Holders of accounts receivable are subject to an obligor's ability and propensity to pay. When accounts receivable become very delinquent, there is an eventual expectation that they will not pay. For companies with small-to-medium accounts receivable a bad loan reserve percentage based on historical bad loans can be applied to decrease the accounts receivable figure. If accounts receivable is a core component of the business operation, then more sophisticated techniques may be appropriate. For example, a valuation that I completed involved an appliance and electronics retailer that sold three-fourths of its products on credit. These sales were booked as accounts receivable. The consumers who purchased these products were of average-to-poor credit quality, with default rates in the upper teens. Defaults followed specific timing patterns typical of consumer credit portfolios. Given the size of the credit sales as a percent of the total revenue and the high default rates, a detailed delinquency and default analysis was integrated into the valuation model.

Inventories

Finished products ready for sale and materials that are ready to be made into products are accounted for as inventory. Three categories usually comprise inventory:

1. *Raw materials:* unprocessed materials
2. *Work in process (WIP):* products in production (i.e., between a raw material and a finished good).
3. *Finished goods:* complete, ready-to-sell products

The major valuation challenge with inventories is timing, which is captured by two different accounting methods. The first method is *first-in-first-out* (FIFO), which is the only method of inventory accounting that IFRS allows. When an item is sold, its value moves from the inventory account on the balance sheet to the cost of goods section of the income statement. Under FIFO, the amount by which that inventory account should be reduced is based on the cost of making the oldest of the same product in inventory.

Under the *last-in-first-out* (LIFO) method, the last product made in inventory represents the value that is removed from the inventory account. Often a company is constantly producing and selling products, allowing LIFO-based inventory valuation to use only the latest product costs for their products. Critics of LIFO contend that the method allows lower inventory valuation and higher cost of goods sold than in actuality. For this reason, IFRS does not allow LIFO-based valuation. In order to compare the results of two valuation models, their inventory valuation methodologies must be the same.

Other Current Assets

Any other item that is liquid within the next 12 months is considered a current asset. Typical other current assets are prepaid expenses, which are items or services that have been paid for but not yet received. These can include:

- Vendor deposits
- Salary advances
- Prepaid rent
- Insurance premiums

Property, Plant and Equipment (PP&E)

The most tangible items within a company are often categorized under property, plant, and equipment. Land, warehouses, production plants, and equipment items of varying sizes are grouped into this category. Specific examples depend on the type of company that is under consideration. For example, an airline company would have multiple planes, repair equipment, warehouses, and hangars under this category. Alternatively, an energy company would primarily list its property and energy plants.

A key point to keep in mind is that PP&E is listed at book value. This is typically thought of as *gross PP&E*. Plant and equipment lose value over time due to wear and tear, otherwise known as *depreciation*. This depreciation is accumulated over time and netted out of gross PP&E to arrive at *net PP&E*. Until an asset is disposed of, its book value is listed under gross PP&E and its accumulated depreciation is netted out. Net PP&E is counted toward the value of the assets.

Notice in the previous paragraph that *land* was not included as an item that loses value over time. Under IFRS, land is not depreciated as part of PP&E.

Intangibles

If PP&E categorizes the tangible assets of the firm, *intangibles* categorizes the intangible assets of a company. What is an *intangible*? Items such as patents, copyrights, trademarks, licenses, other forms of intellectual property rights, and goodwill are examples of intangible assets. Essentially, they are items with value that do not have a tangible form.

Intangibles are challenging to value since they often can be unique; however, they are treated similarly to PP&E in that they can lose value over time. Patents expire, technology can be replaced, and overall intangible value erodes over time. For these reasons, intangible values are amortized over a specific useful life, similar to depreciation. Gross intangibles are kept on the balance sheet along with accumulated intangible amortization. Net intangibles are counted toward the value of the assets.

Goodwill is an exception for intangibles. IFRS 3 and SFAS 142 ended the amortization of goodwill. It is, however, periodically reviewed for impairment.

Other Long-Term Assets and Receivables

Oftentimes a company has some type of long-term investment, such as bond or note investment. This section of companies' balance sheets has come under quite a bit of scrutiny since the advent of the mortgage-backed security (MBS) credit crisis that originated in 2007. Purchasers of MBSs and other structured finance securities typically list these assets on the balance sheets in this section. Overall, two general methods of valuing long-term assets are to use market values or to create an intrinsic valuation based on expected cash flow. Intrinsic valuation can be very challenging given the complexity of some of these assets; however, systems and consulting companies exist that are able to process very detailed valuations of such assets.

MODEL BUILDER 4.1: STARTING THE BALANCE SHEET WITH ASSETS

1. Insert a worksheet after the Income Statement sheet and name it **Balance Sheet**.
2. In cell A1, enter the text **Balance Sheet**.
3. Similar to the other sheets, we will create the balance sheet as a projection and require the dates that we are projecting. As an example, the first three cells of this section on the Balance Sheet sheet should have the following values in the corresponding cells:

   D2: =Vectors!D9
   E2: =Vectors!E9
   F2: =Vectors!F9

   This referencing pattern should continue for range G2:Z2. Also, complete a similar referencing pattern for row 3. The first three cells of this section are shown below:

   D3: =Vectors!D10
   E3: =Vectors!E10
   F3: =Vectors!F10

   Continue this referencing pattern for range G3:Z3. Refer to Figure 4.4 to make sure you are completing this step correctly.

	A	B	C	D	E	F	G	H	I	J
1	*Balance Sheet*									
2				Projected ---->						TV Year
3				12/31/2007	12/31/2008	12/31/2009	12/31/2010	12/31/2011	12/31/2012	12/31/2013

FIGURE 4.4 The dates and timing are continued on the Balance Sheet sheet.

4. We will start at the top of the balance sheet with assets, specifically current assets. Enter the text **Assets** in cell B5 as a label. Then enter the following text in the corresponding cells to get the labels down for current assets:

B6: **Surplus Funds**
B7: **Minimum Cash**
B8: **Marketable Securities**
B9: **Accounts Receivable**
B10: **Inventory (units)**
B11: **Inventory Unit Purchases**
B12: **Inventory Dollar Purchases**
B13: **Inventory (dollars)**
B14: **Other Current Assets**
B15: **Current Assets**

5. With the labels complete, we should now insert one year of historical information. Enter the following values in the corresponding cell references:

D7: **10**
D8: **4**
D9: **17**
D10: **5**
D11: **0**
D12: **0**
D13: **10**
D14: **1**

Also enter the formula **=SUM(D6:D9,D13:D14)** in cell D15. This will total the historic current assets. Copy and paste that formula over the range D15:J15. Thus far the Balance Sheet sheet should look like Figure 4.5.

6. We go back to the Vectors sheet and create the assumptions for the balance sheet. These assumptions will have been based on historical or expected performance. Studies similar to what we did for revenue should be done to understand expected performance. Also, for this model many of the assumptions are based on revenue, which may or may not be the case in other analyses. Also, while we will try to automate the model so that accounting standards are followed, make sure that

	A	B	C	D
1	**Balance Sheet**			
2				
3				12/31/2007
4				
5	Assets			
6	Surplus Funds			
7	Cash and Near Cash			10.0
8	Marketable Securities			4.0
9	Accounts Receivable			17.0
10	*Inventory (units)*			*5.0*
11	*Inventory Unit Purchases*			*0.0*
12	*Inventory Dollar Purchases*			*0.0*
13	Inventory (dollars)			10.0
14	Other Current Assets			1.0
15	Current Assets			42.0

FIGURE 4.5 The current assets in the balance sheet start to take form.

the assumptions entered make accounting sense. Let's start this by going to the Vectors sheet and entering the following text in the corresponding cells:

B19: **Balance Sheet Items**
B20: **Minimum Cash (% of Revenue)**
B21: **MS (% of Revenue)**
B22: **AR (% of Revenue)**
B23: **Inventory (% of Revenue)**
B24: **Other CA (% of Revenue)**
B25: **Other LTA (% of Revenue)**
B26: **AP (% of Inventory Purchases)**
B27: **Other CL (% of Revenue)**
B28: **Other LTL (% of Revenue)**
B29: **Other Equity (% of Revenue)**

7. As with the income statement section of the Vectors sheet, we need to set up the possible scenarios with the labels created in the previous step. Enter the following formulas in the corresponding cells:

B50, B81, B112: **=B19**
B51, B82, B113: **=B20**
B52, B83, B114: **=B21**
B53, B84, B115: **=B22**
B54, B85, B116: **=B23**
B55, B86, B117: **=B24**
B56, B87, B118: **=B25**

	A	B	C	D	E	F	G	H	I	J
50		**Balance Sheet Items**								
51		Cash (% of revenue)			5.0%	1.0%	1.0%	1.0%	1.0%	1.0%
52		MS (% revenue)			2.0%	2.0%	2.0%	2.0%	2.0%	2.0%
53		AR (% of revenue)			8.0%	8.0%	8.0%	8.0%	8.0%	8.0%
54		Inventory (% of sales units)			10%	10%	10%	10%	10%	10%
55		Other CA (% of revenue)			1.0%	1.0%	1.0%	1.0%	1.0%	1.0%
56		Other LTA (% of revenue)			10.0%	10.0%	10.0%	10.0%	10.0%	10.0%
57		AP (% of inventory purchases)			30.0%	30.0%	30.0%	30.0%	30.0%	30.0%
58		Other CL (% of revenue)			3.0%	3.0%	3.0%	3.0%	3.0%	3.0%
59		Other LTL (% of revenue)			5.0%	5.0%	5.0%	5.0%	5.0%	5.0%
60		Other Equity (% of revenue)			1.0%	1.0%	1.0%	1.0%	1.0%	1.0%

FIGURE 4.6 Proxy values for the Vectors sheet should be entered in order to generate values as we construct the model.

> B57, B88, B119: =B26
> B58, B89, B120: =B27
> B59, B90, B121: =B28
> B60, B91, B122: =B29

8. We should also put proxy numbers in for the values each period, for each scenario. Given the large number of hard-coded numbers to enter for each scenario, refer to the complete model on the CD-ROM. Figures from the balance sheet section of each scenario in the Vectors sheet can be copied and pasted directly into the model you are building. Figure 4.6 shows an example of what the base case section should look like for the balance sheet items.

9. Just as was completed for the income statement items on the Vectors sheet, we must implement formulas in the live scenario section so that the correct values are referenced in the model, depending on the scenario the user has selected. Enter the following formula in cell E20:

=CHOOSE(ctrl_ScenNmbr,E51,E82,E113,E144)

Copy and paste this formula over the range E20:J29.

10. Back on the Balance Sheet sheet, we now create formulas to project out the balance sheet items based on the Vector assumptions just entered and the projected revenue from the income statement. Enter the following formulas in the corresponding cells:

E7: ='Income Statement'!E5*Vectors!E19
E8: ='Income Statement'!E5*Vectors!E20
E9: ='Income Statement'!E5*Vectors!E21

Copy and paste these formulas across to column J. For instance, cell E7 should be copied and pasted over the range E7:J7, cell E8 should be copied and pasted over the range E8:J8, and so on.

11. Rows 10 through 13 are dedicated to calculating inventory. The first formula to enter is in cell E10:

='Income Statement'!E5*Vectors!E23

This quantifies the number of units to expect in inventory based on sold units. Next, we have to realize that we made an assumption about how many units we sold and should consider that in order to achieve those sales we need to produce the units. Therefore, we look at how many units are expected to be sold, plus how many extra were kept in inventory. This logic is expressed in the formula that should be entered in cell E11:

='Income Statement'!E5+'Balance Sheet'!E10-'Balance Sheet'!D10

We can then convert the units purchased to a dollar amount based on the cost of each unit. Do this by entering the following formula in cell E12:

=E11*'Income Statement'!E8

We can also value our inventory based on its cost value. Enter the following formula in cell E13:

=E10*'Income Statement'!E8

Copy and paste all of the formulas from this step over to column J while maintaining their respective rows.

12. Now that we know our inventory, we can jump back to the income statement to complete the cost of goods sold calculation. Go to the Income Statement sheet and enter the following formula in cell E9:

='Balance Sheet'!D13-'Balance Sheet'!E13+'Balance Sheet'!E12

Notice that this formula looks at the difference between last year's inventory and the current period's inventory and adds that amount to the purchased inventory. Think about the values currently in the example model. Inventory declines from 10 to 5.57 from 12/31/2007 to 12/31/2008, suggesting that $4.43 worth of inventory was sold. However, in order to justify the sales figures that we are posting, we must have purchased goods that were sold. We did, and this is captured in cell E12. Copy and paste cell E9 over the range E9:J9.

13. Go back to the Balance Sheet sheet and enter the following formula in cell E14:

='Income Statement'!E7*Vectors!E24

Copy and paste the formula over the range E14:J14. Thus far the current assets section of the Balance Sheet sheet should look like Figure 4.7.

	B	D	E	F	G	H	I	J
5	**Assets**							
6	Surplus Funds		0.00	62.92	136.68	236.71	350.50	470.92
7	Cash and Near Cash	10.0	11.03	2.43	2.68	2.95	3.26	3.39
8	Marketable Securities	4.0	4.41	4.86	5.36	5.91	6.52	6.78
9	Accounts Receivable	17.0	17.64	19.45	21.44	23.64	26.06	27.12
10	*Inventory (units)*	*5.0*	10.50	11.03	11.58	12.16	12.76	13.02
11	*Inventory Unit Purchases*	*0.0*	110.50	110.78	116.31	122.13	128.24	130.44
12	*Inventory Dollar Purchases*	*0.0*	58.57	62.23	69.27	77.09	85.80	92.51
13	Inventory (dollars)	10.0	5.57	6.19	6.89	7.67	8.54	9.23
14	Other Current Assets	1.0	2.21	2.43	2.68	2.95	3.26	3.39
15	Current Assets	42.0	40.8	98.3	175.7	279.8	398.1	520.8

FIGURE 4.7 The balance sheet current assets should start taking form. Note that items in italics are not assets, but calculations to help establish asset values.

14. For now we are going to skip over implementing PP&E and intangibles since Chapter 5 will be dedicated to those concepts. This brings us to our expectation for other long-term assets and receivables. As we do not know of any management plans to acquire or dispose of these assets, we will assume they will maintain a historical level commensurate to their revenue. Earlier, in cell B24 on the Vectors sheet, we created the label **Other LTA**, which stands for *Other Long-Term Assets*. The percentages we entered in row 25 are our percent of revenue expectations for other long-term assets and receivables. To implement this projection, enter the following text, value, and formula into the corresponding cells on the Balance Sheet sheet:

B25: **LT investments & receivables**
D25: 8.04
E25: =‘Income Statement’!E7*Vectors!E25

Copy the formula in E25 and paste it over the range E25:J25.

15. We will wrap up the asset side of this Model Builder by summing the total assets. Enter the label **Total Assets** in cell B26 of the Balance Sheet sheet. Enter the following formula in cell D26:

=D15+D19+D23+D25

Copy and paste this formula over the range D26:J26. Refer to Figure 4.8 for a view of how the model should look thus far.

WHAT THE COMPANY OWES

If assets can be thought of as what the company owns, liabilities are what the company owes. Every item that the company owns is either owned and paid for by people who have an interest in the company (equity) or was paid for by a creditor (liability). Similar to assets, liabilities are organized by current liabilities, which are

	A	B	C	D	E	F	G	H	I	J
5		Assets								
6		Surplus Funds			0.00	62.92	136.68	236.71	350.50	470.92
7		Cash and Near Cash		10.0	11.03	2.43	2.68	2.95	3.26	3.39
8		Marketable Securities		4.0	4.41	4.86	5.36	5.91	6.52	6.78
9		Accounts Receivable		17.0	17.64	19.45	21.44	23.64	26.06	27.12
10		Inventory (units)		5.0	10.50	11.03	11.58	12.16	12.76	13.02
11		Inventory Unit Purchases		0.0	110.50	110.78	116.31	122.13	128.24	130.44
12		Inventory Dollar Purchases		0.0	58.57	62.23	69.27	77.09	85.80	92.51
13		Inventory (dollars)		10.0	5.57	6.19	6.89	7.67	8.54	9.23
14		Other Current Assets		1.0	2.21	2.43	2.68	2.95	3.26	3.39
15		Current Assets		42.0	40.8	98.3	175.7	279.8	398.1	520.8
16										
17										
18										
19										
20										
21										
22										
23										
24										
25		LT Investments and Receivables		8.0	22.05	24.31	26.80	29.55	32.58	33.89
26		Total Assets		138.04	270.90	313.27	381.38	460.29	559.51	677.92

FIGURE 4.8 The asset side of the Balance Sheet sheet takes form. Note that we will complete the PP&E and intangibles section in Chapter 5, and that some values in this figure will not appear in a model being built according to the Model Builder steps.

due within 12 months, and long-term liabilities, which are due over a period greater than 12 months.

Accounts Payable

When goods and services are purchased but not immediately paid for, a payable is generated. For the company, this is a debt they owe, although it typically does not bear interest. There are few valuation issues with accounts payable. One possibility is that the amounts reflected include a discount for early payment and the early payment does not actually take place. This would underestimate accounts payable by a small percent.

The other issue for accounts payable is that when a company becomes distressed it might try to finance its business through accounts payable, essentially taking goods and services on credit and not paying for them, nor paying an interest expense. A detrimental strategy such as this should be clear to ratings analysts, who will probably downgrade the company, making it more costly and difficult for the company to borrow. This is a red flag as it perpetuates the distress cycle and could lead to the downfall of a company.

Short-Term Borrowings, Credit Facilities, and Revolvers

A company typically tries to match its assets and liabilities so that there is little discrepancy between revenue generation and funding. Unfortunately, projections can be imprecise and there are times when small amounts of funding (relative to long-term debt) may be necessary to keep operations flowing smoothly. These amounts are considered short term in nature as they are loans that are expected to be repaid within a year or sooner. Short-term debt can be a direct loan from a bank or a drawdown from an established credit facility or revolving account.

The difference between a direct loan and a credit facility is cost and time. A direct loan may be slightly less expensive to implement, but can take longer depending on approval. This can also cause problems during distressed times as approval can be denied. Usually companies set up credit facilities, where there is a preapproved amount of credit that can be drawn down. The trade-off is cost. A credit facility will charge an undrawn amount on the credit line and then an increased amount on drawn balances. For financial modeling purposes, we would have to track both of these charges.

More importantly, for financial modeling, short-term debt often serves as the liability and equity side plug when the projection model creates more assets than liabilities and equity. Some may wonder how a situation could occur where more assets than liabilities and equity are created. A simple way to conceive of this is to imagine running a stress scenario where capital expenditures are expected to exceed base-case forecasting—a situation that occurs frequently. Usually, a set amount of long-term debt is structured for capital expenditures. In a stress situation where capital expenditures are higher than expected, gross PP&E increases. The funding of this increase on the balance sheet must come from somewhere, with short-term debt being the most likely candidate.

Current Portion of Debt

Principal and interest on debt, both long and short term, that is due within the next 12 months is considered the *current portion* of debt. This is classified under current liabilities. On a complete balance sheet, the current portion of debt is a very important figure. There needs to be enough liquidity in the company or earnings potential to service the debt. In particular, cash is required to service the immediate debt payments. If this cannot be done, the firm risks defaulting on its debt and possibly being forced into bankruptcy and, ultimately, liquidation by debt holders.

One needs to be very careful when using a projection model and determining the payment ability of a firm. For instance, we could look at cash on hand in a given period and compare it to the current portion of debt, but relying on cash may not be sustainable. Perhaps the company sold off an asset in a particular period that generated cash. Unless the debt is ultimately paid off, selling off assets is an *unsustainable* method of paying down debt. We may want to look at other sources of funds for debt payment, particularly earnings before interest, taxes, depreciation and amortization (EBITDA). This cash would be available for us to pay down interest. After taxes, dividends, and capital expenditures, we can then use the remaining cash to pay down principal. In Chapter 6, we will look at debt-repayment capacity in much more detail.

Ultimately, we are building a financial projection model for analysis. In the core model, the Balance Sheet sheet will not include the current portion of debt since we will actually try to pay debt over the course of each period. We will still be able to see repayment capacity once the debt sheet is created in Chapter 6.

Other Current Liabilities

As with current assets, there are usually smaller or unique items to a company that do not quite fit in other categories. A common example is salaries payable, which is money that is due to employees but not yet paid. More specific current liabilities exist depending on industry. For instance, in the airplane industry there is often a line item for air traffic liability. These are amounts paid for by passengers and cargo clients, but prior to the service date of the travel or shipment.

Long-Term Borrowings

A company can fund itself in two ways: with money that the owners of the company already have (equity), or by borrowing money from others (debt). When a company seeks debt financing, it can either ask creditors for a corporate loan directly or seek funding from the capital markets via a bond issuance. Overall, debt financing has its advantages and disadvantages compared to equity, which we will examine in detail in Chapter 6.

For now, we should realize that long-term debt shows up on the balance sheet and is considered a liability. Repayment of that liability is a major concern for both the company and the lender. Since many focus a great deal of time on debt, the example model will have an entire sheet, called the *Debt sheet*, dedicated to determining the debt schedule, the repayment capacity, and the tracking of ongoing balances. The long-term borrowings section of the Balance Sheet sheet will reference the balances from the Debt sheet to obtain the correct balances of the long-term borrowings at any given time.

MODEL BUILDER 4.2: CONTINUING THE BALANCE SHEET WITH LIABILITIES

1. Go to the Balance Sheet sheet and enter the following labels in the corresponding cells:

   B29: Liabilities
   B30: Accounts Payable
   B31: ST Borrowings
   B32: Other Current Liabilities
   B33: Current Liabilities

2. For now, we will establish proxy numbers for the current liabilities on the balance sheet. Enter the following values in the corresponding cells:

D30: **15**
D31: **0**
D32: **3**

3. In cell D33, enter the following formula:

=SUM(D30:D32)

Copy and paste this formula over the range D33:J33.

4. In steps 6 to 8 of Model Builder 4.1, we entered the necessary assumptions on the Vectors sheet for a few of the liabilities on the Balance Sheet sheet. We will now put those to use with the following formulas:

E30: = **E12*Vectors!E26**
E32: =**'Income Statement'!E7*Vectors!E27**

Copy and paste these formulas from the E column to the J column. For instance, cell E30 should be copied and pasted over the range E30:J30. See the example model or Figure 4.9 if this is unclear. Also, keep in mind that we purposely skipped row 31 as this is the short-term debt row, which will be the liability and equity side plug to balance the balance sheet. We will come back to this in Chapter 7, when we finish off the balance sheet.

5. Move down the Balance Sheet sheet and enter the label **LT Borrowings** in B35. Also enter a value of 0 in cell D35. We will not fill in any projection formulas at this time since we will examine long-term debt in much more detail in Chapter 6.

6. We will finish off this Model Builder section by entering the text **Total Liabilities** in cell B36. Also enter the following formula in cell D36:

=D33+D35

Copy and paste this formula over the range D36 through J36. The Balance Sheet sheet should look like Figure 4.10 at this point.

	A	B	C	D	E	F	G	H	I	J
29		Liabilities								
30		Accounts Payable		15.00	17.57	18.67	20.78	23.13	25.74	27.75
31		ST Borrowings								
32		Other Current Liabilities		3.00	6.62	7.29	8.04	8.86	9.77	10.17
33		Current Liabilities		18.00	44.10	26.0	28.8	32.0	35.5	37.9

FIGURE 4.9 The current liabilities section of the Balance Sheet sheet.

	A	B	C	D	E	F	G	H	I	J
29		Liabilities								
30		Accounts Payable		15.00	17.57	18.67	20.78	23.13	25.74	27.75
31		ST Borrowings								
32		Other Current Liabilities		3.00	6.62	7.29	8.04	8.86	9.77	10.17
33		Current Liabilities		18.00	44.10	26.0	28.8	32.0	35.5	37.9
34										
35		LT Borrowings								
36		Total Liabilities		18.00	79.10	52.8	47.5	42.5	39.5	37.9

FIGURE 4.10 The liabilities section of the Balance Sheet sheet. Note this figure shows values that will not appear yet on a model that is following the Model Builder steps. The values will populate upon completion.

WHAT THE COMPANY HAS ALREADY PAID FOR

The final section of the balance sheet accounts for amounts owed to the equity holders. While debt holders are part of the firm's value, they hold a lien against the firm and are limited in earnings (and loss). Equity holders invest amounts with greater risk, but have a greater upside than debt holders. Overall, equity holders' returns are dictated directly by the performance of the company, whether they receive their return in the form of dividends or capital gains.

The most standard equity item is common stock, which is listed at issuance price. Common stock is the lowest denomination of equity and represents a fractional share in the market value of the equity in the company. Notice that it is not a fractional share in the market value of the company since debt must be netted out to understand equity value. Debt holders have priority over cash flow and therefore should be removed from the equity holder value. For instance, if the firm were being liquidated, the debt holders would be paid first and then funds would be dispersed to equity holders. Since debt holder amounts are taken away from equity holders, those amounts do not create shareholder value.

Other forms of equity include preferred stock, convertible preferred stock, and minority interest. Preferred stock is technically listed as equity, but it has many attributes of a liability. As with a liability, it typically has a fixed dividend payment based on a percentage, it can sometimes be called debt, and it can sometimes be structured so it converts to common shares. However, it is equity since it is listed as equity and has priority below debt and can sometimes be structured with a capital gains sharing mechanism (although it should never enjoy the full capital gains benefit that common shares receive).

Another type of equity is minority interest. This can often be a complex section of a balance sheet. Minority interest is determined by the percentage of interest one party has in another party. Typically, when one party has 20% or less interest in another company there is a minority interest.

If this sounds confusing, the best way to think about minority interest is to look at the situation where only two companies exist and one has a 20% interest in the other company, while the other company has an 80% interest in the first company. Let's denote Company A as having the minority 20% interest in Company B and Company B as having an 80% interest in Company A. This situation could have been created by Company B acquiring an 80% interest in Company A, thereby causing a consolidated approach according to IFRS. A consolidated accounting approach means that all of the assets from Company A are brought onto the balance sheet of Company B. As Company B does not own all of the assets, they must report a 20% minority interest in their liabilities and equity section of the balance sheet. Other forms of interest in other companies exist, which is dictated by IFRS based on ownership percentages.

The final form of equity that is extremely important is retained earnings. When a company earns money, as reported by the income statement, it eventually flows through as net income. The company then has the choice, depending on the Board of Directors' vote, to dividend that money out to equity holders, or to retain that money internally for use or distribution later. Any retained earnings from the past year are added to the current retained earnings to get the balance. Unless money is released as a dividend, funds are retained. Figure 4.11 shows the first of many connections between the income statement and the balance sheet.

Retained earnings are very important because they are the major link between the income statement and the balance sheet. From a financial modeling viewpoint, this link causes headaches because it is a source of circularity in the model that we must adjust for if we model the company with certain periodicities in mind. We will learn about this circularity more and see how this is efficiently calculated and automated in Chapter 7.

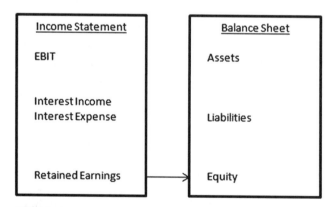

FIGURE 4.11   Retained earnings is a direct link from the Income Statement sheet to the equity section of the Balance Sheet sheet.

MODEL BUILDER 4.3: CONTINUING THE BALANCE SHEET WITH EQUITY

1. Still on the Balance Sheet sheet, label the equity section by entering the text **Equity** in cell B39.
2. Create the following labels in the associated cell references:

   B40: **Minority Interest**
   B41: **Total Common Equity**
   B42: **Retained Earnings**
   B43: **Total Shareholder Equity**

3. We should also enter historical values for 2007. Enter the following values in the corresponding cell references:

   D40: **0**
   D41: **100**
   D42: **20.04**

4. For Minority Interest and Common Equity, we will assume values for now. Enter the following values in each of the associated cells in the range:

   E37:J37: **0**
   E38:J38: **100**

5. Retained Earnings requires a formula that is connected to the Income Statement sheet. Enter the following formula in cell E42:

   ='Income Statement'!E39+D42

   Copy and paste this formula over the range E42:J42.
6. We should sum up the total shareholders' equity by entering the following formula in cell D43:

   =SUM(D39:D42)

   Copy and paste this formula over the range E43:J43.
7. The final part of this section is adding up the liabilities and equity. Enter the text **Total liabilities & equity** in cell B46. Enter the following formula in cell D46:

   =D36+D43

   Copy and paste this formula over the range D46:J46. The equity section of the Balance Sheet sheet should look like Figure 4.12.

	A	B	C	D	E	F	G	H	I	J
39		**Equity**								
40		Minority Interest		0.00	0.00	0.0	0.0	0.0	0.0	0.0
41		Total Common Equity		100.00	100.00	100.0	100.0	100.0	100.0	100.0
42		Retained Earnings		20.04	91.79	160.5	233.9	317.8	420.0	540.0
43		Total Shareholder Equity		120.04	191.79	260.47	333.89	417.80	519.99	640.00

FIGURE 4.12 The equity section of the Balance Sheet sheet. As with other figures, some values may populate later as the model develops.

TOOLBOX: BE CAREFUL WITH GROWTH

Although the actual Excel functions in this chapter's Model Builder exercises were neither new nor advanced, there are common errors that many novice financial modelers make. The first is to use a growth formula to project an item, when the item's assumptions are based on a *percentage* of revenue analysis. For instance, if cost of goods sold was historically analyzed and found on average to be 30% of revenue, then in a base case the projected period's revenue should be multiplied by 30% to estimate cost of goods sold. The common error is to implement a method similar to revenue growth by multiplying last year's cost of goods sold by (1 + .3).

Another error occurs when people try to back into a figure from a growth rate. For example, say one wanted to calculate last year's revenue given a growth rate of 10% and a current revenue estimation of 875. The common mistake is to multiply the 875 by .9. This is wrong as it will yield 787.50, which when grown by 10% equals 866.25. The proper method is to divide 875 by (1 + .1), which will yield 795.45.

CHAPTER 5

Capital Expenditures, Depreciation, Intangibles, and Amortization

A number of items on the balance sheet are of critical importance to a company or have complex interactions with other concepts. In such instances it is best to create separate sheets for these concepts so details can be properly covered and implemented in Excel. *Capital expenditure* is one of these concepts. These are necessary investments a company makes in order to keep the business operational and to further expansion. As technology develops, more and more companies operate with fewer fixed assets than traditional capital expenditures purchase. Instead, their products are intangible items such as intellectual property, patents, and licenses. *Intangible* is another concept that we will want to understand and track in detail separately.

Regardless of whether money is invested in a fixed asset or an intangible, both items lose value over time. This complexity, known as *depreciation* for fixed assets and *amortization* for intangibles, necessitates rigorous technical methods to insure the concepts are properly implemented. Given that many businesses rely on fixed assets and/or intangibles to continue operations, we should look at each of these concepts carefully.

CAPITAL EXPENDITURES

As mentioned earlier, capital expenditures are investments in fixed assets that contribute to corporate operations. Typically, capital expenditures will be made to purchase property, plant, and equipment. Such purchases can be the entire focus of a model since capital expenditures can be significant outlays for a company. The best way to capture capital expenditure costs is by projecting future capital expenditures exactly as they are planned during the forecast period. To accomplish this, we will create detailed capital expenditure schedules that list the amount of capital expenditure on the date that it is expected to take place.

DEPRECIATION

Immediately after a capital expenditure takes place the asset begins to lose value due to normal wear and tear. This depreciation of the asset should be tracked with equal specificity as the original capital expenditure. To understand the depreciation of an asset, one needs to know the book value or cost, the useful life of the asset, and how much (if any) the asset is worth at the end of the useful life. Also, depending on the type of asset and the accounting regime the company follows, the depreciation calculation could be fairly complicated.

IFRS's standard accounting method of choice for calculating depreciation in a given period is known as *straight-line depreciation*. This simple method takes the cost of the asset, less the value at the end of the useful life, otherwise known as the *salvage value*, and divides that amount by the useful life of the asset. As a simple example, take a laptop computer used for a financial modeling training company. If the computer cost \$2,000, had a useful life of three years, and was worth \$500 at the end of the third year, the periodic depreciation would be \$500 ((\$2,000 – \$500)/3). Figure 5.1 depicts the straight-line formula.

Some argue that certain assets do not lose equal amounts of value over time, but rather lose more value in earlier years than later years. This concept is known as *accelerated depreciation* and is used by companies with assets that lose a lot of up-front value, such as vehicles. There are multiple methods of accelerated depreciation depending on how accelerated the depreciation is expected to be. The most basic type of accelerated depreciation is *fixed declining balance depreciation*, which can be accelerated by factors to increase the speed of the depreciation. See Figure 5.2 for the fixed declining balance depreciation formula. Less used types include sum of the year's digits and government depreciation systems such as modified accelerated cost recovery system.

Keep in mind that there are many more types of depreciation that exist. Some of these have been detailed in the Toolbox at the end of this chapter. Also there are some types of depreciation that are asset specific. For example, in project finance transactions one can encounter equipment that depreciates depending on use. Such forms of depreciation require the analyst to thoroughly investigate specific characteristics of the asset.

$$\text{Periodic Straight-Line Depreciation} = \frac{\text{Cost} - \text{Salvage Value}}{\text{Useful Life}}$$

FIGURE 5.1 The straight-line depreciation method equally spaces the depreciable amount of the asset.

$$\begin{array}{c} \text{Periodic Fixed} \\ \text{Declining Balance} \\ \text{Depreciation} \end{array} = \begin{array}{c} \text{(Cost - Total} \\ \text{Cumulative} \\ \text{Depreciation)} \end{array} * 1 - ((\text{Salvage Value/Cost})^{\wedge}\text{Useful Life})$$

FIGURE 5.2 Fixed declining balance depreciation creates a rate based on the salvage value, cost, and usefulness and applies this to each period's remaining asset value.

A BALANCE SHEET OR AN INCOME STATEMENT ITEM?

The answer to the question of whether to classify capital expenditures and depreciation as a balance sheet item or an income statement item is *both*; the effects of capital expenditures and depreciation are found on both the balance sheet and the income statement. However, we must be very careful about the figures that show up on each. On the income statement, depreciation is first seen at the top, prior to EBIT. This is the depreciation for the current period. However, some income statements consolidate depreciation into operating expenses and the actual amounts must be found in footnotes.

Capital expenditures are not directly found on the income statement. However, effects of capital expenditures, such as the disposal of an asset originally created through capital expenditure, could show up on the income statement if there was a gain or loss on the eventual sale.

From a balance sheet perspective, capital expenditure adds to gross PP&E. As each capital expenditure takes place, the gross PP&E number grows. Only when assets are disposed of do their amounts get removed from the gross PP&E figure. However, gross PP&E is not used as part of the total assets calculation. Instead, we must net out all of the depreciation that accumulates for the assets. This means that each asset has periodic depreciation amounts, which are aggregated on the balance sheet under accumulated depreciation. Gross PP&E minus depreciation is equal to net PP&E, which is the value counted toward total assets. Refer to Figure 5.3 for more details on capital expenditures, intangibles, depreciation, and amortization on the income statement and balance sheet.

CONCEPT STATUS

Prior to implementing the first Model Builder that focuses on capital expenditures and depreciation, we should understand a common challenge that will begin to occur. Managing the current status of a concept and the effects of that status in a projection model is a difficulty that financial model builders face. For instance, capital expenditures are usually provided by amount and the expected date of the expenditure. Prior to that date there is no capital expenditure, on the capital

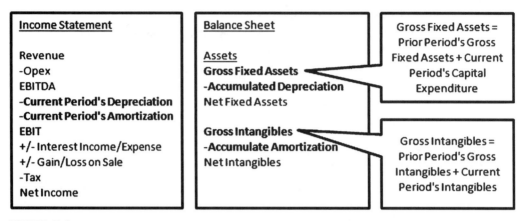

FIGURE 5.3 Capital expenditures, intangibles, depreciation, and amortization appear on both the income statement and balance sheet.

expenditure date there is the capital expenditure, and after that date depreciation begins. Further, depreciation will continue until the useful life of the asset is achieved or the asset is disposed of or impaired, or the accumulated depreciation of the asset is equal to the cost minus the salvage value. As we can see from these examples, both capital expenditures and depreciation have concept states that change over time. Our projection model must be flexible and implemented in such a way that it can adapt to changing characteristics of each concept. Figure 5.4 depicts the thoughts that should go into the concept status.

Capex Characteristics	
Cost	100
Salvage Value	40
Useful Life	3
Method	Straight Line
Capital Expenditure Date	12/1/2010

	12/1/2009	12/1/2010	12/1/2011	12/1/2012	12/1/2013	12/1/2014
Capital Expenditure		100				
Depreciation				20	20	20

Concept Status: Capital expenditure has not occured	Concept Status: No depreciation until period after capital expenditure	Concept Status: Capital expenditure takes place	Concept Status: Depreciation takes place	Concept Status: Depreciation is finished

FIGURE 5.4 Many concepts in financial modeling change status over time.

MODEL BUILDER 5.1: CAPITAL EXPENDITURE SCHEDULES SETUP

1. Insert a sheet and name it **Capex**. There are many standard items to each sheet that we should create, such as the dates and timing and labels.
2. Enter the text **Capex** in cell A1. Then enter the following formulas in their corresponding cell references:

   D2: =Vectors!D9
   D3: =Vectors!D10

   Copy and paste these formulas over to column Z for both rows.
3. The assumptions for capital expenditures and depreciation will be controlled from the Assumptions sheet. We should jump to that sheet and set up assumptions so we can see the formulas work on the Capex sheet. Go to the Assumptions sheet and enter the following text in the corresponding cell references:

   B15: **Capex Assumptions**
   B17: **Capex 1**
   B18: **Capex 2**
   B19: **Capex 3**
   B20: **Capex 4**
   C16: **Depreciation Method**
   D16: **Amt**
   E16: **Capex Date**
   F16: **Useful Life (years)**
   G16: **Salvage Value**

4. We should put proxy values in to create a few capital expenditures that will make the building process easier to implement. Enter the following values in the associated cell references:

   D17: **85**
   D18: **25**
   D19: **10**
   D20: **0**
   E17: **12/31/2008**
   E18: **12/31/2008**
   E19: **12/31/2010**
   E20: **0**
   F17: **4**
   F18: **5**
   F19: **5**
   F20: **0**
   G17: **25**
   G18: **5**

	B	C	D	E	F	G
15	CAPEX Assumptions					
16		Depreciation Method	Amt	Capex Date	Useful Life (years)	Salvage Value
17	Capex 1	Straight Line	85	12/31/2008	4	25
18	Capex 2	Straight Line	25	12/31/2008	5	5
19	Capex 3	Straight Line	10	12/31/2010	5	2
20	Capex 4	Straight Line	0		0	0

FIGURE 5.5 The primary assumptions for the capital expenditures are stored and controlled on the Assumptions sheet.

> G19: **2**
> G20: **0**

Thus far the Assumptions sheet should look like Figure 5.5.

5. Now go back to the Capex sheet and enter the text **Capital Expenditure** in cell B4. Also enter the following cell references in the corresponding cells on the Capex sheet to create labels for the capital expenditure schedules:

> B5: =Assumptions!B17
> B6: =Assumptions!B18
> B7: =Assumptions!B19
> B8: =Assumptions!B20

6. We are now ready to enter the main capital expenditure schedule formula in cell E5:

> =IF(E$3=Assumptions!$E17,Assumptions!$D17,0)

This single formula can be copied and pasted over the range E5:J8. Notice that this formula uses an IF function to test the current date of each column and compares that date against the possible capital expenditure dates. This is what is meant by *concept status*. Depending on the current period and the capital expenditure date, the status of the capital expenditure concept could be either an amount greater than zero or zero. If you are having trouble understanding the dollar signs in the formula, refer to this chapter's Toolbox for more details.

7. We should summarize the capital expenditures. Enter the text **Total Capex** in cell B10. Then enter the following formula in cell E10:

> =SUM(E5:E8)

Copy and paste this formula over the range E10:J10. The Capex sheet should look like Figure 5.6.

	A	B	C	D	E	F	G	H	I	J
1	*Capex*									
2					Projected ---->					TV Year
3				12/31/2007	12/31/2008	12/31/2009	12/31/2010	12/31/2011	12/31/2012	12/31/2013
4		Capital Expenditure								
5		Capex 1			85.00	0.00	0.00	0.00	0.00	0.00
6		Capex 2			25.00	0.00	0.00	0.00	0.00	0.00
7		Capex 3			0.00	0.00	10.00	0.00	0.00	0.00
8		Capex 4			0.00	0.00	0.00	0.00	0.00	0.00

FIGURE 5.6 The upper part of the Capex sheet calculates the amount of capital expenditure on projection dates that the user assumes.

More on Capital Expenditure Schedules

We just implemented the capital expenditure schedule system, and some new financial modelers are asking the question: "What if we have multiple stages of capital expenditure for the same project?" For instance, what if the capital expenditure was a large plant that was to be created in multiple periods? In such cases, my preference is to create separate capital expenditure schedules for each phase. It is easier to work into the current formula and can be better if each phase has its own depreciation schedule.

As an example, take a two-stage project where a generator is built and then an assembly machine. Perhaps the generator is built first and used as soon as it is done to assist with the second capital expenditure. This would mean that the generator begins depreciating prior to the completion of the assembly machine. It would be ideal to separate out the capital expenditures so that the depreciation schedules can be easily distinguished. Otherwise, the two capital expenditures will have blended depreciation schedules, making the formula implementation complicated and the presentation difficult to dissect.

MODEL BUILDER 5.2: DEPRECIATION SCHEDULES SETUP

1. The depreciation schedules will be built directly underneath the capital expenditure schedules. On the Capex sheet, insert the text **Depreciation** in cell B12 and the cell references below to establish labels:

   B13: =Assumptions!B17
   B14: =Assumptions!B18
   B15: =Assumptions!B19
   B16: =Assumptions!B20

2. The example model gives the user the option of selecting one of two of the most common forms of depreciation: straight-line or fixed declining balance. To give the user a choice between these two, we will set up a data validation list on the Assumptions sheet. Prior to that we should create the list contents

◢	B	C
15	**CAPEX Assumptions**	
16		Depreciation Method
17	Capex 1	**Straight Line** ▼
18	Capex 2	Straight Line
		Fixed Declining
19	Capex 3	Straight Line
20	Capex 4	**Straight Line**

FIGURE 5.7 The user has the option to select different depreciation methods for each asset.

on the Hidden sheet. Go to the Hidden sheet and enter the following text in the corresponding cells:

A14: **lst_Depreciation**
A15: **Straight Line**
A16: **Fixed Declining**

Name the range A15:A16 **lst_Depreciation**.

3. Go to the Assumptions sheet and create data validations lists in range C17:C20 using the named range lst_Depreciation as the reference. The completed section is displayed in Figure 5.7.

4. The next formula, which determines the depreciation amount, is complicated. To tackle it we will work on it in sections. Prior to the actual formula instruction we should take a moment to think about the concept status. This is particularly important for depreciation. If we think about the different states for depreciation, we can break it down into three: (1) prior to any capital expenditure, there is no depreciation; (2) the period after a capital expenditure there is depreciation; and (3) once the asset is depreciated to its cost-minus-salvage value, then depreciation ceases. To handle the first part, we should implement the first part of the formula on the Capex sheet in cell E13 (note that the following formula is *not* complete):

=IF(SUM($D5:D5)=0,0

The first part of the formula is an IF function. It references row 5, which is the corresponding capital expenditure schedule for the depreciation schedule we are creating. The IF function checks all of the prior periods for a capital expenditure by adding up the row from the historic period up to the prior period. If there is no capital expenditure in the prior periods, then the SUM function will return a zero, which is equal to zero. The IF will take this TRUE statement and return a zero value for the depreciation. If the use of the dollar sign is confusing, refer to the Toolbox section at the end of this chapter.

If the IF function is FALSE, then we need to continue on through the formula:

**=IF(SUM($D5:D5)=0,0,IF((Assumptions!$D17-Assumptions!$G17)
   <=SUM($D13:D13),0**

The next part of the formula is another IF function. This IF function tests to see whether the asset created by the capital expenditure has already been completely depreciated. It does so by taking the capital expenditure cost and subtracting the salvage value from the Assumptions sheet. If the amount produced from this subtraction is less than or equal to the depreciation taken on the asset thus far, then there should be no more depreciation and a zero is returned. Once again, the use of the dollar sign within the SUM function is integral and the Toolbox section at the end of this chapter should be referenced if this is unclear. The formula then continues with:

**=IF(SUM($D5:D5)=0,0,IF((Assumptions!$D17-Assumptions!$G17)<=SUM
   ($D13:D13),0,IF(inputs_Capex1Dep="Straight Line",SLN (Assumptions!
   $D17,Assumptions!$G17,Assumptions!$F17)**

The logic with this next section is that if the capital expenditure existed in the prior period and all of the depreciation on the asset has not been taken yet, the asset should be depreciated. However, we need one more test since we gave the user the option to depreciate using a straight-line method or a fixed declining balance method. To do this, we use another IF function that checks the named range on the Assumptions sheet where the user selected the depreciation type (inputs_Capex1Dep). If that cell has the value Straight Line, then Excel's built-in straight-line depreciation function, SLN, is used. This function is described in more detail in the Toolbox at the end of this chapter. If the value is different, it means that the user wants to use a fixed declining balance method. We do not need another IF function since the fixed declining balance method is the only other type of method and there can be no more possibilities for the entire formula's return. Prior to implementing the remainder of this formula, we need to create additional functionality for the fixed declining balance calculation.

5. The need for additional functionality for the fixed declining method stems from the calculation's need to know which period of depreciation the asset is experiencing. The mathematical formula uses a compounding calculation to calculate the accelerated figures, which requires us to provide an integer-based compounding number. To do this, we will create a separate section below the depreciation schedules that tracks each asset's depreciation period in integer format. Let's first create labels to guide us. Enter the text **Current Dep Pd** in cell B21 and the following formulas in the corresponding cells:

B22: **=B13**
B23: **=B14**
B24: **=B15**
B25: **=B16**

	B	C	D	E	F	G	H	I	J
21	**Current Dep Pd**								
22	Capex 1			0	1	2	3	4	0
23	Capex 2			0	1	2	3	4	5
24	Capex 3			0	0	0	1	2	3
25	Capex 4			0	0	0	0	0	0

FIGURE 5.8 In order to implement accelerated depreciation schedules we need to track each asset's depreciation period.

6. The formula to determine which time period of depreciation the asset is in needs to check when the asset was created, in order to determine when to start depreciation. The formula also needs to know when to stop counting, which takes place when the asset has taken its full depreciation. Interestingly, we already created this functionality in the first two IF functions of the partial equation in step 7. All we must do is skip the IF function that determines the depreciation method and then finish off the final result if both conditions of the partial equation are false. These additions are shown in the complete formula we should enter in cell E22:

=IF(SUM($D5:D5)=0,0,IF((Assumptions!$D17-Assumptions!$G17)<=SUM ($D13:D13),0,D22+1))

Notice that this formula is essentially a counter. It creates zeroes when the asset is in its first year or earlier and when the asset has taken its full depreciation. However, when those conditions are not met, the formula adds a one to the prior period. This has the effect of creating a cumulative counter. This counter is a cumulative count of the asset's depreciation period. Copy and paste this formula over the range E22:J25. The counter should look like Figure 5.8.

7. We can now finish off the depreciation calculation in cell E13. Go back to that cell and complete the partial equation so that it is the following formula:

=IF(SUM($D5:D5)=0,0,IF((Assumptions!$D17-Assumptions!$G17)<=SUM ($D13:D13),0,IF(inputs_Capex1Dep="Straight Line",SLN(Assumptions! $D17,Assumptions!$G17,Assumptions!$F17),DB(Assumptions!$D17, Assumptions!$G17,Assumptions!$F17,E22))))

The last part of the equation adds in Excel's built-in fixed declining balance function (DB). This function requires all of the information for straight-line depreciation, plus the current depreciation period that we determined in step 6. For more information on the DB function, refer to the Toolbox section of this chapter. Also, make sure to copy and paste the formula created in this step over the range E13:J16.

8. Finally, enter the text **Total Depreciation** in cell B18. Then enter the following formula in cell E18:

=SUM(E13:E16)

	B	C	D	E	F	G	H	I	J
12	**Depreciation**								
13	Capex 1			-	15.00	15.00	15.00	15.00	-
14	Capex 2			-	4.00	4.00	4.00	4.00	4.00
15	Capex 3			-	-	-	1.60	1.60	1.60
16	Capex 4			-	-	-	-	-	-
17									
18	**Total Depreciation**			-	19.00	19.00	20.60	20.60	5.60

FIGURE 5.9 The depreciation associated with each capital expenditure should calculate automatically.

Copy and paste this formula over the range E18:J18. Figure 5.9 shows what this section should look like.

INTANGIBLES

The concept of an intangible is tough to define considering the word itself describes something that cannot be seen or felt. In finance, intangibles have similar characteristics. Many intangibles derive their value from intellectual creations such as patents, licenses, and trademarks. These assets are legal claims to intellectual property that can add significant value to companies. Some industries such as pharmaceuticals, information technology firms, and film companies build their fortunes around intangibles.

One particular type of intangible is known as *goodwill*, which is the difference between book value and market value. Goodwill captures the concept that an entity might be worth more than just the book value of its assets based on its name recognition, reputation, and branding. For instance, Sony charges a premium over competitors for its products and converts its brand and reputation into real value. The market perceives value in the Sony name, which adds to the company's value.

AMORTIZATION

Just as capital expenditures lose value over time, so do intangible assets. Patents can eventually expire, competitors can catch up technologically, and proprietary processes can become outdated or irrelevant. This reduction in value is known as *intangible amortization*. Be very careful with the term *amortization*, since the word draws its roots from the ending of a life or erosion, which can be used with other concepts in finance such as debt. In the case of intangible amortization, we reduce the value of the intangible each year for a specific number of years.

In fact, most accounting methodologies amortize intangibles in an identical manner as straight-line depreciation. Instead the cost is the cost of the intangible, the salvage value is the value, if any, at the end of the useful life, and the useful life is the perceived duration of intangible value. Typically, accelerated forms of amortization are not allowed by accounting boards. IFRS specifically uses straight-line amortization for intangibles.

One exception to intangible amortization is goodwill. Prior to 2002, IFRS amortized goodwill like any other intangible. That practice was stopped and subsequently replaced with the concept that goodwill must be examined periodically for impairment.

MODEL BUILDER 5.3: INTANGIBLES AND AMORTIZATION SCHEDULES

1. We need to set up some assumptions on the Assumptions sheet. Go to that sheet and enter the following text in the corresponding cells:

   I15: **Intangible Assumptions**
   J16: **Amortization Method**
   K16: **Amt**
   L16: **Intangible Date**
   M16: **Life (years)**
   I17: **Intangible 1**
   I18: **Intangible 2**
   I19: **Intangible 3**
   I20: **Intangible 4**

2. We should also enter some initial assumptions that we can work with. Enter the following values in the corresponding cells:

   J17: **Straight Line**
   J18: **Straight Line**
   J19: **Straight Line**
   J20: **Straight Line**
   K17: 10
   K18: 5
   K19: 3
   K20: 0
   L17: **12/31/2008**
   L18: **12/31/2009**
   L19: **12/31/2010**
   M17: 3
   M18: 2
   M19: 2
   M20: 0

Figure 5.10 shows what the assumptions area should look like.

	I	J	K	L	M	N	O
15	**Intangible Assumptions**						
16		Amortization Method	Amt	Intangible Date	Life (years)		
17	Intangible 1	Straight Line	10	12/31/2008	3		
18	Intangible 2	Straight Line	5	12/31/2009	2		
19	Intangible 3	Straight Line	3	12/31/2010	2		
20	Intangible 4	Straight Line	0		0		

FIGURE 5.10   The assumptions for intangibles are created in a similar manner as capital expenditures.

3. Insert a new sheet after the Capex sheet and name it **Intangibles**.
4. On the Intangibles sheet, set up labels for rows by entering the following text and formula references in the corresponding cells:

A1: **Intangibles**
B4: **Intangibles**
B5: =Assumptions!I17
B6: =Assumptions!I18
B7: =Assumptions!I19
B8: =Assumptions!I20
B10: **Total Intangibles**
B12: **Amortization**
B13: =Assumptions!I17
B14: =Assumptions!I18
B15: =Assumptions!I19
B16: =Assumptions!I20
B18: **Total Amortization**

5. Create the dates and timing for this sheet by doing the same Vectors sheet reference in the following cells:

D2: =Vectors!D9
D3: =Vectors!D10

Copy and paste each of these cells across their respective rows to column Z.
6. The next step is to determine the correct amount of amortization in the right time period. This is done with virtually the same formula used for the capital expenditure schedules:

E5: =IF(E\$3=Assumptions!\$L17,Assumptions!\$K17,0)

Copy and paste this formula over the range E5:J8. If you are having difficulty with the dollar signs, refer to the Toolbox at the end of this chapter.

	A	B	C	D	E	F	G	H	I	J
1	*Intangibles*									
2					Projected ---->					TV Year
3				12/31/2007	12/31/2008	12/31/2009	12/31/2010	12/31/2011	12/31/2012	12/31/2013
4		Intangibles								
5		Intangible 1			10.00	0.00	0.00	0.00	0.00	0.00
6		Intangible 2			0.00	5.00	0.00	0.00	0.00	0.00
7		Intangible 3			0.00	0.00	3.00	0.00	0.00	0.00
8		Intangible 4			0.00	0.00	0.00	0.00	0.00	0.00
9										
10		Total Intangibles			10.00	5.00	3.00	0.00	0.00	0.00

FIGURE 5.11 The schedule of intangibles takes the data from the Assumptions sheet and lays it out over the projection period.

7. Total each period's intangible amounts by entering the following formula in cell E10:

=SUM(E5:E8)

Copy and paste this formula over the range E10:J10. These steps should make the Intangibles sheet look like Figure 5.11.

8. The related amortization schedules present the same concept status issues as depreciation. We need to know when the intangible was created or purchased and when the total expected amortization has been taken. This is done using the following formula in cell E13:

=IF(SUM($D5:D5)=0,0,IF(Assumptions!$K17-(SUM($D13:D13))=0,0,SLN (Assumptions!$K17,0,Assumptions!$M17)))

Notice that this formula does not use the named cells, but instead uses relative referencing so the same formula can be used for multiple cells. Also note that the example model has no salvage value for the intangibles. Copy and paste this formula over the range E13:J16.

9. Total up the amortization for each period by entering the following formula in cell E18:

=SUM(E13:E16)

Copy and paste this formula over the range E18:J18. The final part of the Intangibles sheet is depicted in Figure 5.12.

INCOME STATEMENT AND BALANCE SHEET EFFECTS

With schedules created for capital expenditures, depreciation, intangibles, and amortization, we should now integrate these figures into our modeling process. The income

	B	C	D	E	F	G	H	I	J
12	**Amortization**								
13	Intangible 1			0.00	3.33	3.33	3.33	0.00	0.00
14	Intangible 2			0.00	0.00	2.50	2.50	0.00	0.00
15	Intangible 3			0.00	0.00	0.00	1.50	1.50	0.00
16	Intangible 4			0.00	0.00	0.00	0.00	0.00	0.00
17									
18	Total Amortization			0.00	3.33	5.83	7.33	1.50	0.00

FIGURE 5.12　The intangible amortization works similar to depreciation; however, for the most part it is calculated using a straight-line method.

statement is the first section in which we encounter any of these items. Depreciation and amortization are non-cash items that reduce the earnings of a firm. This is due to the idea that when these assets are eventually disposed of the accrued depreciation and amortization must be already accounted for or taken at one single time. Instead, companies are allowed the benefit of spreading this charge over time, which makes sense since items usually lose value over time, not just in one instance. The reduction in earnings due to depreciation and amortization also provides a tax benefit to companies since the amounts are removed prior to paying tax.

On the balance sheet we take a more comprehensive view. Gross fixed assets are tracked each year, which are increased by capital expenditures and decreased by fixed asset disposals. Depreciation for each fixed asset is tracked and added together to form accumulated depreciation. The difference between gross fixed assets and accumulated depreciation is known as the *net fixed assets* of the firm. Similarly, gross intangibles are increased by the intangibles each period and reduced by their disposal. Accumulated amortization is tracked and increased by the amortization each period. The difference between gross intangibles and accumulated amortization produces the net intangible figure. Both net numbers contribute to the total assets of the firm.

MODEL BUILDER 5.4: INTEGRATING CAPITAL EXPENDITURES, DEPRECIATION, INTANGIBLES, AND AMORTIZATION

1. Go back to the Income Statement sheet. Enter the text **Depreciation** in cell B15 and **Amortization** in cell B16.
2. In cell D15, enter the value **5**, and in cell D16, enter the value **2**. These will be our historical assumptions for depreciation.
3. In cell E15 on the Income Statement, enter the following formula:

   =Capex!E18

   Copy and paste this formula over the range E15:J15.
4. In cell E16, enter the following formula:

   =Intangibles!E18

A	B	C	D	E	F	G	H	I	J
1	*Income Statement*								
2				Projected ---->					TV Year
3			12/31/2007	12/31/2008	12/31/2009	12/31/2010	12/31/2011	12/31/2012	12/31/2013
4									
5	Sales units		100.00	105.00	110.25	115.76	121.55	127.63	130.18
6	Sales Price		2.00	2.10	2.21	2.32	2.43	2.55	2.60
7	Sales Revenue		200.00	220.50	243.10	268.02	295.49	325.78	338.94
8	Cost Units		0.50	0.53	0.56	0.60	0.63	0.67	0.71
9	Cost of Goods Sold		70.00	63.00	61.60	68.57	76.31	84.94	91.82
10	**Gross Profit**		130.00	157.50	181.50	199.45	219.18	240.84	247.12
11	SG&A Expense		27.00	30.87	34.03	37.52	41.37	45.61	47.45
12	Operating Expenses		9.30	13.23	14.59	16.08	17.73	19.55	20.34
13	**EBITDA**		93.70	113.40	132.88	145.85	160.08	175.69	179.33
14									
15	Depreciation		5.00	-	19.00	19.00	20.60	20.60	5.60
16	Intangible Amortization		2.00	-	3.33	5.83	7.33	1.50	-
17	**EBIT**		86.70	113.40	110.54	121.02	132.15	153.59	173.73

FIGURE 5.13   Depreciation and amortization are non-cash items that reduce net income on the income statement.

Copy and paste this formula over the range E16:J16. The updated income statement is shown in Figure 5.13.

5. Go to the Balance Sheet sheet and enter the following text in the corresponding cells to create labels:

B17: **Gross Fixed Assets**
B18: **Accumulated Depreciation**
B19: **Net Fixed Assets**
B21: **Gross Intangibles**
B22: **Accumulated Amortization**
B23: **Net Intangibles**

6. Enter the following values to insert historical assumptions:

D17: **85**
D18: **17**
D21: **25**
D22: **5**

7. Let's complete the capital expenditure and depreciation formulas first. These are cumulative figures that use the prior period's value plus the current depreciation or amortization. Insert the following formulas in their corresponding cells:

E17: **=D17+Capex!E10**
E18: **=D18+Capex!E18**

	B	C	D	E	F	G	H	I	J
14	Gross Fixed Assets		**85.0**	195.00	195.0	205.0	205.0	205.0	205.0
15	Accumulated Depreciation		**17.0**	17.00	36.0	55.0	75.6	96.2	101.8
16	Net Fixed Assets		**68.0**	178.00	159.0	150.0	129.4	108.8	103.2

FIGURE 5.14 Gross fixed assets are increased by periodic capital expenditures, while accumulated depreciation is increased by periodic depreciation. The difference between gross fixed assets and accumulated depreciation is net fixed assets.

Copy and paste these formulas over to the J column for each of their respective rows.

8. Net fixed assets are the difference between gross fixed assets and accumulated depreciation. Enter the following formula in cell D19:

=D17-D18

Copy and paste this formula over the range D19:J19. Refer to Figure 5.14 for details on how the balance sheet should be developing.

9. Next we will work on the intangibles and amortization. Enter the following formulas in the corresponding cells:

E21: =D21+Intangibles!E10
E22: =D22+Intangibles!E18

Copy and paste these formulas over to the J column for each of their respective rows.

10. Finally we need to subtract the amortization from the intangibles to get the net figure. Enter the following formula in cell D23:

=D21-D22

Copy and paste this formula over the range D23:J23. Similar to Figure 5.14, Figure 5.15 shows the interaction for intangibles.

TOOLBOX

Understanding Dollar Signs

Seeing dollar signs in formulas can be confusing to new financial modelers if they are unfamiliar with Excel conventions. The technical utility of a dollar sign is to change

	B	C	D	E	F	G	H	I	J
18	Gross Intangibles		**25.0**	35.00	40.0	43.0	43.0	43.0	43.0
19	Accumulated Amortization		**5.0**	5.00	8.3	14.2	21.5	23.0	23.0
20	Net Intangibles		**20.0**	30.00	31.7	28.8	21.5	20.0	20.0

FIGURE 5.15 Gross intangibles are reduced by accumulated amortization to calculate net intangibles.

a reference from a relative reference to an absolute reference. In normal-speak, a dollar sign *locks* a cell reference so the reference does not change when the formula the reference is created in is dragged. As an example, imagine the following formula in cell C5 of any sheet:

=A1+B1

If C5 is dragged or copied to the right one cell, then the formula's references will change to B1+C1. However, if we put dollar signs in front of the rows and columns, such as in the case of $A$1+$B$1, we can lock the reference. Now when cell C5 is dragged or copied to the right one cell the formula's references remain $A$1+$B$1. Figure 5.16 shows the difference between these two methods.

In the previous example we did not actually have to put dollar signs in front of both the row and column references. Since we were dragging the cell to the right, we were moving only across columns. We could have locked the reference by entering $A1+$B1. However, if we dragged cell C5 down one cell, the row reference would change and the formula in cell C6 would be $A2+$B2. We could do the opposite and put dollar signs only in front of the row references, such as A$1+B$1. Now when cell C5 is dragged down the references will not change, but when cell C5 is

Dragging References *without* Dollar Signs Produces a Change In Reference

	A	B	C	D
1				
2				
3				
4			→	
5			=A1+B1	=B1+C1

Dragging References *with* Dollar Signs Does Not Produce a Change In Reference

	A	B	C	D
1				
2				
3				
4			→	
5			=$A$1+$B$1	=$A$1+$B$1

FIGURE 5.16   Using dollar signs changes a reference from relative to absolute.

	A	B	C	D
1				
2				
3				
4			→	
5		↓	=A$1+B$1	=B$1+C$1
6		↓	=A$1+B$1	

FIGURE 5.17 Dollar signing in front of the rows will prevent the row numbers from changing when the reference is dragged down, but will have no effect on the columns when dragged across.

dragged, say, one cell to the right, the formula will change to B$1+C$1. Figure 5.17 shows this dragging example.

Dollar signs are used in this chapter because we want to use one formula for multiple capital expenditure and intangible items on the Assumptions sheet. Each capital expenditure or intangible is organized with different types of information going across columns, with each capital expenditure or intangible having its own row. Therefore, if we want to reference different characteristics of the capital expenditure or intangible, such as amount or date, we would want to have a dollar sign in front of the column, but not row. Conversely, we want to reference the dates on either the Capex or Intangibles sheet in the schedule formulas, but as we drag those formulas down rows we do not want the row reference to change. Therefore, we put dollar signs in front of the rows for this reference, but not in front of the columns since we want to reference a new date each period. Figure 5.18 shows the organization of the assumptions that need to be worked around with dollar signs.

Dollar Signs and Arrays

Dollar signs can also be used with functions that accept arrays. First, what is an array? An *array* is more than one cell of data, which can be a single column list or a matrix of data. For the most part, Excel functions that work with arrays work only with single-column or -row arrays. Many of us are already familiar with functions that work with arrays, such as the SUM or AVERAGE function. All it means is that the function can accept and return a value with multiple continuous cells of data as inputs.

The typical reference for an array is to use the starting cell reference, a colon symbol, and then the ending cell reference. For instance, range C5:G5 would reference cells C5, D5, E5, F5, and G5. Or it could be interpreted as saying "for each cell in the range of cells C5 to G5."

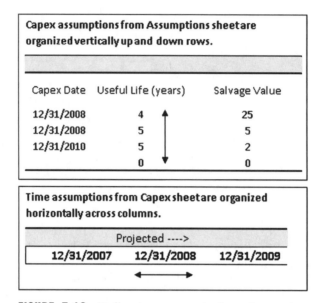

FIGURE 5.18 Dollar signs are required to reference data correctly between the Assumptions and Capex sheets.

As with any cell reference, array references are relative and change as they are dragged. So imagine the following formula in cell G10:

=SUM(C5:G5)

If cell G10 was dragged one column across to cell H10, the formula in cell H10 would read:

=SUM(D5:H5)

Now, many people have guessed that you could write the following to lock down the reference:

=SUM($C$5:$G$5)

This previous formula would be locked down, but what is interesting is that we have the option of locking down only one of the two cell references in the range. For example, in cell G10 we could enter:

=SUM($C$5:G5)

When the previous formula is dragged one column to the right to cell H10, the reference will change to:

=SUM($C$5:H5)

	C	D	E	F	G	H
5	5	8	10	12	8	7
6						
7						
8						
9						
10					=SUM($C$5:G5)	=SUM($C$5:H5)

FIGURE 5.19 The formula in cell G10 returns a sum of 43. When cell G10 is dragged to cell H10, the initial location of the reference is locked and picks up the additional 7, to return a total of 50.

Notice that the first part of the reference is locked, while the second part is not and changes. This will increase the array reference and sum up anything in cell H5, but not move the original starting point. In finance, this method is frequently used to calculate cumulative figures. Figure 5.19 shows this example with numbers to assist in the explanation.

Depreciation Functions: SLN, DB, DDB, SYD

SLN (Straight Line Depreciation)   There are numerous prebuilt depreciation functions in Excel. In this section, we will cover four of the most commonly used ones. The first is the SLN function, which calculates straight-line depreciation. Earlier we provided the mathematical formula for straight-line depreciation. The SLN function's entry parameters are as follows:

=SLN(Cost, Salvage Value, Useful Life)

Always keep in mind the problem absolute referencing causes with this function. The function on its own does not know when to turn off depreciation as it is dragged across time periods. This problem is mitigated by using the formula created in step 4 of Model Builder 5.2.

DB (Fixed Declining Balance Depreciation)   Given that some assets do not depreciate in equal amounts each period, accelerated depreciation calculations try to create an organized method for determining unbalanced depreciation. A common method is the fixed declining balance depreciation method. The entry parameters for this function include:

=DB(Cost, Salvage Value, Useful Life, Current Depreciation Period, Month)

Most of the entry parameters are the same as the SLN function except for the last two. The current depreciation period is the period of depreciation for the asset, *not* the current period of the model. The optional month parameter is if the asset begins and ends depreciation on a partial-year basis. You can select the month numerically if this is the case.

There is a minor problem with the DB function that can become a major problem in financial modeling. The DB function rounds results to the third decimal place. This can cause too much depreciation to be taken. If too much depreciation is taken, then the cost minus the salvage value, less the depreciation, will be a negative number. This can cause errors to propagate throughout a model. The suggested fix for this issue is to recreate the DB function mathematically and not use rounding. This can be done by entering the following formula rather than the DB function:

=(Cost-SUM(Prior Depreciation Amounts))*(1-((Salvage Value/Cost)^
(1/Useful Life)))

DDB (Double Declining Balance Depreciation)   In some cases the fixed declining balance method of accelerated depreciation does not accurately capture the expected depreciation of the asset. To account for this Excel has a host of other depreciation functions. A common alteration to the formula is to accelerate the rate of depreciation by a factor of two, which is known as the *double declining balance method*. The DDB function calculates this amount using the following entry parameters:

=DDB(Cost, Salvage Value, Useful Life, Current Depreciation Period, Factor)

The only new element in this function is the Factor, which is two in the case of double declining or three for triple declining, and so on. I have rarely used this formula and have never had to alter the factor to anything greater than 2. For those who follow U.S. GAAP accounting, you should be mindful that GAAP does not allow accelerated depreciation to dip below the equivalent straight-line depreciation. One could account for this using a MAX function or implement the VDB function, which takes care of this problem.

SYD (Sum of the Years' Digits Depreciation)   The final depreciation method we will discuss is sum of the years' digits. This is an accelerated form of depreciation that is faster than straight line, slower than a fixed declining method in the early periods, but faster in later periods. Conceptually it can be thought of as a more *smoothed* version between straight-line depreciation and fixed declining balance methods. Sum of the years' digits is officially calculated using the following formula:

(2 * (Useful Life − Current Depreciation Period + 1)*(Cost-Salvage Value))/
(Useful Life * (Useful Life + 1))

Alternatively, we could use the SYD function in Excel, which is much easier. The entry parameters for this function include:

=SYD(Cost, Salvage Value, Useful Life, Current Depreciation Period)

CHAPTER 6

Long-Term Debt

*L*ong-term debt is one of the most looked-at items on a balance sheet. It is scrutinized for many reasons: Bankers often issue or monitor long-term debt extended to entities, treasury groups look at their own company's leverage to make sure they are optimally funding the company, and anyone involved in understanding the credit risk of a firm is looking at long-term debt since its characteristics contribute dramatically to default risk. Regardless of perspective or reason, analyzing long-term debt requires thorough explanation and study because it can be very complicated to model debt schedules correctly. Even more complicated is integrating debt schedules into a fully dynamic model. Our approach in this chapter will be to first look at the core concepts of debt and then learn how to implement and integrate long-term debt into the example model through Model Builder examples.

WHAT IS LONG-TERM DEBT?

First, we should understand what bankers issue that constitutes long-term debt. This is usually broken down into two separate subcategories: loans and bonds. Loans are typically issued between a bank and the company. Long-term loans have a maturity greater than 12 months from the analysis date and have detailed documentation that guides the payment of interest and principal each period. This documentation also directs the payment priority when multiple issuances of debt are created. Similarly, bonds with maturities greater than 12 months are liabilities of the company that require interest and principal payments. However, bonds are issued and sold to many different investors and are guided by a document known as a *bond indenture*.

USING DEBT FOR A REASON

As we explore the components of debt instruments in the Model Builder examples, some will ask, "Why go through all this trouble? Why not just fund the entire company with personal funds or equity?" The easy answer is that there may not be enough equity investors to feasibly fund the entire company. A more complicated

	Debt	Equity
Priority of Payment	Debt usually paid over equity	Equity can be locked out after debt
Claim on Firm	Higher priority in liquidation	Priority after debt in liquidation
Tax Shield	Interest tax deductible	Dividends paid after tax

FIGURE 6.1   In most cases, long-term debt is cheaper and more secure than equity.

answer is that debt is cheaper than equity and is therefore an attractive method of funding a company.

Debt is less expensive to fund a company with than equity for a number of reasons. The first and most transparent reason is the tax shield that debt interest enjoys according to major accounting methodologies. Debt interest is removed from taxable income, thereby reducing the effective debt rate. The second reason debt is less expensive than equity is because debt is given priority over equity in terms of the company's cash flow and cannot demand as much compensation for risk as equity holders. Before equity can receive dividends, most debt holders must be paid their interest and, depending on covenants, any principal that is due. The more secure the cash flow, the less risk and therefore the less reward. Figure 6.1 summarizes these differences.

However, risk does exist, particularly if a company is unable to make interest and/or principal payments to debt holders. When this occurs, the company is thought to be in default of its liabilities. Defaulting on liabilities is a precarious situation because most loan or bond documentation gives debt holders powerful rights in relation to the control of the company. Essentially, debt holders are given control to either work out the cash flow problems or send the firm into liquidation in order to recover their debt investment from liquidation proceeds.

We can see from the previous reasoning above why it is incredibly important to model debt correctly. The first step in modeling debt is calculating what is due to debt holders each period. Creating these debt schedules is the basis for multiple auxiliary calculations. The second step is determining how much of what is due can be paid. This can be very complicated, depending on the number of debt issuances a company must service and the priority structure that exists between the debt issuances. The final step is integrating the paid debt schedules into a dynamic cash flow model, which can be challenging when trying to determine interest and principal sources.

MODELING DEBT: DEBT COMPONENTS IN DETAIL

Prior to jumping into a Model Builder to begin our creation and integration of long-term debt in the example model, we should learn about common characteristics of debt. Naturally, there can be variations in the market depending on regional and industry-specific factors, but most debt has the following factors:

- *Issuance date:* This is the date that the debt principal is issued. Interest is calculated from this date forward. For financial modeling, we must be aware that there can be three time perspectives of debt: historical debt that was issued prior to the date the model is built, debt under immediate analysis that is being issued in conjunction with the creation of the model, and also future debt that will be issued in future projection periods. Often entire models are built to examine debt issuances, which means that the issuance dates correspond to the first model date. In such cases, the periodicity is also determined by the periodicity of the debt.

- *Maturity date:* This is the date that the debt is scheduled to return all principal to the investor. Maturity dates are important, but they should not be confused with other metrics of debt exposure and time such as weighted average life and duration.

- *Balance:* The balance is the principal amount of the loan or bond issuance. This amount should not include any interest unless it has been previously capitalized. Also, keep in mind that historical debt may have different current balances than at issuance since the balance may have amortized since issuance.

- *Rate:* The major incentive for someone to issue debt is to earn a return. This is done in the form of interest payments. The rate at which an entity pays interest is a combination of factors. For fixed rate issuances the underlying rate is the risk-free rate. Nearly all entities are not risk free and therefore have default risk. To compensate debt holders for this default risk, a spread is charged over the risk-free rate. This spread is a complex calculation involving the creditworthiness of the firm, expectations regarding future performance, and market opinions.

    Funding a company using a fixed rate can be problematic since the cash flow the company earns could be correlated to market interest rates. Take a financial institution with financial assets as an example. If the institution is funded with a fixed rate and the assets generate cash flow based on a floating rate, the company will be distressed if market rates decrease below the fixed funding rate.

    To cope with differences of rates between income generation and funding, known as *basis risk*, swaps or derivatives can be used or the company can fund itself using floating-rate instruments. Floating-rate debt charges interest based on an index, plus a spread. The index can be a common international one such as LIBOR, or for more localized transactions it would be a regional rate such as the Bank Bill Swap Bid Rate (BBSY) in Australia or Tasa de Interés Interbancaria de Equilibrio (TIIE) in Mexico. Just as with a fixed rate, a floating rate also includes a spread that is charged to capture the credit risk of the entity borrowing funds.

Date	Market Rate	Fixed Rate Locked in First Period with 1.25% Margin	Floating Rate with a 1.25% Margin	Floating Rate with a 1.25% Margin and a Cap at 2.85%
9/1/2009	1.50%	2.75%	2.75%	2.75%
10/1/2009	1.53%	2.75%	2.78%	2.78%
11/1/2009	1.55%	2.75%	2.80%	2.80%
12/1/2009	1.58%	2.75%	2.83%	2.83%
1/1/2010	1.60%	2.75%	2.85%	2.85%
2/1/2010	1.63%	2.75%	2.88%	2.85%
3/1/2010	1.65%	2.75%	2.90%	2.85%
4/1/2010	1.68%	2.75%	2.93%	2.85%

FIGURE 6.2 Market rates change based on the economy, while individual company debt rates can lock in at certain points, float, or use a derivative to limit fluctuations. All corporate rates typically have a risk margin added to them.

Interest rate movements and their effect on debt can be very complex depending on the exact documentation for the debt product. Floating-rate structures can have variable payments or keep the payments the same and have variable terms. Pricing for debt changes depending on market rates and can often incentivize or disincentivize issuance, investment, or debt trading. Figure 6.2 compares fixed and floating rates in relation to debt.

- *Term:* The amount of time between the issuance date and the maturity date is the term. The term of the debt can often dictate the forecast period of the model if the model is being created by a debt banker. The term in the example model is represented in months since, as we saw from the initial date and timing setup, it is easier to work with months in Excel.
- *Payment type:* Debt can pay down or amortize in a number of ways. The most common amortization method is simple level principal amortization. This takes the original principal amount and divides it evenly by the term. Amortization could occur at any interval of time, such as on an annual basis as seen in the example model.

Frequently, companies want to time the amortization of principal that they owe, so it is more manageable to work with revenue inflows. *Bullet amortization* schedules can be created, where specific percentages of debt are due at certain intervals of time. Often, bullet amortizations become *balloon* amortizations where large amounts or balloon payments are due at maturity. These amounts are typically refinanced.

Another major payment style is level payment amortization. This may sound similar to the first type of amortization above, but level payment amortization is focused on the payment, which is composed of both interest and principal

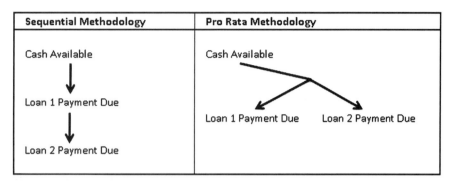

FIGURE 6.3 Sequential debt pays in order while pro rata debt pays at the same time.

components. A level payment is typical of consumer-type debt, where a borrower strives to pay the same amount each month.

■ *Payment priority:* When a company borrows multiple times there can be more than one instrument of debt outstanding at a given time. This creates an issue of payment priority since debt has priority of cash flows over equity. However, which debt instruments have priority of debt over each other? The most standard setup is to borrow funds and then any additional borrowings are subordinate in cash flow priority to the older borrowing. This is known as a *senior subordinate structure*, where senior debt gets its funds first, followed by the subordinate debt. The debt is known to pay in a sequential manner. If there is a shortfall, then the senior loan gets paid prior to the subordinate loan.

An alternative to sequential debt is *pro rata* or *pari passu* debt, which gets its name from the Latin translation "by rate of" or "by change of." Pro rata debt is where there are two or more issuances of debt that have equal priority. The debt is known to pay in a concurrent manner. This means that cash flow is paid to each debt instrument as it is due; but if there is a shortfall, then the shortfall is shared equally, depending on principal balance or possibly what each debt issuance is owed. Refer to Figure 6.3 for a graphical overview of the two methods.

MODEL BUILDER 6.1: SETTING UP DEBT AND CALCULATING WHAT IS DUE

1. We need to get some debt assumptions into the model. Insert a worksheet after the Intangibles sheet and name it **Debt**. Enter the text **Debt** in cell A1 of the newly created sheet.
2. Enter the following text in the corresponding cells to establish labels for the Debt sheet:

A1: **Debt**
B3: **Long-Term Debt Assumptions**
B4: **Debt Issuance**

D4: **Rate**
E4: **Spreads**
F4: **Term**
G4: **Balance**
H4: **Issue Date**
I4: **Maturity Date**
J4: **PMT Type**
K4: **Priority**
L4: **Pro Rata Seq**

3. Notice that we are creating fields for assumptions directly on the Debt sheet rather than the Assumptions sheet. This is because we will be heavily focused on Debt and will want to work in this sheet frequently. If a user is not as concerned by debt, but rather by other areas of the model, she should expand the area of the model that she is most focused on and enter specific assumptions in that area. For now, we will focus on debt and enter initial values for assumptions in the corresponding cells:

B5: **1**
B6: **2**
B7: **3**
E5: **2.35%**
E6: **2.50%**
E7: **2.58%**
F5: **36**
F6: **48**
F7: **60**
G5: **5**
G6: **10**
G7: **20**
H5: **12/31/2008**
H6: **12/31/2008**
H7: **12/31/2008**
I5: **12/31/2011**
I6: **12/31/2012**
I7: **12/31/2013**
L5: **1**
L6: **1**
L7: **1**

Keep in mind that we skipped a few columns. Those columns were skipped because the assumptions will get their values from data validation lists that we need to create first. Another nuance that some might notice is we put hard-coded values in for both term and maturity date. Theoretically, when the term changes,

A	B	C	D	E	F	G	H	I	J	K	L
Debt											
Long-Term Debt Assumptions											
Debt Issuance	Rate			Spreads	Term	Balance	Issue Date	Maturity Date	PMT Type	Priority	Pro Rata Seq
1				2.35%	36	5	12/31/2008	12/31/2011			1
2				2.50%	48	10	12/31/2008	12/31/2012			1
3				2.58%	60	20	12/31/2008	12/31/2013			1

FIGURE 6.4 Since debt is often a key factor in a model, the debt assumptions will be located directly on the debt sheet.

the maturity date should change or vice versa. For now, let's leave them both as hard-coded values and keep in mind that they should be consistent. Thus far the model should look like Figure 6.4.

We should also go through and name each assumption. Name the following cells with the corresponding names:

E5: debt_Debt1Spd
E6: debt_Debt2Spd
E7: debt_Debt3Spd
F5: debt_Debt1Term
F6: debt_Debt2Term
F7: debt_Debt3Term
G5: debt_Debt1BegBal
G6: debt_Debt2BegBal
G7: debt_Debt3BegBal
H5: debt_Debt1BalDate
H6: debt_Debt2BalDate
H7: debt_Debt3BalDate
I5: debt_Debt1MatDate
I6: debt_Debt2MatDate
I7: debt_Debt3MatDate
L5: debt_Debt1PRSeq
L6: debt_Debt2PRSeq
L7: debt_Debt3PRSeq

4. Let's create the information needed for the data validation lists by first going to the Hidden sheet. On the Hidden sheet enter the following text in the corresponding cells:

A18: lst_PaymentType
A19: Level
A20: Bullet
A22: lst_Priority

A23: **Sequential**
A24: **Pro Rata**

Name the range A19:A20 **lst_PaymentType** and range A23:A24 **lst_Priority**.

5. We can now go back to the Debt sheet and create data validation lists. In cells J5, J6, and J7, create data validation lists using lst_PaymentType as the source for each list. Similarly, in cells K5, K6, and K7, create data validation lists using lst_Priority as the source for each list. Set the J values to Level and the K values to Sequential for now. Name the following cells with the corresponding names:

J5: **debt_Debt1PayType**
J6: **debt_Debt2PayType**
J7: **debt_Debt3PayType**
K5: **debt_Debt1Priority**
K6: **debt_Debt2Priority**
K7: **debt_Debt3Priority**

6. We will next create a data validation for the rates. This is a special list since it is contained on the Vectors sheet and should be referenced directly there. However, we have yet to create any interest rate information on the Vectors sheet and should do that first. Go to the Vectors sheet and enter the following text in the corresponding cells:

B33: **Interest Rates**
B34: **10Y U.S. Treasuries**
B35: **Euribor**
B36: **3M Libor**
B37: **1M Libor**

Name the range B34:B37 **lst_InterestRates**.

7. Since interest rates can change in sensitivity analysis, we should also create labels for each of interest rates for each scenario below the current/live scenario. Enter the following formula in the cell references below:

B64, B95, B126: **=B33**
B65, B96, B127: **=B34**
B66, B97, B128: **=B35**
B67, B98, B129: **=B36**
B68, B99, B130: **=B37**

8. Refer to the assumptions entered on the Vectors sheet of the CD-ROM for each scenario (Base Case, Upside Case, and Downside Case) interest rate value. This should be done particularly if you want to follow along and compare numerical results between the version you are building and the complete example

	A	B	C	D	E	F	G	H	I	J
33		**Interest Rates**								
34		10Y U.S. Treasuries			3.00%	3.50%	4.00%	4.50%	5.00%	5.50%
35		Euribor			4.50%	4.50%	4.50%	4.50%	4.50%	4.50%
36		3M Libor			6.00%	6.00%	6.00%	6.00%	6.00%	6.00%
37		1M Libor			4.20%	4.20%	4.20%	4.20%	4.20%	4.20%

FIGURE 6.5 The interest rates are stored on the Vectors sheet and also can change between scenarios.

model. These values can always be changed later. This section should look like Figure 6.5.

9. We need to create the functionality to change the interest rates in the current/live scenario, when the scenario is changed on the Assumptions sheet. This is done by entering the following formula in cell E34:

=CHOOSE(ctrl_ScenNmbr,E65,E96,E127,E158)

Copy and paste this formula over the range E34:J37.

10. With the interest rate assumptions entered, we can go back to the Debt sheet and create data validation lists for the user to select an index for each debt issuance. On the Debt sheet, create data validation lists in cells D5, D6, and D7 using the named range lst_InterestRates as the source of the list. Select **1M Libor** as the initial value for each cell in range D5:D7. Make sure to name the following cells with the corresponding names:

D5: debt_Debt1Rate
D6: debt_Debt2Rate
D7: debt_Debt3Rate

11. We are close to actually doing some debt calculations, but have more prep on the Debt sheet. Dates and timing are incredibly important for debt, and just as with other sheets we should reference the dates and timing from the Vectors sheet. On the Debt sheet, enter the following references in the corresponding cells:

D11: =Vectors!D9
D12: =Vectors!D10

Copy and paste cell D11 over range D11:Z11 and cell D12 over range D12:Z12.

12. The next step is creating the first debt issuance. As mentioned earlier, we will approach this conceptually by first determining how much debt is due. The formulas in this section can get complicated because of the numerous variations that debt can exhibit, but we will take a step-by-step approach and break down complicated formulas into understandable segments. Also the principal formulas will have to be left incomplete temporarily since their full functionality depends

on a balanced model where we know how much surplus cash exists. We will come back to finish these formulas in Chapter 7. Readers should be cognizant that we will focus on Debt 1 as a primary example and that many of the steps can be repeated for Debt 2 and Debt 3. There will be a few instances when formulas will differ between debt issuances, but these will be pointed out in detail. Let's start the actual debt calculations by entering the following text in the corresponding cells:

B15: **Debt 1**
B25: **Debt 2**
B35: **Debt 3**
B16: **Debt 1 Rate**
B26: **Debt 2 Rate**
B36: **Debt 3 Rate**
B17, B27, B37: **Interest Due**
B20, B30, B40: **Custom Prin Amort %**
B21, B31, B41: **Principal Due**

13. Each debt issuance's interest rate is selected by the user on the Debt sheet. For Debt 1, the user selects an index in cell D5 and enters a spread value. Each period the projected index's rate could change depending on the assumptions from the Vectors sheet. We need to create functionality that looks up the correct interest rate from the Vectors sheet depending on the index selected on the Debt sheet and the time period.

This can be accomplished using the OFFSET MATCH combination, our most powerful lookup method. This method was first seen in Chapter 2, when we created a formula that returned the number of months between periods in cell B8 of the Hidden sheet. This cell changed when the user selected a periodicity in cell D10 on the Assumptions sheet. This method was also described in detail in Chapter 2's Toolbox.

For the case of the interest rates, we will offset the interest rates in the current/live section of the Vectors sheet by a value that is returned by matching the user-selected interest rate against all rates. On the Debt sheet, enter the following formula in cell E16:

=OFFSET(Vectors!E$33,MATCH(debt_Debt1Rate,lst_InterestRates,0),0)+ debt_Debt1Spd

Breaking this formula apart, we see that the OFFSET sets its reference on cell E32 of the Vectors sheet. Notice that this cell is directly above the possible interest rates for the first projection period. The next part of the formula uses the MATCH function to return the ordinal value of the index the user selected on the Debt sheet (debt_Debt1Rate) in the list of all possible interest rates (lst_InterestRates). Since this is an exact MATCH, do not forget to finish off the

MATCH function with the 0 parameter at the end. To finish off the OFFSET function, make sure to include a 0 at the end for the column parameter. Since this formula will be dragged across each period we do not want to offset any columns; we want to offset only vertically to get the correct rate depending on the selected index. Finally, the last bit of the formula adds the spread for Debt 1. Copy and paste this formula over the range E16:J16. Replicate this formula for Debt 2 and Debt 3 in rows 26 and 36 respectively. Make sure to change all references so they are applicable to the correct tranche of debt. Figure 6.6 visually depicts these connections.

14. Let's test this new functionality and explain some of the flexibility of implementing such a rate-lookup system. On the Debt sheet, change the Debt 1 Rate in cell D5 from 1M Libor to **3M Libor**. This should change the interest rates in range E16:J16 so that they reflect the 3M Libor assumption from the Vectors sheet, plus the spread on the Debt sheet in cell E5.

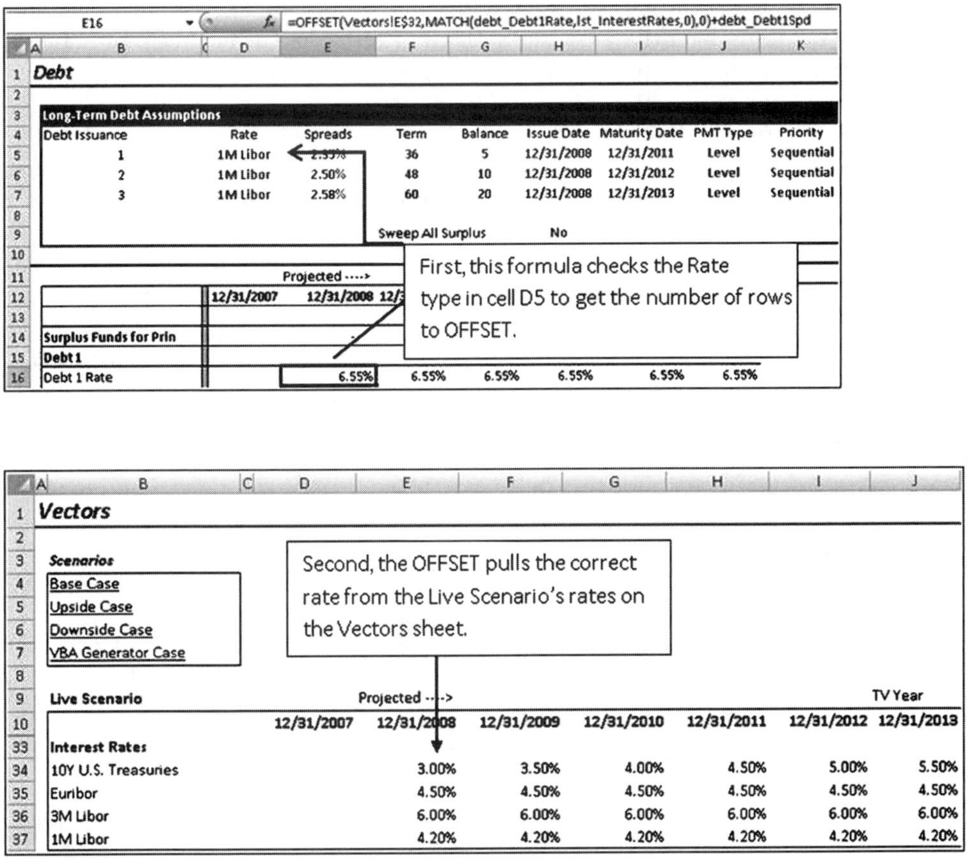

FIGURE 6.6 The OFFSET MATCH combination works well to manage interest rates.

What if a user wanted to store more than just four rates in the model? A powerful benefit of the method we implemented is the scalability of using named ranges, referencing, and lookup functions. Go to the Vectors sheet and insert a row between rows 34 and 35. Enter a new interest rate index by entering the text **BBSY** in cell B35. We will want to have versions of this rate for each scenario, so insert rows between 66 and 67, 98 and 99, and 130 and 131. Note that these instructions assume the reader inserts each row starting from the top of the sheet; otherwise, the cell references above may be slightly different.

For each newly inserted row, enter the text **BBSY** for each B column reference. Next, enter proxy values for each scenario. These should be made up since this is a test of functionality and not part of the complete example model. Back on row 35, enter the lookup functionality created by the CHOOSE function and reference each scenario's interest rates depending on the scenario number from the Hidden sheet (which the user selected from the Assumptions page). Now, go back to the Debt sheet and select the data validation list in D5. BBSY should appear as the second rate on the available interest rates. When it is selected, the rates for Debt 1 on the Debt sheet should reflect the current scenario's BBSY assumptions that are populated in the current/live section of the Vectors sheet. This addition is depicted in Figure 6.7.

It is very important to understand that the data validation list picked up the new interest rate because it was inserted *between* the boundaries of the named range lst_InterestRates. While we could introduce functionality for picking up new values in named ranges that are entered at the end of the named ranges, we will use the simpler method of inserting new items between named ranges. Also keep in mind that by entering the new interest rate name the ordinal values of the items on the list below the newly inserted item increase by 1. This is all taken care of automatically through the use of the OFFSET MATCH combination on the Debt sheet.

Some readers may also notice that we discussed fixed-rate issuance earlier in this chapter, but seem to have implemented only a floating-rate system. The current setup of the model is quite easy to integrate fixed rates. Use the same

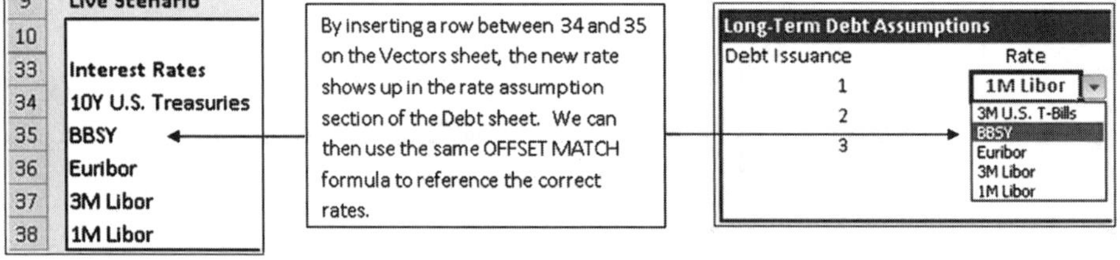

FIGURE 6.7 By using a combination of data validation lists and lookup functions we can easily scale the model to accept additional data points.

method as previously, where a row is inserted on the Vectors sheet between cells B34 and B37, name it **Fixed Rate**, and enter the same fixed-rate assumption each period. Make sure to zero out the spread on the Debt sheet for fixed-rate issuances, unless your intention is to put a fixed base rate and then a margin on the Debt sheet.

At this point, in order to adhere to the example model provided on the CD-ROM, you should delete any additional interest rates that you added to test the scalability. If you choose to leave the additional interest rates in the model, there will be a number of references on the Vectors sheet that will differ from the text.

15. Now that we have an interest rate each period to reference, we are nearly set to calculate the interest due. However, the interest due is composed of two parts, the interest rate and the principal balance outstanding. We should take a moment to create the periodic balances for the debt. The periodic balance for each debt issuance tracks the balance, which could change as principal is repaid. This will be done below all of the debt schedules on the Debt sheet. Enter the following text and references in the corresponding cells to set up labels for the debt balances:

B47: **BOP Balances**
B48: **=B15**
B49: **=B25**
B50: **=B35**
B52: **EOP Balances**
B53: **=B15**
B54: **=B25**
B55: **=B35**

BOP in *BOP Balances* stands for *beginning of period*; *EOP* stands for *end of period*. Be very careful with debt balances since amortization and possible interest capitalization can change balances between periods. Also, be cognizant to never reference items in the future. For instance, once we create the EOP Balance for Debt 1 we should never reference the EOP Balance in the period that is being used to calculate it. This is a common mistake and will create circular references.

16. Next we can get the correct beginning-of-period balance for Debt 1 by thinking about the concept status and entering the following formula in cell D48 on the Debt sheet:

=IF(D12<debt_Debt1BalDate,0,C53)

This formula checks the concept status by referencing the current period's date (cell D12) and seeing whether it is less than the issuance date (debt_Debt1BalDate). If this is the case, we are in a time period prior to issuance and there is no beginning balance (0). Otherwise, the beginning balance is last year's ending balance, which we will create in the next step. Copy and paste this formula over the range D48:J48.

17. Determining the end-of-period balance is more challenging. We will enter the full formula now, but it will reference cells that we have not created yet. The logic will be explained now and further as concepts that relate to this formula are introduced. Enter the following formula in cell D53 on the Debt sheet:

=IF(D12<debt_Debt1BalDate,0,IF(D12=debt_Debt1BalDate,debt_Debt1 BegBal,D48-D22+D19))

Let's break this formula down by each section. First, an IF function is used just as in the BOP Balance section in order to determine the concept status. If the current period's date is less than the issuance date, then there is no balance. However, we quickly deviate from the BOP Balance formula by immediately implementing another IF function that tests the current date to see whether it is equal to the issuance date. If this is the case, then the end-of-period balance is whatever the user entered as the beginning balance of Debt 1 in cell G5. If we are in a period greater than the issuance date, then we should see what the beginning balance of the loan is (cell D48) and subtract out any principal amortization paid (cell D22) and add any unpaid or capitalized interest (cell D19). Unpaid interest and principal payment will be addressed later in this chapter. Copy and paste this formula over the range D53:J53. This process can be replicated for Debt 2 and Debt 3 by making sure to change all assumptions and schedule references to the applicable columns and rows. Figure 6.8 shows the creation of the first few periods of balances.

A	B	C	D	E	F
11				Projected ---->	
12			12/31/2007	12/31/2008	12/31/2009
47	BOP Balances				
48	Debt 1		-	-	5.00
49	Debt 2		-	-	10.00
50	Debt 3		-	-	20.00
51					
52	EOP Balances				
53	Debt 1		0.00	5.00	
54	Debt 2		0.00	10.00	
55	Debt 3		0.00	20.00	
56					
57					

FIGURE 6.8   The debt balances should be tracked from a beginning-of-period and end-of-period viewpoint.

18. We can now go back to the interest due section on the Debt sheet and enter the following formula in cell E17:

=E48*E16

Copy and paste this formula over the range E17:J17. This formula multiplies the beginning-of-period balance by the current periodic interest rate. A key word in the previous sentence was *periodic*. Notice that this model is set up to an annual periodicity. If it is changed to anything else, the rates need to be adjusted on the Vectors sheet so they reflect the correct periodicity. One can attempt to automate this process with entering only annual rates and using a divisor based on the periodicity, but it is not very complex to just enter the correct periodic rate on the Vectors sheet. One other point is that the interest amount is temporarily going to be excessively high each period since the debt balance does not change each period, because we have yet to create the principal amortization. This section can be replicated for Debt 2 and Debt 3 at this point.

19. Paying interest will be discussed later in this chapter, so we should now turn to principal due calculations. The first section we should develop is in the instance of custom bullet amortization, where percentages of original balance are due during the projection period. For this we will create a row of percentage assumptions that the user can customize. Enter 0.00% for now in each cell in the ranges E20:J20, E30:J30, and E40:J40.

20. The principal due formula will be one of the most complex formulas in the entire example model. It will be created in multiple steps that will continuously add functionality. The most basic functionality that we want to create is calculating the correct principal due given two possible amortization methods: level principal or bullet principal. Enter the following formula in cell E21 on the Debt sheet:

=IF(debt_Debt1PayType="Level",MIN(debt_Debt1BegBal/(debt_Debt1Term/ ctrl_Periodicity),D53),min(E20*debt_Debt1BegBal,D53))

This formula first looks to the user-selected principal payment type (debt_ Debt1PayType) and checks whether a level principal method is selected. If this is the case, then the principal is calculated by dividing the beginning balance of Debt 1 (debt_Debt1BegBal) by the monthly term (debt_Debt1Term), further divided by the numerical periodicity (ctrl_Periodicity). This figure is within a MIN function that takes the minimum of the previously calculated principal amount and the prior period's principal balance. This MIN function is necessary for two reasons: (1) When there is no balance, there is no principal payment due, and (2) if the principal balance goes off schedule due to principal prepayment, then the MIN function ensures that no more principal is paid in a given period than the principal balance at the beginning of the period. No one will pay more than they owe. Note that it is my habit to reference the prior period's end-of-period principal balance, which is essentially the same as the current period's principal balance. These references can be used interchangeably based on your preference.

| | E21 | | | f_x | =IF(debt_Debt1PayType="Level",MIN(debt_Debt1BegBal/(debt_Debt1Term/ctrl_Periodicity),D53),E20* debt_Debt1BegBal) |

	B	C	D	E	F	G	H	I	J	K	L
12			12/31/2007	12/31/2008	12/31/2009	12/31/2010	12/31/2011	12/31/2012	12/31/2013		
13											
14	**Surplus Funds for Prin**			-	13.46	24.33	58.73	82.06	90.41		
15	**Debt 1**										
16	Debt 1 Rate			6.55%	6.55%	6.55%	6.55%	6.55%	6.55%		
17	Interest Due			-	0.33	0.22	0.11	-	-		
18	Interest Paid										
19	Interest Unpaid										
20	Custom Prin Amort %			0.00%	0.00%	0.00					
21	Principal Due			-	1.67	1.6					
46											
47	**BOP Balances**										
48	Debt 1			-	-	5.00	3.3				
49	Debt 2			-	-	10.00	7.5				
50	Debt 3			-	-	20.00	16.0				
51											
52	**EOP Balances**										
53	Debt 1			0.00	5.00		1.67	0.00	0.00	0.00	
54	Debt 2			0.00	10.00		5.00	2.50	0.00	0.00	
55	Debt 3			0.00	20.00		12.00	8.00	4.00	0.00	

The sheet should be developing as shown here. Notice that the principal due comes one period after issuance and that the formula caps the due amount using a MIN function.

FIGURE 6.9 The principal due is currently based on the user-selected amortization methods and is capped by the prior period's balance.

Also, if you are unfamiliar with the MIN function, refer to the Toolbox at the end of this chapter. For a graphical depiction, refer to Figure 6.9.

The outer part of the formula is the IF function. If the IF function that tests whether the principal payment type is set to level principal method is FALSE, then a bullet percentage method is implemented. This is done by multiplying the user-entered percentage (cell E20) by the original balance of the loan (debt_Debt1BegBal). A MIN function is still necessary here because the debt schedule could go off schedule due to prepayments.

21. An additional feature we will add to this function is to turn off principal calculations when the debt is reduced to a very small level. When principal is prepaid, it sometimes throws debt off by very small decimal amounts. If these small balances persist, then there could be issues in later projection periods. As a check against this we can implement a precision factor to zero out calculations. Essentially, a precision factor allows us to tell the model to stop calculating when a value is reduced to a very, very small amount. Rather than hard coding this feature into formulas, we will create a precision level on the Assumptions sheet and use it throughout the model. Go to the Assumptions sheet and enter the text **Precision Level** in cell B12. Enter the value **.0001** in cell D12 and name that cell **inputs_Precision**. Now, go back to the Debt sheet and modify the formula in cell E21 to reflect the following:

=IF(D53<inputs_Precision,0,IF(debt_Debt1PayType="Level",MIN(debt_ Debt1BegBal/(debt_Debt1Term/ctrl_Periodicity),D53),min(E20* debt_Debt1BegBal,D53)))

This addition to the formula checks the prior period's end-of-period balance to see whether it is less than the precision factor, which is nearly zero. If the balance is that low, then the principal payment is assumed to be 0. This protects against situations where there are thousandths of a penny in balance that could perpetuate a payment unnecessarily. The precision factor can be changed on the Assumptions sheet to a value that the model user is comfortable with or to a level that an auditor requires.

At this point, you can copy and paste the formula in cell E21 over the range E21:J21 with the understanding that this formula will change later. For this section, hold off completing the principal due for Debt 2 and Debt 3. There are minor changes between the tranche formulas that will be discussed later in this chapter.

PAYING LIABILITIES

So far we have calculated what is due for the long-term debt interest and principal. The more complicated step is determining how much can be paid, depending on the corporation's cash flows. This seems relatively simple in theory: If there is enough cash to pay the liability, pay the liability; otherwise, pay what is possible with the cash flow. We will see in Model Builder 6.2 that this theory is not too difficult to initially implement, but when we introduce the possibility of varying payment priorities, it becomes complex.

Getting the Correct Order

The ordering of liability payments within a company is extremely important. Altering payment priority can completely change the risk profile and investment-worthiness of a lending decision. The most standard form of payment priority is *sequential*, where each liability is paid in order or seniority. The most senior liability gets paid first, the immediate junior liability gets paid next, and so on. This process continues until everyone is paid or until there is no more cash and certain creditors receive partial payments or no funds at all. Within this process junior creditors should get paid a higher interest rate than creditors more senior to themselves. This is proper risk pricing since the more junior a creditor is the more risk of default exists. Refer to Figure 6.10 for a graphical representation of this concept.

A common alternative to sequential payment priority is pro rata or pari passu priority. A pro rata payment priority is typical for syndicated or bilateral funding, where two or more parties have the same priority of payment. However, if there is a shortfall or prepayment, how should the funds be divided? The division of loss or excess is done on a pro rata or proportional basis. In many cases, the proportion is based on the liability principal balance. This can be detected when reading loan documents and coming across wording such as: "The payment should be made *concurrently* on a *pro rata basis* based on...." An alternative to using principal balance as the basis for the pro rata division is the terminology "based on each

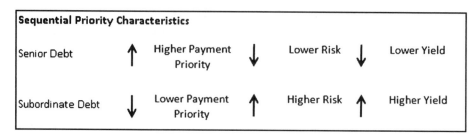

FIGURE 6.10   There are common risk and reward trade-offs to sequential debt structures.

liability's due amount." In the case of interest payments, this would suggest that the pro rata proportion is based on interest due amounts.

To understand the effects of payment priority, we will go through an example of paying liabilities using a sequential payment structure, a pro rata payment structure based on principal balance, and a pro rata payment structure based on interest due. Let us assume we have two loans with the following characteristics:

Loan 1 Principal Balance: $500
Loan 1 Interest Rate: 8%
Loan 2 Principal Balance: $250
Loan 2 Interest Rate: 10%

The interest payments due for the first period would be $40 for Loan 1 and $25 for Loan 2. Assume that we had $75 to pay our liabilities. In such a case, both loans are able to receive their full interest payment since the combined liabilities are $65. However, now assume a stress scenario and that the cash available is reduced to $50. Under a sequential payment priority where Loan 1 is senior to Loan 2, Loan 1 would receive its full $40 of interest, while Loan 2 would receive only $10 of the $25 due. Loan 2 would bear the full brunt of the $15 shortfall in debt service. As the first loss lender, Loan 2 is riskier, which is why it is getting paid a higher interest rate. These calculations are shown in Figure 6.11.

Let's suspend reality for a minute and hold all assumptions the same, but change the payment priority to pro rata based on loan balance. The reason I suggest we are suspending reality is that the interest rates most likely would be more in line with each other in a pro rata situation, although in certain bilateral negotiations each lender's rates may be unknown to the other. Regardless, under a pro rata situation where the first loan represents 67% of the combined principal outstanding and the second loan is the other 33%, a sharing of the loss in the $50 cash flow case would take place. Loan 1 would be paid only $33 ($50 * 67%), while Loan 2 would be paid $17 ($50 * 33%). Notice in this situation the $15 shortfall is allocated on a pro rata basis between the two loans. These calculations are shown in Figure 6.12.

Sequential Methodology		
Loan 1	$	500
Loan 1		8.00%
Loan 2	$	250
Loan 2		10.00%
Cash Available	$	50
Loan 1 Interest Due:	$	40
Loan 1 Interest Paid:	$	40
Loan 2 Interest Due:	$	25
Loan 2 Interest Paid:	$	10

FIGURE 6.11 A sequential pay structure will show loss at the subordinate level first.

We can now try a third method of payment priority: pro rata using the interest due amounts as the proportion. Under this situation, Loan 1 has a proportional share of 62% ($40 interest due out of $65 of total interest due), whereas Loan 2 has a share of 38% ($25 interest due out of $65 of total interest due). Using the same example we have used for the previous two payment priority methodologies, under this payment priority Loan 1 would be paid $31, whereas Loan 2 receives

Pro Rata Methodology Using Principal for Proportional Calculation				
Loan 1	$	500	Proportional Share	66.67%
Loan 1		8.00%	(based on balance)	
Loan 2	$	250	Proportional Share	33.33%
Loan 2		10.00%	(based on balance)	
Cash Available	$	50		
Loan 1 Interest Due:	$	40		
Loan 1 Interest Paid:	$	33		
Loan 2 Interest Due:	$	25		
Loan 2 Interest Paid:	$	17		

FIGURE 6.12 A pro rata pay structure shares loss depending on the proportional share calculation.

Pro Rata Methodology Using Int Due for Proportional Calculation				
Loan 1	$	500		
Loan 1		8.00%		
Loan 2	$	250		
Loan 2		10.00%		
Cash Available	$	50		
Loan 1 Interest Due:	$	40	Proportional Share	61.54%
Loan 1 Interest Paid:	$	31	(based on int due)	
Loan 2 Interest Due:	$	25	Proportional Share	38.46%
Loan 2 Interest Paid:	$	19	(based on int due)	

FIGURE 6.13 Depending on the proportional share calculation the sharing of loss can be different.

$19. Simply by changing the payment priority methodology we can alter the cash flow that each lender receives. Figure 6.13 summarizes these calculations.

Mechanics of Calculating the Correct Amount

Once we know how much should be directed to each party, we should make sure to institute a method that ensures the correct amount is actually paid each period. Calculations done by hand are fine with the standalone examples in the previous section, but we need to implement a system of logic that will return the correct amount to be paid each period. This can be done with the following statement: "Pay the lesser of what is available and what is due."

This statement can be applied to most examples, although determining what is available and what is due can occasionally get very complicated. As an example, let's use Loan 1's interest due amount of $40 above. If we had $50 available to pay the $40 interest due, then we would pay the lesser of $50 and $40, which is $40. If we had $30 available to pay the $40 interest due, then we would pay the lesser of $30 and $40, which is $30. Any way we work it, with this situation we will either pay the due amount, or, in a shortfall situation, all of the money available. Figure 6.14 shows how this calculation is set up (we will explain this calculation further in the next Model Builder).

An issue that we should discuss is the money that is available. In a corporation, what funds are available to pay debt service? This is an interesting question for financial modelers since we want to set up our model to draw upon the correct funds at the correct time. In the case of interest due to borrowers, we should recall

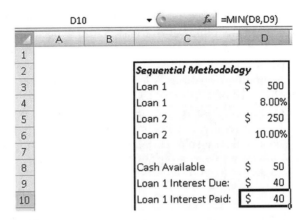

FIGURE 6.14 This calculation shows how to implement the theory of paying the lesser of what is available and what is due.

from most accounting methodologies that any amounts of interest paid are tax deductible, while principal is not. This suggests that the funds to pay interest come from a source pretax. If we work backward through the income statement, we have *net income, taxes paid, earnings before tax,* and then *interest expense/income.* Right before interest expense/income the funds available to the firm are *earnings before interest and taxes* (EBIT).

Careful readers may say, "But prior to EBIT there could be non-cash items removed such as depreciation and amortization. Also, there could be cash on hand. Aren't there really more funds available?" Those readers are correct. There is more cash available if you add back the non-cash items and the cash on hand that period, but this could be an aggressive assumption depending on perspective. Lenders may think using earnings before interest, taxes, depreciation and amortization (EBITDA) is aggressive, particularly with capital-intensive companies, since the depreciation and amortization amounts will have to be replaced to keep the business in operation. From a short-term point of view, the difference between EBTIDA and EBIT is there in cash, but in the long term it is not viable to keep using that cash.

Similarly, if cash on hand is used to pay debt service, there could be anomalies in the figure that are only temporary. For instance, if a company sold off assets in one period and tried to use that amount as debt service coverage, it would be unsustainable unless it kept selling off assets at the same level. If this took place, it would probably impair the business from operating and reduce the ongoing cash flow to the firm that could be used for debt repayment. Also, if a minimal amount of cash is needed to run the company, the cash on hand may not be truly available for debt service. For our purposes, we will be conservative and use EBIT as the source of funds for interest debt service.

Principal is a different matter since it is paid after tax. This can get complicated since there are a number of items that may need to be paid after tax. Capital expenditure is perhaps the most important. Certain capital expenditures could be put on hold in times of distress, but that investment is typically necessary to keep a company running over time. Another major item after tax is equity payment or dividends. In times of distress or leading up to distress, dividends should be locked out and debt repaid. Just from these two we see that the person using the financial model must be careful where he draws his principal repayment funds from. In our case, we will calculate surplus cash after funding the company and use that amount to pay required amortization; if funds are still left over, then we will implement a cash sweep to prepay debt.

MODEL BUILDER 6.2: PAYING THE CORRECT LIABILITY AMOUNT

1. The first payment we will make will be the interest payments. We will start with easy formulas by implementing the simplest form of payment priority—sequential. Prior to entering formulas, we should take a moment to add some additional labels by entering the following text in the corresponding cells:

   B18, B28, B38: **Interest Paid**
   B19, B29, B39: **Interest Unpaid**
   B22, B32, B42: **Principal Paid**
   B23, B33, B43: **Principal Unpaid**

2. With labels complete, we can now start entering the first interest paid formula. Enter the following formula in cell E18 on the Debt sheet to create the interest payment for Debt 1:

   =MIN('Income Statement'!E17-'Income Statement'!E19+'Income Statement'! E25-'Income Statement'!E28,E17)

   Earlier we used the MIN function to prevent calculating too much principal to be due. In this case, we are using the MIN function to translate the statement "Pay the lesser of what is available and due" directly into an Excel function. Notice that the sources of the funds for the first interest payment are being calculated using EBIT, less nonoperating expenses, plus interest income, less short-term debt interest. At this point, we have not calculated the interest income or short-term debt interest, but will come back to those calculations in Chapter 7. The MIN function takes the lesser of those funds and the interest due. Copy and paste this formula over the range E18:J18.

3. We will now implement the same formula for Debt 2, but there will be a slight difference. Let's enter the following formula in cell E28 and then discuss the difference:

=MIN('Income Statement'!E17-'Income Statement'!E19+'Income Statement'!
  E25-'Income Statement'!E28-E18,E27)

The difference is that there is an additional item subtracted from what is available. Notice we subtract cell E18, which is Debt 1's interest paid amount. This is because we have implemented a sequential payment structure and funds that have been paid to Debt 1 are not available to Debt 2. Copy and paste this formula over the range E28:J28.

4. We should then enter the last interest paid formula in cell E38:

=MIN('Income Statement'!E17-'Income Statement'!E19+'Income Statement'!
  E25-'Income Statement'!E28-E18-E28,E37)

Notice the pattern of subtracting out the senior debts' interest payments (Debt 1 and Debt 2). By calculating what can be paid in such a way we will never misplace cash and use it for other sources that should not have access. Models that do not subtract out senior debt payments from cash available to junior layers, whether intentional or not, are creating fictitious cash in the model.

5. If we know how much interest is due and how much can be paid, we should take a moment to calculate whether there is any unpaid interest. This calculation is just interest due minus interest paid. Enter the following formula in cell E19, still on the Debt sheet:

=E17-E18

Copy and paste this formula over the range E19:J19. This amount is very useful for creating internal validations to quickly see whether any interest payment is missed and also for capitalizing unpaid interest. Recall that we referenced row 19 in row 53, the balance calculation, so that any unpaid interest was added to that period's balance. This is the full interest capitalization implementation. The model should be developing as seen in Figure 6.15.

6. We should also remember to enter the unpaid interest formulas for Debt 2 and Debt 3. Enter the following formulas in the corresponding cell references:

E29: =E27-E28
E39: =E37-E38

Copy and paste these formulas to column J in their respective rows.

7. The remaining steps are focused on principal payments and can get very complicated, so it is important to pay close attention to the growth and final outcome of formulas. The first step we need to do for principal is creating a space for the funds available to pay the principal. Since we have yet to finish the balance sheet we do not know how much surplus funds there are to pay the principal. We will label and put proxy values in for now until we complete the surplus funds

⊿ A	B	K	D	E	F	G	H	I	J	K	L
1	**Debt**										
2											
3	**Long-Term Debt Assumptions**										
4	Debt Issuance		Rate	Spreads	Term	Balance	Issue Date	Maturity Date	PMT Type	Priority	Pro Rata Seq
5	1		1M Libor	2.35%	36	5	12/31/2008	12/31/2011	Level	Sequential	1
6	2		1M Libor	2.50%	48	10	12/31/2008	12/31/2012	Level	Sequential	1
7	3		1M Libor	2.58%	60	20	12/31/2008	12/31/2013	Level	Sequential	1
8											
9											
10											
11				Projected ---->						TV Year	
12			12/31/2007	12/31/2008	12/31/2009	12/31/2010	12/31/2011		12/31/2012	12/31/2013	
13											
14											
15	Debt 1										
16	Debt 1 Rate			6.55%	6.55%	6.55%	6.55%	6.55%	6.55%		
17	Interest Due			—	0.33	0.22	0.11	—	—		
18	Interest Paid			—	0.33	0.22	0.11	—	—		
19	Interest Unpaid			—	—	—	—	—	—		

FIGURE 6.15 Thus far we have covered enough to set up debt and make interest payments. Note that your version will have different figures until principal amortization is implemented.

field in Chapter 7. On the Debt sheet, enter the following text in the corresponding cell:

B14: **Surplus Funds for Prin**

Also in each cell within the range E14:J14 enter a value of **100**. This will be a proxy value until we complete the surplus funds calculation.

8. Now we have two primary formulas to complete: principal due and principal paid. We never completely finished the principal due formula in Model Builder 6.1 because when a cash sweep is implemented we need to understand payment priorities for the distribution of excess cash. Now that we know more about payment priorities we can complete the formula.

The first formula to focus on is principal due. The challenge with principal due is that when there is surplus cash, it is often used to accelerate the pay down of long-term debt. This may or may not be the case, so we need to implement an option for the user to allow all of the surplus cash to be due for principal prepayment. To do this, we need to create a few administrative items.

On the Debt sheet, in cell F9, enter the text **Sweep All Surplus**. Cell H9 will contain a Yes/No selection, which we will create as a data validation list. Go to the Hidden sheet and enter the following text in the corresponding cells:

D12: **lst_YesNo**
D13: **Yes**
D14: **No**

Name the range D13:D14 **lst_YesNo**. Go back to the Debt sheet and in cell H9 create a data validation list using the named range lst_YesNo as the source.

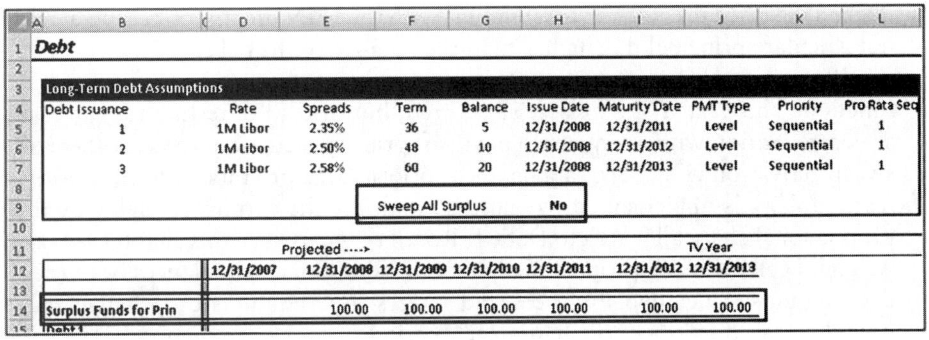

FIGURE 6.16 The cash sweep and surplus funds available for principal payment are added to the sheet.

Name cell H9 **debt_CashSweepOn**. When debt_CashSweepOn is set to Yes, we will take all of the surplus cash and use that to pay down debt. This means that the principal due formula will draw from the entire surplus in each period of row 14 on the Debt sheet. For now, keep the cash sweep off by selecting **No**. Keep in mind that right now we have proxy values in row 14, which will be altered in Chapter 7. The new features are highlighted in bold black boxes in Figure 6.16.

9. With the cash sweep option implemented we are primed to complete the principal due formula that we started in Model Builder 6.1. The complete formula will follow with a detailed explanation of each new addition, which is in bold in the formula. On the Debt sheet in cell E21, modify the existing formula so that it reads:

=IF(AND(debt_CashSweepOn="Yes",debt_Debt1Priority="Sequential"),
MIN(E14,D53),IF(AND(debt_CashSweepOn="Yes",debt_Debt1Priority=
"Pro Rata"),MIN(E14*E60,D53),IF(D53<inputs_Precision,0,IF(debt_Debt1
PayType="Level",MIN(debt_Debt1BegBal/(debt_Debt1Term/ctrl_
Periodicity),D53),E20*debt_Debt1BegBal))))

This is clearly one of the most complex formulas in the model. There are multiple nested IF, AND, and MIN functions. Also there is a reference to a pro rata section that we have not completed yet, so if pro rata is selected as the payment priority method for this loan this formula will return an error. Let's begin from the very beginning of the formula and work through each IF function. The first IF function immediately uses an AND function in order to evaluate two conditions. The first condition is whether the cash sweep is activated; the second condition is whether the payment priority is set to sequential or pro rata. If the cash sweep is on and the payment priority is set to sequential, then the minimum of the surplus funds (cell E14) and the prior period's end-of-period balance (cell E53) is returned. In a sequential payment priority structure with a cash sweep activated, any remaining surplus cash will first be due to the most senior debt

(Debt 1). Notice that we cap this amount with the MIN function since we would not calculate principal due higher than the balance of the debt.

If the first IF function is false, then another test is set with a nested IF function. The next IF is similarly structured, but instead of testing for the cash sweep activation with a sequential payment priority method, it tests for the cash sweep activation with a pro rata payment priority. If a pro rata payment priority methodology is implemented, we need to multiply the surplus available by the proportional share allocated to Debt 1. Recall that earlier in this chapter we saw we could calculate this proportional amount using principal balances or interest due amounts. Since debt balances and interest due amounts can change each period we need to track this figure each period. In our example model we will set up pro rata proportional shares based on debt balance. This will be done in Model Builder step 10. For now, we can reference where we will do that calculation (cell E60). If we constrain the surplus available by the proportional share, we are correctly calculating the amount available. We must still worry about exceeding the principal balance of the debt, so we use a MIN function.

Finally, if the cash sweep is not activated, then our principal due amount is the previously explained calculation that is dependent on whether a level or bullet payment methodology is selected. Copy and paste the formula over the range E21:J21.

10. A critical element that is incomplete in the last formula is the reference to cell E60, where the pro rata proportional share is calculated. The formula that we will enter in cell E60 will be a special type of formula known as an *array* formula. This is an intermediate-to-advanced use of Excel and is explained in more detail in the Toolbox later in this chapter. Let's learn about this formula by entering the following formula on the Debt sheet in cell E60:

=IF(E48<=inputs_Precision,0,E48/(SUM(IF(debt_Debt1PRSeq=$L$5:$L$7, E$48:E$50,0))))

You will immediately notice that this will cause an error. This is because the formula is an array formula and references multiple cells at a time. In order to tell Excel that we are entering an array formula we must hold down **CTRL-SHFT** and then press **ENTER** to correctly enter an array formula. This will cause the curly braces to appear as seen here:

{=IF(E48<=inputs_Precision,0,E48/(SUM(IF(debt_Debt1PRSeq=$L$5:$L$7, E$48:E$50,0))))}

The formula first checks the balance of Debt 1 at the beginning of the period. If it is less than the precision level, then the debt is paid off and there should be no proportional share to Debt 1. However, if Debt 1 has a balance, we need to compare that to the other debt balances in order to determine the proportional share due to Debt 1. Although this may seem like a simple division of

	E60				f_x	{=IF(E48<=inputs_Precision,0,E48/(SUM(IF(debt_Debt1PRSeq=$L$5:$L$7,E$48:E$50,0))))}				
	A	B	C	D	E	F	G	H	I	J	K
59		**Pro Rata Shares (Balances)**									
60					0.00%	14.29%	12.42%	8.93%	0.00%	0.00%	
61					0.00%	28.57%	27.95%	26.79%	23.81%	0.00%	
62					0.00%	57.14%	59.63%	64.29%	76.19%	100.00%	

FIGURE 6.17   The pro rata share percentages are critical to calculating the correct pro rata amounts.

Debt 1's balance by the total debt balances at the beginning of the period, there is a chance that all of the debt is not pro rata. Figure 6.17 shows this new addition.

This is where debt structures can get very complicated. We could have Debt 1 being a senior debt issuance and Debt 2 and Debt 3 as pro rata subordinate issuances. This would mean Debt 1 would have priority over cash flow, but Debt 2 and Debt 3 are pari passu and must share anything left over. Similarly, Debt 1 and Debt 2 could theoretically be pari passu and share the first amounts, while Debt 3 is sequential and must take subordinate cash flows. To overcome this problem it is best to implement a pro rata sequencer.

We create the basic pro rata sequencer in range L5:L7 on the Debt sheet. It is currently set to all 1's as a proxy. Keep in mind that the pro rata sequencer does nothing when a sequential payment priority method is set (which should be the current default state of the model). When we activate pro rata payment priority, we need to establish which debt is pro rata with the others. If all of the values in the pro rata sequencer are set to 1, then all of the debts are pro rata with each other. However, if the first loan is a senior and takes sequential priority over two pari passu issues, then the pro rata sequencer should be set to 1,2,2, indicating the first tranche is senior to two pari passu tranches. The default setting of 1,1,1 is entered in the example model and shown in Figure 6.18.

The actual assumption entry in range L5:L7 has little functionality. It is the conditional sum we created in the following part of the formula entered in cell E60:

SUM(IF(debt_Debt1PRSeq=$L$5:$L$7,E$48:E$50,0)))

This section of the formula sums results returned by an IF function that evaluates Debt 1's pro rata sequence (debt_Debt1PRSeq) against all of the pro rata sequences. It will at least be equal to itself, so at minimum the denominator will include the balance of Debt 1, which will produce 100% as the denominator to its own balance as a numerator. However, if other debt issuances share priority with Debt 1, then those balances will be returned by the IF function and then summed by the SUM formula. Copy and paste the formula in cell E60 over the range E60:J62. We should also label this section **Pro Rata Shares (Balances)** by entering that text in cell B59.

Pro Rata Seq

1

1

1

FIGURE 6.18 The pro rata sequencer is used to tell the formulas which loan issuances are pro rata with each other.

11. We can now complete the principal paid section. Enter the following formula in cell E22 on the Debt sheet:

=IF(debt_Debt1Priority="Sequential",MIN(E14,E21),MIN(E14*E60,E21))

If the payment priority is sequential, then the formula takes the lesser of what is available (cell E14) and what is due (cell E21). Otherwise, a pro rata payment priority is assumed, where the proportional share in cell E60 is multiplied to the surplus funds in order to determine how much cash is available for debt service. This amount is capped by the principal due calculation, using a MIN function. Copy and paste this formula over the range E22:J22.

12. Similar to interest, we should track whether there is unpaid principal. Go to cell E23 and enter the following formula:

=E21-E22

Copy and paste this formula over the range E23:J23. This completes Debt 1's principal calculations. We will next replicate the calculations for Debt 2 to show the similarities and differences when working with more than one issuance of debt.

13. The complete formula for Debt 2's principal due amount should be entered as follows in E31 on the Debt sheet:

=IF(AND(debt_CashSweepOn="Yes",debt_Debt2Priority="Sequential"),
    MIN(E14-E22,D54),IF(AND(debt_CashSweepOn="Yes",debt_Debt
    2Priority="Pro Rata"),MIN(E14*E61,D54),IF(D54<inputs_Precision,0,

IF(debt_Debt2PayType="Level",MIN(debt_Debt2BegBal/(debt_Debt2Term/ctrl_Periodicity),D54),E30*debt_Debt2BegBal))))

This formula is nearly identical to Debt 1's except for the following key differences:

- Any assumption that used the naming "Debt1," such as debt_Debt1Priority, is switched to Debt2, as in debt_Debt2Priority.
- Sequential calculations must remove Debt 1's principal payment. For example, the MIN function that calculates the principal due amount subtracts cell E22, which is Debt 1's principal paid amount.
- All references to Debt 1 information such as balances and pro rata share percentages must be changed to Debt 2.
  Copy and paste the formula over the range E31:J31.

14. For principal paid, the differences are the same, but for the formula in cell E32:

=IF(debt_Debt2Priority="Sequential",MIN
(E14-E22,E31),MIN(E14*E61,E31))

We can see that the primary differences are the references for Debt 2 and the subtraction of any principal paid to Debt 1. Copy and paste this formula over the range E32:J32.

15. Complete the process for Debt 2's principal unpaid and the pro rata share percentages. Be careful when dragging some references since there are many uses of named ranges that are specific to each debt issuance. These may require changing the formula's references by hand.

16. Once Debt 2 is complete, do the same for Debt 3, making sure to take into account the principal payments for Debt 1 *and* Debt 2. Also change all references so they refer to Debt 3 assumptions and calculations.

17. A figure that will help us understand cash flow is how much money remains after principal is repaid. In cell B45 on the Debt sheet, enter the text **Surplus Funds Post Prin**. In cell E45, enter the following formula:

=E14-E22-E32-E42

Copy and paste this formula over the range E45:J45. The debt section for Debt 1 should now look like Figure 6.19.

Limitations on the Implemented System

The system that is set up in the example model is robust, but definitely has room for modification and expansion to adapt to analysis needs. The following limitations and suggestions for expansion should be noted:

1. To keep the initial stages of the Model Builder exercises easier the interest calculations were done using only a sequential payment priority. If a true pro

	A	B	C	D	E	F	G	H	I	J
11					Projected ---->					TV Year
12				12/31/2007	12/31/2008	12/31/2009	12/31/2010	12/31/2011	12/31/2012	12/31/2013
13										
14	Surplus Funds for Prin				100.00	100.00	100.00	100.00	100.00	100.00
15	Debt 1									
16	Debt 1 Rate				6.55%	6.55%	6.55%	6.55%	6.55%	6.55%
17	Interest Due				-	0.33	0.22	0.11	-	-
18	Interest Paid				-	0.33	0.22	0.11	-	-
19	Interest Unpaid				-	-	-	-	-	-
20	Custom Prin Amort %				0.00%	0.00%	0.00%	0.00%	0.00%	0.00%
21	Principal Due				-	1.67	1.67	1.67	-	-
22	Principal Paid				-	1.67	1.67	1.67	-	-
23	Principal Unpaid				-	-	-	-	-	-

FIGURE 6.19 The debt section is nearly complete with principal payments now being calculated.

rata payment system were introduced, it would more likely be the case that interest payments were also set up in a pro rata fashion. This can be easily implemented in the example model by examining the pro rata option formulas for principal paid and applying them to the interest paid section. An additional pro rata sequencer and percentage share section can be incorporated for the interest. Also keep in mind that even if there is a switch to pro rata, there should still be priority of the interest payments over the principal payments. Most likely the interest will be paid prior to tax, whereas the principal is paid using after-tax, remaining funds.

2. There can be rare instances in a pro rata situation when the formulas that were implemented in Model Builder 6.2 will break down. The formulas in that section assume that if there are pro rata issuances of debt, they will have very similar characteristics in regard to payments. If there are significant differences between payment terms for pro rata issuances of debt, there might be a need to modify the formulas. For example, take two loans that are pari passu to each other as an example. If one of the loans had a custom amortization schedule where a principal payment was not due in a given year and the other had a payment due, there could be problems if there were a shortfall of cash in that year. Let's say Loan 1 has a pro rata share percentage of 70%, whereas Loan 2 has a pro rata share percentage of 30%. Further assume Loan 1 has a custom amortization schedule where there is no principal payment due in the current period; however, Loan 2 has a principal payment due of $50. The final assumption to assume is that the cash available for Loan 2 is $100. Our formula in this case would calculate the principal paid at $30 for Loan 2 for the current period. This would mean there would be $20 of unpaid principal, which would theoretically be retained or released to equity. No debt holder would stand for such an arrangement! The formula would have to be modified, most likely using an IF function, to see whether there is another payment due and adjust the payment appropriately.

3. A similar problem with the pro rata calculation can occur if there is a large mismatch between balances and principal payments due. This could lead to paying less principal for a loan than required, even when there are funds available. The modifications for this are similar to point 2, where an IF function would ensure payment in odd circumstances.

4. Currently, the user must enter any sequential loans in order from top to bottom on the Debt sheet. This will work fine as long as the users know that this must be done and that if pro rata loans enter into the capital structure they must use the pro rata sequencer in an ordinal matter (e.g., 1,2,2 is the correct order for two pro rata loans subordinate to a senior loan, not 2,2,1).

5. Payments are assumed to take place on the dates in the forecast period. Interest is assumed to be charged over the course of the full payment period, whereas principal payments come in on that same period. If, say, an annual system is set up, but quarterly principal payments are being made, a model user might want to average out the balance since the interest due will be less than in a pure annual payment scheme. Overall, this is not preferred since the model should be set to a periodicity that is in line with the debt payments.

6. Using both sequential and pro rata payment methodologies in the same scenario (e.g., 1,2,2) with the cash sweep activated requires a modification of the example model formulas. This is because the example formula does not subtract out the sequential cash flow from the cash available. Creating this functionality is quite complicated as you must set up an array formula to reference the correct sequential issuance and use that as an indicator to determine the principal paid that should be subtracted.

MODEL BUILDER 6.3: INTEGRATING LONG-TERM DEBT INTO THE INCOME STATEMENT AND BALANCE SHEET

1. There are a few more steps to complete the long-term debt section of the model. First we should jump to the Income Statement sheet where interest expense is removed from net income. Enter the text **Interest Expense** in cell B27 on the Income Statement sheet and then enter the following references for labels:

   B29: =Debt!B15
   B30: =Debt!B25
   B31: =Debt!B35

2. Since all of the calculations are already done for us, we need only to reference the interest amounts from the Debt sheet. Note that we are referencing the interest due component of each debt issuance. This is because if we were to get very technical with the model and develop it more, we would have the interest due be the interest expense for the period and any unpaid amounts accruing

in an accrued interest account. Given the target level of the model, we will just reference the interest due section of the balance sheet. Enter the following references in the corresponding cells:

E29: =Debt!E17
E30: =Debt!E27
E31: =Debt!E37

Copy and paste these formulas from column E to column J while maintaining the same row. For example, cell E29 should be copied and pasted over range E29:J26, and cell E30 over range E30:J30. Be careful not to just drag cell E29 down and across since it will not reference the correct rows.

3. Enter the text **Total Interest Expense** in cell B32. Then enter the following formula in cell E32:

=SUM(E28:E31)

Copy and paste this formula over the range E32:J32. Note that this SUM function captures row 28, which will be completed in Chapter 7. Also keep in mind that in Chapter 3 we entered the formula for EBT, which subtracts row 32 from EBIT. This section is directly how interest expense impacts earnings. Figure 6.20 shows these additions to the Income Statement sheet (keep in mind your figures are most likely different from the figure for total interest expense since we have yet to explain short-term debt, which is part of this calculation).

4. On the Balance Sheet sheet, we need to update the liability section to include the long-term debt calculations. Enter the following formula in cell E35 on the Balance Sheet sheet:

=Debt!E53+Debt!E54+Debt!E55

Copy and paste this formula over the range E35:J35. This new section to the Balance Sheet sheet is shown in Figure 6.21.

	B	C	D	E	F	G	H	I	J
27	Interest Expense								
28	ST Debt			0.53	0.53	-	-	-	-
29	Debt 1			-	0.33	0.22	0.11	-	-
30	Debt 2			-	0.67	0.50	0.34	0.17	-
31	Debt 3			-	1.36	1.08	0.81	0.54	0.27
32	Total Interest Expense			0.53	2.89	1.80	1.26	0.71	0.27
33	EBT		85.20	109.64	105.26	119.17	134.16	160.28	185.72

FIGURE 6.20 The long-term debt interest is an expense taken out of net income, prior to tax.

	B		D	E	F	G	H	I	J
35	LT Borrowings		**0.00**	35.00	26.83	18.67	10.50	4.00	0.00
36	Total Liabilities		18.00	79.10	52.8	47.5	42.5	39.5	37.9

FIGURE 6.21 The debt balances from the Debt sheet are long-term liabilities on the balance sheet.

TOOLBOX

MIN, MAX

The MIN function on its own is very simple; it stands for the word *minimum* and takes the least-valued number out of the entered range of numbers. The entry parameters for MIN are:

MIN(value 1, value 2, value 3 . . .)

As you can see, it will return the value that is smaller than all of the other values. For finance, MIN can be thought of as a *cap creator*. For instance, if you have a 6.0% interest rate cap and the current market rate is 7.0% and you created a formula with MIN(interest rate cap, market rate), the interest rate cap would be returned. If the market rate went below the interest rate cap, then the market rate would be returned.

The opposite of taking a minimum is taking a *maximum*. The function for that is MAX. Essentially, MAX does the opposite of MIN, even in respect to finance theory. MAX can be thought of as a *floor creator*.

AND, OR

AND and OR functions are logical functions. That statement seems to underscore the difficulty in working with these functions since they can be confusing. An AND function evaluates up to 255 separate conditional tests and returns a TRUE if all of the tests are TRUE. If one or more tests are FALSE, then a FALSE is returned. The entry parameters for AND include:

AND(conditional test 1, conditional test 2, conditional test 3 . . .)

To demonstrate this in an example, imagine we had a row with "Yes" or "No" denoting whether a reserve account was active and a row with periodic dates. Now, for each period, suppose we wanted to return a TRUE if the reserve account was active and the projection date was greater than an assumption date. Looking at the setup in Figure 6.22, we could use AND by writing:

AND(D3="Yes",D2>$A$3)

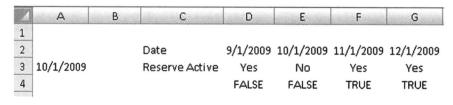

FIGURE 6.22 The AND function evaluates both the Yes/No and the date to return a TRUE or FALSE depending on whether BOTH conditions are TRUE.

A variation on this is if we were concerned about only one of the conditions being TRUE. In that case, we would use an OR function. An OR function returns a TRUE if just one conditional test is TRUE. A FALSE is returned when all conditional tests are FALSE. The entry parameters for OR are identical to AND:

OR(conditional test 1, conditional test 2, conditional test 3 . . .)

We can modify the example above by switching the AND to an OR. Notice the difference in the resulting TRUE and FALSE returns by instituting the change. This difference is shown in Figure 6.23.

One particular challenge financial modelers have is working with AND and OR functions effectively. On their own they are relatively simple functions, but how do we extract the full value from them? This is done by using AND and OR with IF functions. An IF function evaluates a reference for a TRUE or FALSE value and then returns different results depending on whether TRUE or FALSE was the result of the original evaluation. Since AND and OR functions return a TRUE or FALSE, we can use them in combination with IF functions.

Working with our prior example, let's add a row for income. In the first case we will want to have the income returned if the reserve account is active and if the current date is past a certain assumption date. We can use the combination of an IF and AND function as seen in Figure 6.24.

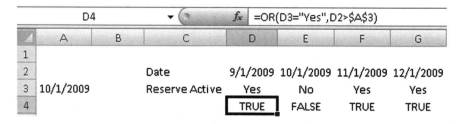

FIGURE 6.23 Changing the AND to an OR produces different TRUE or FALSE returns because with an OR function only one condition of the two must be met.

	D5		▼	f_x	=IF(AND(D3="Yes",D2>$A$3),D4,0)	
	A	B	C	D	E	F	G
1							
2			Date	9/1/2009	10/1/2009	11/1/2009	12/1/2009
3	10/1/2009		Reserve Active	Yes	No	Yes	Yes
4			Income	200	250	275	280
5			Realized income	0	0	275	280

FIGURE 6.24 Using an IF function with AND or OR allows multiple conditional tests to be evaluated and meaningful results returned.

Array Functions

Array functions are a powerful way to use Excel. An *array* is a series of data. For our purposes, we must realize that it is *any set of data greater than one cell*. This can be in column, row, or matrix form. The term *function* refers to an Excel function. Combining these two words, we have the concept of an Excel function that works with arrays or multiple cells of data.

Readers might be confused because some functions work with arrays of data that do not seem very special, such as SUM, AVERAGE, MIN, and so on. Array functions are special types of Excel functions that differentiate themselves in one of two ways:

- They return multiple values using the exact same formula and are entered by first highlighting multiple cells and then entering a single formula. LINEST is an example of this as it returns 10 key statistical values based on a single formula reference.
- They are regular formulas that reference multiple cells without the use of an Excel function. For example, imagine we had a loan amortizing and wanted

	D20		▼	f_x	{=MIN(IF(C16:C20=0,B16:B20,10000))}	
	B	C	D	E	F
16	1	1000			
17	2	800			
18	3	400			
19	4	0			
20	5	0	4		

FIGURE 6.25 In this formula, we use an IF function that returns the period if the balance is equal to zero, or a very large number if it is not. Then the MIN function returns the lowest of those values, which will be the period that the loan pays off.

to know the period that it paid off. We can use a mathematical formula that evaluates all of the cells where there is a balance. Since there are going to be multiple cells where the balance is zero, we want to examine each cell and then take the minimum period number of the ones that are zero. This formula is shown in Figure 6.25.

A key concept to keep in mind is that array functions must always be entered by holding down **CTRL-SHFT** and then pressing **ENTER**. This will create the curly braces around the function and inform Excel that an array function is being used.

CHAPTER 7

Balancing the Model

We are now at a very interesting stage in the model-building process, where we need to tie together all of our seemingly independent calculations and produce a truly dynamic model. So far, we have had a few linkages between the Income Statement, Balance Sheet, Capex, Intangibles, and Debt sheets, but nothing really unifying all of them. In this chapter we will revisit the Income Statement and Balance Sheet sheets to connect any incomplete items, calculate a few skipped-over concepts, and ultimately balance the balance sheet.

The concept of balancing the model reverts back to the accounting theory discussed in Chapter 4. The most relevant principle from that chapter is that *assets must equal liabilities plus shareholders equity at all times*. In cases where our projections temporarily deviated from this principle, we identified surplus funds as the asset-side plug and short-term debt as the liability-side plug. Figure 7.1 reviews these concepts.

One challenge of implementing the plugs is that, aside from just being used to calculate the difference when our main accounting principle is unbalanced, the plugs contribute to the difference through interest expense and income. All forms of cash, including surplus funds, would most likely be kept in a highly liquid, safe investment such as guaranteed investment contracts or marketable securities. These investments will earn a small, but potentially useful amount of income. Similarly, short-term debt is not free and will require the company to pay interest. These interest amounts flow through the income statement and affect retained earnings. This change in equity further changes the balance sheet and sets up a circular problem.

Our process in this chapter will be to first set up the interest calculations for cash and short-term debt. Once that is done, we are ready to implement the balancing mechanism, which balances the balance sheet. After creating a dynamic, balanced model, we will try a few assumptions to make sure that the model makes sense, prior to proceeding further.

MODEL BUILDER 7.1: CALCULATING CASH AND SHORT-TERM DEBT INTEREST

1. The first step that will greatly assist our development of this section is putting proxy values in for surplus funds and short-term debt. This will prevent annoying

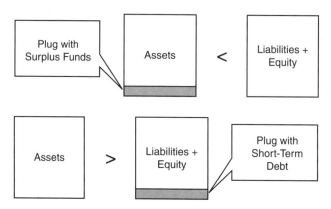

FIGURE 7.1   Plugs are used in projection models to adhere to the standard accounting principle of assets equaling liabilities plus equity.

#DIV/0! errors and make our formula creation visually easier. For now, put a value of **1** for each period for the Surplus Funds For Prin on the Debt sheet (range E14:J14). Also put values of **1** for each period for the ST borrowings section on the Balance Sheet sheet (range E31:J31). These temporary states of the model are shown in Figure 7.2.

2. We need to set up one reference on the Balance Sheet sheet before focusing on the Income Statement sheet. On the Balance Sheet sheet, enter the following formula in cell E6:

=Debt!E45

Copy and paste this formula over the range E6:J6.

From the Debt sheet

A	B	C	D	E	F	G	H	I	J
11				Projected ---->					TV Year
12			12/31/2007	12/31/2008	12/31/2009	12/31/2010	12/31/2011	12/31/2012	12/31/2013
13									
14	Surplus Funds for Prin			1.00	1.00	1.00	1.00	1.00	1.00
15	Debt 1								

From the Balance Sheet sheet

	B	C	D	E	F	G	H	I	J
29	Liabilities								
30	Accounts Payable		15.00	17.57	18.67	20.78	23.13	25.74	27.75
31	ST Borrowings		0.00	19.92	0.00	0.00	0.00	0.00	0.00

FIGURE 7.2   To make it easier to implement new formulas, we should put proxy values in each period, for both plugs.

3. We need to set down the basic assumptions for cash and short-term debt interest. We are primarily concerned with the interest rate settings for each of these items. A secondary concern is the absolute amount of short-term debt that is being created. Go to the Assumptions sheet and enter the following text in the corresponding cells:

B22: **Cash and Short-Term Debt Assumptions**
B24: **Surplus Funds**
B25: **Cash**
B26: **Marketable Securities**
B27: **Short-Term Funds**
B28: **Short-Term Funds Limit**
C23: **Rate**
D23: **Spread**

4. Each of the interest-bearing items (Surplus Funds, Cash, Marketable Securities, and Short-Term Debt) will be assigned an index based on the indexes available on the Vectors sheet. Essentially, we are setting up the same rate-referencing system as we did for long-term debt. Create data validation lists in C24:C27 using the named range lst_InterestRates as the source. Set each one initially to **1M Libor**.
5. Enter a value of **0.125%** for each cell in range D24:D26. These will be the spreads or margins over the index rate that the cash items are earning. For short-term debt we will assume a higher spread. Enter the value **1.15%** in cell D27. Thus far, the new section on the Assumptions sheet should look like Figure 7.3.
6. Go to the Income Statement sheet and enter the following text in the corresponding cells to establish labels for the section we will work on:

B21: **Interest Income**
B22: **Surplus Funds**

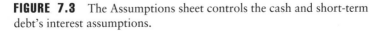

	A	B	C	D
21				
22		**Cash and Short-Term Debt Assumptions**		
23			Rate	Spread
24		Surplus Funds	**1M Libor**	**0.125%**
25		Cash	**1M Libor**	**0.125%**
26		Marketable Sec.	**1M Libor**	**0.125%**
27		Short-Term Debt	**1M Libor**	**1.150%**
28		Short-Term Debt Limit		

FIGURE 7.3 The Assumptions sheet controls the cash and short-term debt's interest assumptions.

B23: **Cash**
B24: **Marketable Securities**
B25: **Total Interest Income**
B28: **ST Debt**

7. We will complete the interest income prior to the short-term debt. The first item to add is any historical interest income amounts. Because surplus funds is merely a projected figure, there should be no historical amounts for it. Enter the following values and formulas in the corresponding cells:

D23: .30
D24: .20
D25: =SUM(D19:D21)

Copy and paste the formula in cell D25 over the range D25:J25.

8. A challenge with implementing this section is that we will require balances in order to get figures to propagate in these cells. To set this up properly, the easiest method is to assume there are balances on the balance sheet and as we complete the balance section later the interest sections will be populated with values. To do this, enter the following formula in cell E22 on the Income Statement sheet:

**=AVERAGE('BalanceSheet'!D6:E6)*(OFFSET(Vectors!E$33,MATCH(inputs_
SuplusFundsRate,lst_InterestRates,0),0)+inputs_SurplusFundsSpd)**

Let's break this lengthy formula apart in three separate pieces. The first piece is an AVERAGE function that refers to the surplus funds balance for the prior and current period. As mentioned earlier, we do not have balances yet, but when we do, these will be the basis for multiplying by an assumed interest rate. The real question for this piece of the formula is: Why do we use the AVERAGE function? The reason is that we do not know exactly when the surplus funds were created. In a model that is set to annual periodicity, it is unlikely that all of the surplus funds were created exactly at the beginning of the period. Most likely they came in over time. For this reason, we take an average of the balances between the prior period and the current period to create a balance estimate. If the model is set to a more specific periodicity, or the model user knows exactly when the funds came in, the AVERAGE function can be eliminated and a more specific balance reference used.

The second piece of the formula is an OFFSET MATCH combination—something with which we are very familiar by now. It matches the user-indicated surplus funds rate (inputs_SurplusFundsRate) against the list of possible interest rates (lst_InterestRates). This is highly similar to the formula used to determine the rate for long-term debt issuances in Chapter 6.

The third piece of the formula is very easy. It is the spread (inputs_SurplusFundsSpd) on top of the selected index. This part is a straightforward addition formula. Copy and paste this formula over the range E22:J22.

9. Repeat this process for cash and marketable securities. Enter the following formulas in the corresponding cells:

   E23: =AVERAGE('BalanceSheet'!D7:E7)*(OFFSET(Vectors!E$33,MATCH
   (inputs_CashRate,lst_InterestRates,0),0)+inputs_CashSpd)
   E24: =AVERAGE('BalanceSheet'!D8:E8)*(OFFSET(Vectors!E$33,MATCH
   (inputs_MSRate,lst_InterestRates,0),0)+inputs_MSSpd)

   Copy and paste each of these cells over to column J for each respective row.
10. Short-term debt interest is calculated in a similar manner. Still on the Income Statement sheet, enter the following formula in cell E28:

    =AVERAGE('BalanceSheet'!D31:E31)*(OFFSET(Vectors!E$33,MATCH
    (inputs_STFundsRate,lst_InterestRates,0),0)+inputs_STFundsSpd)

    Copy and paste this formula over the range E28:J28. Thus far the new area on the Income Statement sheet should look like Figure 7.4.
11. We are very close to installing the balancing mechanism. Prior to this, we need to make sure everyone has the exact same calculations. To ensure this, repeat step 1 for the complete example model that is on the CD-ROM. If you are following along by building your model in a step-by-step process, your total assets and total liabilities plus equity should be identical to the example model at this point. If not, compare all assumptions. A good troubleshooting method is to check each section of the balance sheet to see whether your numbers are the same. If there is a difference in one of those sections, it will give you a hint as to the area that you should focus your attention on.

    This is not suggesting that the total assets should equal total liabilities plus equity. In fact, they should not since we have yet to install the balancing mechanism. This step is to make sure that all other calculations are the same. Otherwise, if your model does not balance it could be due to a host of missed or erroneous prior calculations that would be difficult to troubleshoot with the balancing method installed. It is much easier to troubleshoot problems *prior to balancing* by putting in hard-coded proxy values for surplus funds and short-term debt

	A	B	C	D	E	F	G	H	I	J
22		Surplus Funds			-	1.36	1.36	2.25	7.05	12.27
23		Cash		0.30	0.45	0.29	0.11	0.12	0.13	0.14
24		MS Securities		0.20	0.18	0.20	0.22	0.24	0.27	0.29
25		Total Interest Income		0.50	0.64	1.85	1.69	2.62	7.46	12.70
26										
27		Interest Expense								
28		ST Debt			0.53	0.53	-	-	-	-

FIGURE 7.4 The plugs contribute to interest income and expense that is taken into account on the income statement.

and identifying differences in sections of the balance sheet between the model provided on the CD-ROM and the model that you are building.

If you are having a difficult time getting your model to produce similar results as the example model, it is acceptable to save a version of the example model, put the 1 values in the surplus fund and short-term debt sections above, and use that model to continue this Model Builder. If you do choose to use this method, many of the upcoming steps will be already completed for you.

12. Assuming that all calculations are correct in your model, go to the Balance Sheet sheet. Enter the following text in the corresponding cells:

B48: **Surplus Cash**
B49: **Required Short-Term debt**

13. We want to quantify the differences between the assets without the surplus funds plug, and the liabilities plus equity without the short-term debt plug. If we did a simple subtraction of the two, we could possibly get a negative number, depending on which figures we subtracted first. What we should do is set up an absolute system where only positive numbers are returned. If surplus funds are positive, it means that there should be no need for short-term debt. Conversely, if short-term debt is positive, it means that there should be no surplus funds available. We basically want to create a floor at zero. In the previous chapter, we learned that a MAX function can be used to create a floor. Enter the following formula in cell E48:

=MAX((SUM(E30,E32,E35,E39,E40,E41,E42)+SUM(Debt!E22,Debt!E32, Debt!E42))-SUM(E7,E8,E9,E13,E14,E19,E23,E25),0)

Copy and paste this formula over the range E48:J48.

14. Repeat this process for cell E49, but enter the following formula where the references are reversed:

=MAX(SUM(E7,E8,E9,E13,E14,E19,E23,E25)-(SUM(E30,E32,E35,E39,E40, E41,E42)+SUM(Debt!E22,Debt!E32,Debt!E42)),0)

Copy and paste this formula over the range E49:J49. The new section on the Balance Sheet sheet should look like Figure 7.5.

	B		D	E	F	G	H	I	J
46	**Total Liabilities & Equity**		**138.04**	**270.90**	**313.27**	**384.69**	**439.68**	**515.09**	**608.42**
47									
48	Surplus Cash			0.00	71.09	2.78	112.26	228.57	350.80
49	Required Short-Term Debt			19.92	0.00	0.00	0.00	0.00	0.00

FIGURE 7.5 The plugs need to be calculated so that they can be fed back into the system to determine their final amounts.

15. We are soon going to link up everything. The problem is that we will have a circular reference when we do this. If you think about it, we have determined how much surplus or short-term debt we need to balance the model. However, in that same period, the interest income or expense is dependent on the figure that gets plugged. But, the figure that gets plugged is dependent on the interest income or expense since it is connected to retained earnings! This circularity can be solved in two ways: setting Excel to calculate with iterations or using loops in VBA code to optimize the problem. Since the VBA code is more advanced and will be explained in Chapter 12, we will first implement a solution using iterations. To do this, we must set Excel to calculate with iterations.

For Excel 2003 or earlier: Go to **Tools** and select **Options**. On the Options dialogue box there should be a tab called Calculation. Select the **Calculation** tab; there is a checkbox for Enable Iterations, followed by a field for Maximum Iterations, and Maximum Change. Just check the box **Enable Iterations**. Press **OK**.

For Excel 2007: Go to the Office button and select **Excel Options** in the bottom-right area. Select the **Formulas** menu. On the upper-right section of the Formulas menu there should be a checkbox for Enable Iterative Calculation, followed by a field for Maximum Iterations, and Maximum Change. Just check the box to **Enable Iterative Calculation**. Press **OK**. The area from Excel 2007 is show in Figure 7.6.

16. Go to the Debt sheet and enter the following reference in cell E14:

='Balance Sheet'!E48

Copy and paste this formula over the range E14:J14.

17. Back on the Balance Sheet sheet, enter the following reference in cell E31:

=E49

Copy and paste this formula over the range E31:J31.

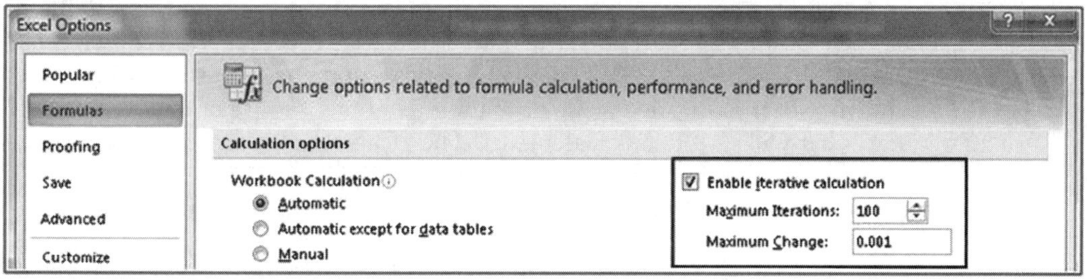

FIGURE 7.6 Iterative calculation is activated under Excel Options. It allows Excel to iterate through circular references.

18. At this point the model should be balanced. Verify this by adding up all of the total assets for each period and comparing that figure to the total liabilities plus equity. You might also want to check each period to make sure that the assets equal the liabilities plus equity. There are a few things that are very important to realize about what we have just done:

   a. The model is mathematically correct, but I cannot stress enough that this does not mean your *analysis* is correct! One participant in a corporate valuation course that I was teaching in Nigeria exclaimed, "This is voodoo accounting!" Although I won't take it to that level, I will say we are making assumptions here to adhere to accounting principles. We need to verify that our results are reality based. For instance, in a previous model that I worked on for a large holding company transaction, every stress scenario worked. The model was very large and it took me a while to figure out why, but it all came back to the short-term facility plug that the model builder had set up. In the stress cases, this plug was reaching levels from $300 million to $400 million. Unfortunately, the company had only $175 million in short-term facility available. So, in a worst-case scenario the model was still showing everyone getting paid because all of the shortfalls were being covered by the short-term facility plug. In reality, the company would have gone into default because it would not have been able to access such large amounts of short-term debt. We will see how we can set up the model to warn ourselves about this issue in the Internal Validation section of Chapter 8.

   b. Plugs sometimes come under criticism for their simplicity. Allowing only either a surplus or drawing down on one source such as short-term debt seems limited. Plugs can be set up to be more complicated, though. One can direct a certain amount of shortfall on the liability and equity side to multiple sources such as debt and equity. In such a way we can maintain management's expected capital structure plan. We can also hook up the debt plug to other sources of debt such as a liquidity facility, where there are drawdowns and repayments with surplus.

   c. The other issue with plugs is that there is a circular reference that we have allowed on the sheet, opening the possibility of error. It is a correct circular reference in that we understand exactly how it is operating and it gets us to an acceptable answer. We can verify there is a circular reference by looking at Excel's status bar. The status bar is the bar in the far bottom-left that normally says "Ready." When Excel's calculation settings are set to manual and the sheet is uncalculated, or if there is an active circular reference, the status bar will say "Ready Calculate." The "Calculate" means that the sheet is not calculated. If you are unfamiliar with Excel's calculation settings, refer to the Toolbox at the end of this chapter. The problem with a circular reference is that even if Excel's calculation setting is set to Automatic, the status bar will still display "Calculate." On its own it is not a problem, but what if we accidentally create another circular reference? We may see the error, but troubleshooting it will be difficult given the purposeful circular reference that we just implemented. This is why I lean toward using VBA subroutines to solve circularities or optimize models. Those subroutines can enter the correct value in any cell we want as a hard-coded figure rather than maintaining a circular reference. We will see how to do this in Chapter 12.

d. Overall, plugs should be used sparingly. The projections of a company should be set up in a logical manner from the start. For instance, it would be unusual to increase capital expenditures by a significant amount and not plan on funding it, thus allowing the liability and equity plug to pick up the slack. Our models should reflect carefully laid-out scenarios where we provide as much logical data as possible and rely on plugs for minor aberrations.

WORKING WITH THE MODEL

At this point we have a working, dynamic model that can balance itself by utilizing either surplus cash or short-term debt. We should now try changing a few assumptions to see their effects on the model:

- *Cash sweep:* We should see the effect of turning the cash sweep on, since its current setting is *off*. First, let's look at what is happening when the cash sweep is turned off. We can see in the example model that we have a shortfall of funds the first period, followed by surplus funds in 2009 and beyond. Looking at 2009 as a focal point, we can see that we have 8.17 of scheduled principal due in that year. Fortunately, there is plenty of surplus cash to pay this principal (71.09). After paying the principal, we are left with 62.92, which is the surplus cash displayed on the balance sheet.

  Now, if we activate the cash sweep by switching cell H9 on the Debt sheet to "Yes," we will see a dramatic change. In this case, we have built in an acceleration of debt, meaning that all of the surplus funds are distributed to the debt holders. Looking at the Debt sheet, we see that all of the debt is paid off. The example set here would be an acceleration of debt caused by some breach of a covenant. Make sure to set cell H9 back to "No" before proceeding on to the next assumption change. Figure 7.7 depicts where the change should be made.

- *Revenue growth:* Our next example is changing the revenue growth vectors, which are the most influential factors in the model. First, we should take a few notes regarding the current state of the model. The default scenario is set to Base Case, which produces $1,257.74 of surplus funds post–principal paydown from December 2009 to December 2013 (sum up range F6:J6 on the Balance Sheet sheet). Note that all three debt issuances get their interest and scheduled principal paid on time (look at the Interest and Principal paid and unpaid rows on the Debt sheet).

  Now, switch the scenario on the Assumptions sheet (cell D31) to Downside Case. Look at Figure 7.8 to see the scenario selector that should be changed. Assuming that the Downside Case assumptions that are used in the example model

A	B	C	D	E	F	G	H	I	J
1	**Debt**								
2									
3	**Long-Term Debt Assumptions**								
4	Debt Issuance		Rate	Spreads	Term	Balance	Issue Date	Maturity Date	PMT Type
5		1	1M Libor	2.35%	36	5	12/31/2008	12/31/2011	Level
6		2	1M Libor	2.50%	48	10	12/31/2008	12/31/2012	Level
7		3	1M Libor	2.58%	60	20	12/31/2008	12/31/2013	Level
8									
9					Sweep All Surplus		Yes ▾		
10							Yes		
							No		
11				Projected ---->				TV Year	
12			12/31/2007	12/31/2008	12/31/2009	12/31/2010	12/31/2011	12/31/2012	12/31/2013
13									
14	Surplus Funds for Prin			-	12.96	18.95	42.93	71.67	86.74
15	Debt 1								
16	Debt 1 Rate			6.55%	6.55%	6.55%	6.55%	6.55%	6.55%
17	Interest Due			-	0.33	-	-	-	-
18	Interest Paid			-	0.33	-	-	-	-
19	Interest Unpaid			-	-	-	-	-	-
20	Custom Prin Amort %			0.00%	0.00%	0.00%	0.00%	0.00%	0.00%
21	Principal Due			-	5.00	-	-	-	-
22	Principal Paid			-	5.00 ←	-	-	-	-

FIGURE 7.7 Switching the cash sweep on takes all surplus cash and applies it to the debt in the payment manner selected in the debt assumptions.

are implemented in the model you are using, there should be some considerable differences. Go back to the Balance Sheet sheet and sum up the surplus funds post-principal. You will notice this has decreased greatly to $954.08.

If a scenario was used where a growth got worse, a few things could happen that the analyst might have to customize. The first is that in such a downside case there might be covenants to protect the senior tranches of debt. Subordinate tranches would probably be locked out of principal payments until the more senior tranches are paid.

Scenario Controls

Global Scenario Selector	Base Case ▾
	Base Case
	Upside Case
	Downside Case
	VBA Generator Case

FIGURE 7.8 Changing the scenario to a stress case produces less revenue and has dynamic impacts on the modeling results of many sections. Note that "VBA Generator Case" will not show up on your drop-down list yet. It will be implemented in Chapter 12.

The other issue that sometimes occurs is the use of a short-term facility to pay current portions of long-term debt. In our model setup, we have restricted principal paydown to occur only when there are surplus funds available. In some models you may notice the model builder has allowed the short-term facility to cover interest or principal payments on long-term debt. This is a concern because you are essentially swapping debt and possibly prolonging a cash flow problem that is leading toward default.

All of the results from dropping revenue make sense. In the downside case, we lowered revenue and increased expenses, which stresses the cash flow. This is evident in our model when we examine the reduced surplus funds. Make sure to switch back to the base case after finishing this analysis.

- *Increased capital expenditure:* Next we will see a very tangible effect on cash flow. First, notice the surplus funds for 2010 of $99.39. Now, we are going to hold all assumptions constant, but increase the third capital expenditure in 2010. This area is shown in Figure 7.9. If we do not adjust funding for this project, then there are going to be problems affording it. This should be easy to spot in the model.

Change the third capital expenditure on the Assumptions sheet (cell D19) from $10 to **$175**. Now, take a look at the surplus funds in 2010. You will notice that they have been reduced to zero. In fact, not only have surplus funds been reduced to zero, but debt goes unpaid. What is happening is that the capital expenditure costs money and there is barely enough from earnings, long-term financing, equity, or cash on hand to pay for it. Doing this causes severe stress on the firm's ability to keep to scheduled principal repayments. In 2010, principal payments are missed because there are limited surplus funds to pay them.

We can now use the model as an optimization tool. We can determine how much we can increase the third capital expenditure until there is no unpaid scheduled principal. Decrease the third capital expenditure to **$108**. You will

	B	C	D
14			
15	**CAPEX Assumptions**		
16		Depreciation Method	Amt
17	Capex 1	Straight Line	85
18	Capex 2	Straight Line	25
19	Capex 3	Straight Line	10
20	Capex 4	Straight Line	0

FIGURE 7.9 Increasing capital expenditures while holding everything else constant will impact the affordability of other liabilities.

notice that all of the scheduled principal can be paid. Perhaps it is not optimized, so we should test out increasing the third capital expenditure to **$109**. This causes unpaid debt. If we were to keep going back and forth, perhaps using a divide-and-conquer algorithm (dividing the previous correct attempt and the current wrong attempt by half until an optimal solution is found), we would find that $108.20 could be spent on capital expenditure and all the debt could be paid. Later, we will see that there are ways to automate the search process using tools built into Excel such as Goal Seek and Solver. Make sure to switch the third capital expenditure back to **10** prior to proceeding.

THE MODEL AS AN ANALYSIS TOOL

Now that we have completed most of the plumbing in the model to get it to a dynamic stage, we will rapidly increase our ability to use it for analysis. Whereas this book heavily focuses on how to create a dynamic model, the real value an analyst provides is in using the model appropriately. To ensure that the model is being used appropriately, we should build in validation tests that check to make sure logical results are being returned. Chapter 8 focuses on validating the model through commonly seen calculations that check the cash flow movements of important items related to the company's viability, such as working capital. These items are summarized in the cash flow statement, which can be used in a financial model as a reconciliation tool.

TOOLBOX: EXCEL'S CALCULATION MODES

In many of my valuation modeling classes I have often received the question, "I'm dragging the formula over exactly as you are saying, but nothing is changing on my screen." The most common response and solution to that is to check the calculation mode setting.

For Excel 2003 and earlier: Go to **Tools—Options** and select the **Calculation** tab. On the Calculation tab there should be an option button for three different calculation settings, each described here:

- *Automatic:* recalculates the entire workbook any time a change is made to the workbook. Default mode of most Excel workbooks and models.
- *Automatic without Tables:* recalculates the entire workbook any time a change is made to the workbook, except for data tables that a user created. If you are unfamiliar with data tables, it is not necessary to learn them if you decide to learn VBA. Data tables are useful for scenario analysis, but hamper calculation time when used frequently. The slow calculation time is why an option exists to recalculate everything except the tables. The other reason is that a user might want data stored in the table that is reflective of a past scenario.

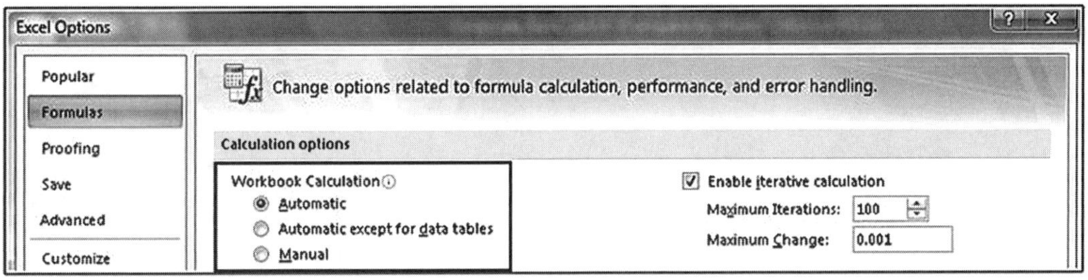

FIGURE 7.10 In Excel 2007, we can switch the calculation mode under Excel Options—Formulas.

- *Manual:* recalculates the entire workbook only when the user presses **F9**. Changes made to immediate cells or ranges of cells will be calculated after **Enter** is pressed, but connected links or dragged items will not change until **F9** is pressed.

For Excel 2007 users: The same possible calculation modes are available, but they must be accessed by clicking on the **Office** button, pressing the **Excel Options** button, selecting **Formulas,** and choosing one of the three option boxes under the Workbook Calculation section in the upper-left area of the dialogue box. Figure 7.10 shows the area to change the Workbook Calculation mode.

CHAPTER 8

Reconciling Cash Flow

Most of the core calculations that generate cash flow in from assets and those that set up our liabilities and equity are done. However, there are numerous calculations necessary to understand more about the company's performance and financial health. Primarily, we should trace cash that is flowing through the company to see how much is earned or used through operations, investing, and financing. In particular, when assessing the viability of a company we should pay particular attention to operational cash flow, which is partially comprised of working capital needs or excess. Once we know more about the sources and uses of cash, we should also take time to implement internal validations that make sure the calculations backing these cash flow figures are absolutely correct.

THE CASH FLOW STATEMENT

The last major financial statement that we have yet to discuss or implement is the cash flow statement. As alluded to in the opening paragraph, this statement organizes the cash flows of a company by operational, investing, and financing activity. The cash flow statement provides an analyst with a picture of the sources and uses of cash in a company. It is relatively simple to set up since nearly all of the calculations are references to sections already calculated in the model. No new conceptual calculations are necessary. Figure 8.1 shows a graphical representation of the cash flow statement in relation to other parts of the model.

Financial modelers use cash flow statements in two ways. First, if one does not balance the surplus cash in a similar manner as we did on the Debt and Balance Sheet sheets in Chapter 7, he or she will typically use the cash at the end of the period on the cash flow statement to balance the model. Although this is an acceptable and common means of balancing a model, it adds a layer connectivity that is not needed. The cash flow statement is really just referencing other parts of the model, and to balance a model one needs to interact only with the Income Statement, Balance Sheet, and supporting sheets.

If a financial modeler implements a balancing system similar to what we have done in Chapter 7, which is common, then the cash flow statement can be used to reconcile cash. Any change in all of the cash items on the balance sheet between

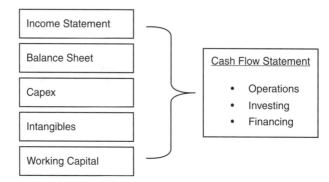

FIGURE 8.1 The cash flow statement is created from other sheets that have already been created in the model.

periods should be identical to the change in cash from the cash flow statement. If there is a difference, it means either items are missing from the cash flow statement or other parts of the model are miscalculating. With this check in place, the cash flow statement becomes an invaluable tool for troubleshooting a model.

WORKING CAPITAL

One goal that we are getting closer to is ultimately corporate valuation. A large part of corporate valuation modeling is understanding the cash flow of a company—particularly cash flow related to operations. Within operational cash flow, an important set of calculations that are often separated are those that allow us to calculate working capital needs.

We should be very clear with semantics at this point:

- *Working capital needs:* the difference between the current period's working capital and the prior period's working capital.
- *Working capital:* in a single period, the difference between current assets and current liabilities. Typically, cash is excluded from this calculation, unless cash is an integral part of the company's day-to-day business or the company operates in country where high cash balances (possibly in different currencies) are necessary due to exchange rate and/or inflation problems.
- *Current assets:* all assets that are liquid within 12 months.
- *Current liabilities:* all liabilities that are due within 12 months.

Working capital is sometimes confusing because people reference it in two ways: first as working capital needs and second as cash change. What is the difference

Calculating Working Capital Needs and Cash Change

	2009	2010		
Current Assets				**Cash Change**
Accounts Receivable	150	0		150
Inventory	0	300		-300
Current Liabilities				
Accounts Payable	0	200		200
Other Current Liabilities	400	0		-400

Working Capital	-250	100		

Working Capital Need	350	**Total Cash Change**	-350

FIGURE 8.2 Working capital should be assessed by the change in cash; the opposite is thought of as the working capital needs.

between these two concepts? Let's use an example. Imagine that we had the current assets and current liabilities in Figure 8.2.

We could take the difference between current assets and current liabilities each period and then take the difference between the current and prior period. In this case, we would have a positive number. This positive number represents the working capital that is needed to keep the business operational. Without this cash flow, we would not have been able to fund the purchase of inventory, which is highly critical, nor pay down our other current liabilities, where nonpayment could lead to default.

Another thing to look at is the cash change method. The question a financial analyst needs to ask is: "What is the impact on cash?" This is often a confusing concept for people to get quickly. For instance, when inventory increases from 0 to 300 in our example, the cash impact is –300. This is because for us to create 300 of inventory we need 300 of cash. Conversely, the opposite happens for liabilities. When accounts payable increases from 0 to 200, our cash change is positive because we have received a good or service without laying out any cash.

MODEL BUILDER 8.1: CALCULATING WORKING CAPITAL

1. Working capital is a useful calculation to separate out since it will be used for the cash flow statement, free cash flow, and for the analyst's judgment of operational performance. Some financial modelers choose to do this calculation within the cash flow statement, but given its importance we will create a separate sheet for the working capital. Insert a sheet after the Debt sheet and name it **Working Capital**.

2. Enter the text **Cash Change Method** in cell A2. This is to advise model users that we will be calculating the change in cash as described in the paragraph preceding Model Builder 8.1.

3. Set up the dates and timing for the sheet by entering the following formulas in the corresponding cells:

E2: =Vectors!E9
E3: =Vectors!E10

Copy and paste these formulas over to column Z, within their respective rows. Notice we start with the first projection period since we do not have any information prior to the first historical period. There would be no way to calculate the cash change for the historical year without the year prior to the historical year's information.

4. We should establish labels for the upcoming working capital calculations. Something new to our model is that this is the first time that negative numbers will appear and remain part of the calculations. It is easier to work with changes in cash by viewing reductions in cash as negative values. Enter the following text in the corresponding cells:

C4: (Inc.)/Dec. in Acct. Rec.
C5: (Inc.)/Dec. in Inventory
C6: (Inc.)/Dec. in Other Current Assets
C7: Inc./(Dec.) in Acct. Pay.
C8: Inc/(Dec.) in ST Debt
C9: Inc./(Dec.) in Other Current Liab.
C10: Net Working Capital Cash Change

5. Our first actual calculations will focus on the current assets. Enter the following formulas in their corresponding cells:

E4: ='Balance Sheet'!D9-'Balance Sheet'!E9
E5: ='Balance Sheet'!D13-'Balance Sheet'!E13
E6: ='Balance Sheet'!D14-'Balance Sheet'!E14

Copy and paste these formulas over to column J while maintaining the formula within its respective row.

6. We should calculate the cash change for the current liabilities. Enter the following formula in cell E7:

='Balance Sheet'!E30-'Balance Sheet'!D30

Copy and paste this formula over the range E7:J9.

A B	C	D	E	F	G	H	I	J
1	**Working Capital**							
2	Cash change method		Projected ---->					TV Year
3			12/31/2008	12/31/2009	12/31/2010	12/31/2011	12/31/2012	12/31/2013
4	(Inc.) Dec. in Acct. Rec.		-0.64	-1.81	-1.99	-2.20	-2.42	-1.05
5	(Inc.) Dec. in Inventory		4.44	-0.63	-0.70	-0.78	-0.87	-0.69
6	(Inc.) Dec. in Other Current Assets		-1.21	-0.23	-0.25	-0.27	-0.30	-0.13
7	Inc. (Dec.) in Acct. Pay.		2.57	1.10	2.11	2.35	2.61	2.01
8	Inc. (Dec.) in ST Debt		19.92	-19.92	0.00	0.00	0.00	0.00
9	Inc. (Dec.) in Other Current Liab.		3.62	0.68	0.75	0.82	0.91	0.39
10	**Net Working Capital Cash Change**		**28.69**	**-20.80**	**-0.09**	**-0.08**	**-0.07**	**0.53**

FIGURE 8.3 The Working Capital sheet provides a detailed look at cash necessary to keep the core business operational.

7. Sum up the columns for each period to see the net working capital cash change by entering the following formula in cell E10 and copying and pasting it over the range E10:J10:

=SUM(E4:E9)

Figure 8.3 shows what the completed section should look like.

MODEL BUILDER 8.2: BUILDING THE CASH FLOW STATEMENT

1. The cash flow statement is a separate worksheet in the example model. Insert a new worksheet after the Working Capital sheet and name it **Cash Flow Statement**. On the Cash Flow Statement sheet, enter the text **Cash Flow Statement** in cell A1.
2. We will need historical information, so we should create the dates starting with the historical period. Enter the following formulas in the corresponding cells:

D2: =Vectors!D9
D3: =Vectors!D10

Copy and paste these formulas over to column Z in their respective rows.
3. The first section that we will complete is cash flow from operations. Enter the following text to create labels in the following corresponding cells:

B5: **Operations**
B6: **Net Income**
B7: **Depreciation & Amortization**
B8: **Change in Working Capital**
B9: **Cash from Operations**

4. We start cash flow from operations with net income from the year. We will directly reference the income statement to get this number. Still on the Cash Flow Statement sheet, enter the following reference in cell E6:

='Income Statement'!E36

Copy and paste this formula over the range E6:J6.

5. Net income is not the operational cash flow because non-cash items have been removed. In our example model, we have two forms of non-cash items: depreciation and amortization. Real cash flow is not reduced by these items and should therefore be added back to the operational cash flow. Enter the following formula in cell E7:

='Income Statement'!E15+'Income Statement'!E16

Copy and paste this formula over the range E7:J7.

6. Earlier in this chapter we identified working capital as an integral part of operations. If there is a need to fund working capital, then this must be removed from the cash flow. Similarly, if there is an excess amount of cash from working capital, this can add to the cash flow. Enter the following formula in cell E8:

='Working Capital'!E10

Copy and paste this formula over the range E8:J8. Notice that since we used the cash change method on the Working Capital sheet we can directly reference that sheet here. Some financial models build the working capital calculation into this section of the cash flow statement.

7. Since we are working with positive values representing cash flow in and negative values representing cash flow out, we can sum the values for each period to get to our total cash flow from operations. Enter the following formula in cell E9 and copy and paste it over the range E9:J9:

=SUM(E6:E8)

Refer to Figure 8.4 for the current development of cash flow from operations section of the cash flow statement.

8. The next section of the cash flow statement focuses on investing activities. Enter the following text in the corresponding cells:

B11: **Investing**
B12: **Disposal of Fixed Assets**
B13: **Capital Expenditures**
B14: **Intangible Acquisition**

		12/31/2007	12/31/2008	12/31/2009	12/31/2010	12/31/2011	12/31/2012	12/31/2013
1	**Cash Flow Statement**							
2			Projected ---->					TV Year
3								
4								
5	Operations							
6	Net Income		76.75	73.68	83.42	93.91	112.19	130.01
7	Depreciation and Amortization		—	22.33	24.83	27.93	22.10	5.60
8	Change in Working Capital		28.69	(20.80)	(0.09)	(0.08)	(0.07)	0.53
9	**Cash from operations**		105.45	75.21	108.17	121.76	134.22	136.14

FIGURE 8.4 The cash flow from operations section helps us determine the operational viability of the firm over a forecast period.

B15: **Sale of LT Investments**
B16: **Purchase of LT Investments**
B17: **Cash from Investing**

9. The first entry of the cash flow from investing section, disposal of fixed assets, may be confusing since we have not covered it. It's mainly here to demonstrate how the model can be scaled up to include more granular detail. At some point one may want to add items or concepts not discussed. One of the best places to start is determining where it is on the cash flow statement and where the cash would come from. In this case, an asset disposal would have cash flow through the income statement, depending on a gain or loss on sale. Since this is a scalable section not covered by the example model, we can put in proxy values of 0 right now for each cell in the range E12:J12.

10. The more obvious investing activities are capital expenditures. Here we can directly reference the Capex sheet. Enter the following formula in cell E13:

=-Capex!E10

Copy and paste this formula over the range E13:J13. Notice that there is a negative sign in front of the formula. This is because capital expenditures are always cash flow out and we used positive values in their calculation on the Capex sheet.

11. Just as intangibles were very similar in calculation to capital expenditures, their setup on the cash flow statement is as well. Enter the following formula in cell E14:

=-Intangibles!E10

Copy and paste this formula over the range E14:J14.

12. The next part of the cash flow from investing section is a bit different from any that we have seen thus far. This part is where we see whether there is cash flow, cash flow out, or both from the sale or purchase of long-term investment. As

	A	B	C	D	E	F	G	H	I	J
15		Sale of LT Investments			—	—	—	—	—	—
16		Purchase LT Investments			(14.01)	(2.26)	(2.49)	(2.75)	(3.03)	(1.32)
17		**Cash from Investing**			(134.01)	(7.26)	(15.49)	(2.75)	(3.03)	(1.32)

FIGURE 8.5 Certain items benefit from a more detailed look at the differences between periods. Here we can see when a purchase or a sale occurred, not just a net number.

model builders, we have the choice to consolidate the sale or purchase of assets to one row or split it into two. What's the difference, you might ask? One row is easier to implement since it is just the difference between the two periods. However, two rows give us the flexibility to see whether we had both a sale and a purchase or one or the other. Leaning toward a more detailed approach, enter the following formula in cell E15:

=MAX('Balance Sheet'!D25-'Balance Sheet'!E25,0)

This formula takes the difference between the prior year and the current year's long-term investments. If the number is positive, it means there was a net sale of assets, but if it is negative, it means there is a net purchase of assets. Since we are focused only on sales in row 15 we use a MAX function as a floor to prevent any negative values from being introduced into this row. Some readers will wonder, "If we have only one line for long-term investments on the balance sheet, why does it matter to split it into two separate rows?" This is a valid point; the method of handling multiple investments is just being shown for demonstration purposes. Copy and paste this formula over the range E15:J15. Figure 8.5 shows how this section is developed.

13. To do the purchase of long-term investments, enter the following formula in cell E16:

=MIN('Balance Sheet'!D25-'Balance Sheet'!E25,0)

Copy and paste this formula over the range E16:J16. Notice that we use the MIN function to create a cap at zero. Since a purchase of long-term investments is cash flow out, this number should be only negative. Once again, it is merely for demonstration purposes because in our model we have only one line for long-term investments on the balance sheet.

14. We now sum up all of the cash changes for investing with the following formula in cell E17:

=SUM(E12:E16)

Copy and paste this formula over the range E17:J17. Figure 8.6 shows the development of the investing section of the cash flow statement.

	A	B	C	D	E	F	G	H	I	J
11		Investing								
12		Disposal of Fixed Assets			—	—	—	—	—	—
13		Capital Expenditures			(110.00)	—	(10.00)	—	—	—
14		Intangible Acquisition			(10.00)	(5.00)	(3.00)	—	—	—
15		Sale of LT Investments			—	—	—	—	—	—
16		Purchase LT Investments			(14.01)	(2.26)	(2.49)	(2.75)	(3.03)	(1.32)
17		**Cash from Investing**			(134.01)	(7.26)	(15.49)	(2.75)	(3.03)	(1.32)

FIGURE 8.6 Cash flow from investing is important since the investments may be required to keep the business running in the future. Also, we might want to see whether a lot of funds were derived from the sale of any assets rather than from operational income.

15. The final section we need to work on is cash flow from financing. Enter the following text in the corresponding cells:

   B19: **Financing**
   B20: **Dividends Paid**
   B21: **Inc. LT Borrowings**
   B22: **Dec. LT Borrowings**
   B23: **Inc. Common Stock**
   B24: **Dec. Common Stock**
   B25: **Cash from Financing**

16. Financing brings in cash and costs cash. The first financing item is a cost: dividends paid. Enter the following formula in cell E20:

   =-'Income Statement'!E38

   Copy and paste this formula over the range E20:J20. As with capital expenditure and intangibles, notice that a negative sign is put in front of the value since it is cash flow out.

17. Next we will focus on long-term debt. We will take a similar approach to the sale and purchase of long-term investments and create two separate rows for long-term debt: one for increases and the other for decreases. In cell E21, enter the following formula:

   =MAX('Balance Sheet'!E35-'Balance Sheet'!D35,0)

   Once again, we use the MAX function as a floor to prevent negative numbers, since any increase in long-term debt will be a positive. Also be careful with the order of subtraction. For assets, we subtract the current period from the prior period. For liabilities, we subtract values from the prior period from the current period. Copy and paste this formula over the range E21:J21.

18. Create opposite functionality for decreases by enter the following formula:

=MIN('Balance Sheet'!E35-'Balance Sheet'!D35,0)

Copy and paste this formula over the range E22:J22.

19. The same concepts will be applied for common stock. Enter the following formulas in the corresponding cells:

E23: =MAX('Balance Sheet'!E41-'Balance Sheet'!D41,0)
E24: =MIN('Balance Sheet'!E41-'Balance Sheet'!D41,0)

Copy and paste these values over to column J in their respective rows.

20. Finally, in cell E25, sum up the cash flow changes from financing by entering the following formula:

=SUM(E20:E24)

Copy and paste this formula over the range E25:J25. The final section, cash flow from financing, is shown in Figure 8.7.

21. We can now add each of the cash flow changes from the three cash flow sections: operations, investing, and financing. Enter the following formula in cell E27:

=E9+E17+E25

Copy and paste this formula over the range E27:J27. Also enter the text **Net Changes in Cash** in cell B27 to label this row.

22. At this point, the cash flow statement is done, allowing us to assess where cash is coming in from or going out to. However, since we balanced our model entirely on other sheets, we may want to see whether we accounted for everything by reconciling the cash flow movements from the cash flow statement with the cash balances on the balance sheet. To create such a comparison, we need to calculate

	A	B	C	D	E	F	G	H	I	J
19		**Financing**								
20		Dividends Paid			(5.00)	(5.00)	(10.00)	(10.00)	(10.00)	(10.00)
21		Inc. LT Borrowings			35.00	—	—	—	—	—
22		Dec. LT Borrowings			—	(8.17)	(8.17)	(8.17)	(6.50)	(4.00)
23		Inc. Common Stock			—	—	—	—	—	—
24		Dec. Common Stock			—	—	—	—	—	—
25		**Cash from Financing**			30.00	(13.17)	(18.17)	(18.17)	(16.50)	(14.00)

FIGURE 8.7 The financing activities of a firm are very important since the capital structure of a company is a prominent indicator of financial health.

the cash balance as projected by the cash flow statement and compare it to the total cash each period from the balance sheet. Enter the following text in the corresponding cells to label the rows in this section:

B29: **Cash Balance from CF Statement**
B30: **Cash Balance from Balance Sheet**
B31: **Difference**

23. We need to complete row 30 prior to 29 since there is some historical information necessary. Row 30 is a sum of the cash from the balance sheet. This includes all sources of cash: surplus funds, cash on hand, and marketable securities. Enter the following formula in cell D30:

='Balance Sheet'!D6+'Balance Sheet'!D7+'Balance Sheet'!D8

Copy and paste this formula over the range D30:J30. This formula adds up each of the cash items. For the historic period, you will notice there is no surplus cash. This is fine since it is just adding a zero and has no effect on the calculation.

24. We will take the historic cash amount and adjust it by the net change in cash from the cash flow statement. We will then take each prior period's calculated cash using this method and add the net change in cash for each new period. These figures should be identical to those on the balance sheet. In cell E29, enter the following formula:

=MAX(D32+E29,0)

Copy and paste this formula over the range E29:J29. Note that the MAX function is used as a floor to prevent negative cash, which in this model would be calculated as short-term debt.

25. The final calculation is a comparison of the two rows. Enter the following formula in cell E31:

=E29-E30

Copy and paste this formula over the range E31:J31. There should be no difference between the cash change calculated from the cash flow statement and that on the balance sheet. If there is, you should take a logical troubleshooting approach of seeing what value the difference is and trying to find that value within the model. This calculation is particularly useful when new concepts are integrated into the model as it forces model builders to categorize the cash flow in order to reconcile cash. Figure 8.8 shows the cash reconciliation between the balance sheet and the cash flow statement.

	A	B	C	D	E	F	G	H	I	J
26										
27		Net Changes in Cash			1.43	54.78	74.51	100.85	114.69	120.82
28										
29		Cash Balance from CF Statement			15.44	70.22	144.73	245.58	360.27	481.09
30		Cash Balance from Balance Sheet		14.00	15.44	70.22	144.73	245.58	360.27	481.09
31		Difference			—	—	0.00	0.00	0.00	0.00

FIGURE 8.8 Tracking and assigning all cash flow movements in the model is a useful way to ensure the model is calculating correctly.

PREVENTING ERROR THROUGH INTERNAL VALIDATION

Now that we have all three financial statements and our core calculations complete, we should make sure that our model is working correctly. There can be innumerable tests in a model to validate its performance, but the key ones that we will focus on in the example model include:

- *Assets = liabilities + equity:* The model must always adhere to the number-one accounting principle; every period, total assets must equal total liabilities plus equity.
- *Unpaid debt principal:* If scheduled principal goes unpaid, we should be able to identify such a scenario quickly.
- *Unpaid debt interest:* Similar to principal, if interest goes unpaid, we should be able to identify it quickly.
- *ST funds limit breach:* In Chapter 7 we mentioned that while we may have a balanced model we should always verify that it reflects reality. Although a company can have unlimited surplus cash, companies have limited access to debt, and the short-term debt plug should be either limited or flagged if it exceeds the commitments that are available to the company.
- *Cash check:* In this chapter we reconciled cash using the cash flow statement. If there is a difference between the balance sheet cash and the cash flow statement, we should be able to identify this quickly.

MODEL BUILDER 8.3: IMPLEMENTING INTERNAL VALIDATIONS

1. Since the model user will primarily operate the model from the Assumptions sheet, we should set up the internal validations on that sheet. This way, when model users change an assumption, they can quickly see whether the model has a problem. On the Assumptions sheet, in the following cells, enter the corresponding text:

   L3: **Internal Validation**
   L4: **Assets = Liab + SH Equity**
   L5: **Unpaid Debt Principal**

L6: **Unpaid Debt Interest**
L7: **ST Funds Limit Breach**
L8: **Cash Check**

2. Each one of these validations will be a conditional test on the problem at hand. Depending on the conditional test setup, it can produce an "OK" or an "ERROR." Readers may notice the cell-formatting changes in the example model depending on whether "OK" or "ERROR" appears. This is achieved through a feature called *conditional formatting*, which is described at the end of this chapter in the Toolbox. Let's start with the first test by entering the following formula in cell O4:

=IF(ROUND(SUM('Balance Sheet'!E26:I26),0)=ROUND
(SUM('Balance Sheet'!E46:I46),0),"OK","ERROR")

Working through this formula we encounter a new function: ROUND. This function rounds values to a number of decimal places provided by the user in the function. If you are unfamiliar with this function, you should reference the Toolbox at the end of this chapter. Otherwise, if we pick this formula apart we see that the formula sums up all of the periods' total assets and then rounds them so there are no decimals. The same is done for all of the periods' total liabilities and equity. An equal sign is used to see whether those two calculated values are equal. If they are equal, a TRUE value is returned, which is used by an IF function. The IF function returns an "OK" if a TRUE is returned or an "ERROR" if a FALSE is returned. The ROUND function is necessary because there can be very minute differences between values in the projected balancing. The two comparison fields from the Balance Sheet sheet are shown in Figure 8.9.

3. The next two tests are related to the long-term debt, since this is the focus of many peoples' analysis. Enter the following formulas in the corresponding references:

O5:
=IF(SUM(Debt!E23:I23,Debt!E33:I33,Debt!E43:I43)>0,"ERROR","OK")
O6:
=IF(SUM(Debt!E19:I19,Debt!E29:I29,Debt!E39:I39)>0,"ERROR","OK")

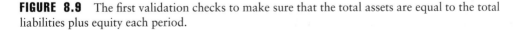

	B	C	D	E	F	G	H	I	J
26	Total Assets		138.04	270.90	313.27	381.38	460.29	559.51	677.92

	B	C	D	E	F	G	H	I	J
46	Total Liabilities and Equity		138.04	270.90	313.27	381.38	460.29	559.51	677.92

FIGURE 8.9 The first validation checks to make sure that the total assets are equal to the total liabilities plus equity each period.

These two formulas are very similar. The first one sums up the total unpaid principal for each debt issuance (rows 23, 33, and 43 on the Debt sheet) and checks to see whether that value is greater than 0. If it is, it returns an "ERROR"; otherwise, an "OK" is returned. Nearly identical is the unpaid interest check that looks to the total unpaid interest for each debt issuance (rows 19, 29, and 39 on the Debt sheet).

4. The short-term debt limit is the next test. This requires an additional field to be entered on the Assumptions sheet. Go to cell D28 on the Assumptions sheet and enter a value of **100**. Name cell D28 **inputs_STFundsLimit**. Now go back up to cell O7 on the Assumptions sheet and enter the following formula:

=IF(MAX('Balance Sheet'!E31:J31)>inputs_STFundsLimit,"ERROR","OK")

This test takes the maximum short-term debt balance from any period on the balance sheet and checks to see whether that value is greater than the short-term funds limit. If it is, there is a breach and an "ERROR" value is produced. Otherwise, the short-term debt is within its limits and the test passes with an "OK." Refer to Figure 8.10 for detail.

5. The final test we will implement is the Cash Check. Enter the following formula in cell O8:

=IF(ROUND(SUM('Cash Flow Statement'!E31:I31),0)=0,"OK","ERROR")

This formula sums up the differences between the cash flow–calculated cash balances and the balance sheet–calculated cash balances. It uses a round function in case there are a few decimals' difference and checks to see whether that value is equal to zero. If it is, that means there is no meaningful difference between the

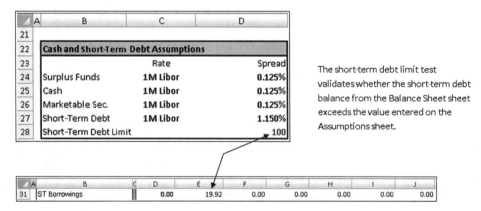

FIGURE 8.10   The short-term debt test checks the short-term debt balance on the balance sheet to make sure it does not exceed the limit set on the Assumptions sheet.

two balances and the cash reconciliation is "OK." Otherwise an "ERROR" is produced.

OTHER VALIDATIONS

The validations and reconciliation methods presented in this chapter are common ones to monitor. As your model develops, you might want to include tests that are specific to important items in your model. For instance, if you create a section on convertible debt, you might want to monitor the current stock price and interest rates to compare against the terms of the convertible debt. The test would then be focused on whether any of the convertible debt is in the money or not. Further actions could be built on the results of this test, such as assuming conversion and equity dilution. We will see in Chapter 10 that we can also automate some of the items for tests, such as the downloading of current stock prices or interest rates from the Web.

TOOLBOX

Conditional Formatting

A useful feature of Excel is the ability to alter the formatting of a cell or range of cells depending on the value of the cell or range of cells. This feature is known as *conditional formatting* since the formatting depends on conditions that the user enters. Conditional formatting is easy to use since it is a prebuilt tool in Excel, but its operation and features differ greatly between Excel 2003 and Excel 2007.

For Excel 2003 and earlier: Conditional formatting can be accessed by going to **Format—Conditional Formatting** and starting the process by selecting **Formula Is**.

For Excel 2007: Conditional formatting received a major overhaul in Excel 2007. There are now a host of new options. To access conditional formatting, go to the **Home** ribbon, **Styles** box, and select **Conditional Formatting**. The drop-down that appears provides multiple options, which are shown in Figure 8.11.

The first two options are an organization of conditional formatting rules. The first of those options is called "Highlight Cells Rules." Within this section, the user can select from a multitude of rules that will highlight a cell or range of cells with a selected format depending on the value or conditional test of values in the cell or range of cells.

The second option is called "Top/Bottom Rules." Within this section, the user can select from rules that will change the formatting of a range of cells depending on the value of each cell compared to the other values in the range. For example, one of the options is "Above Average." This rule will examine the active range that is highlighted, determine the arithmetic average, and highlight any cells in that range where the value is greater than the average.

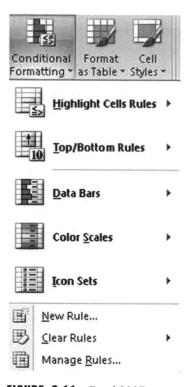

FIGURE 8.11 Excel 2007 provides multiple conditional formatting options.

There are three more options below "Highlight Cells Rules" and "Top/Bottom Rules." These provide highly specialized graphic formatting that is dependent on cell values compared to one another. Similar to "Top/Bottom" rules, these rules will change the color or create different icons depending on the values of cells in the active range.

Finally there are three options at the very bottom of the initial drop-down box. These allow a user to create a new rule from scratch, clear existing rules, or edit and manage existing rules.

ROUND

The ROUND function is a simple function that does exactly what the name implies: It rounds values to a decimal place the user enters. The entry parameters for the ROUND function are:

ROUND(value, # of decimal places)

For instance, the ROUND function is used with the following entry parameters:

=ROUND(5.244,0)

The return value for this function would be 5. This is because the function was instructed to round 5.244 to the 0 decimal place; since the tenths decimal place is 2, the value is rounded down to 5. Keep in mind that the decimal place parameter is all that matters for rounding the value preceding it.

For example, the following function is used:

=ROUND(5.499,0)

The return value for this function would still be 5, which is correct. ROUND does not first round the tenths decimal place up to 5 and then round the whole number up to 6.

CHAPTER 9

Free Cash Flow, Terminal Value, and Discount Rates and Methods

We have built a dynamic model and discussed important sections in detail, but we have yet to consolidate our work to derive a corporate value. This chapter lays out the theory and technical implementation of deriving a corporate value. Overall, we will take an intrinsic, cash flow–based approach to determining the value. This is similar to the valuation of many financial instruments, where cash flow is projected and then discounted back to the present day to determine the present value. This *discounted cash flow* (DCF) methodology can be applied when discussing securities pricing, project valuation, and nearly any other investment opportunity valuation.

The challenge of using a DCF methodology for corporations is determining what constitutes cash flow, what the company is worth beyond the forecast period, and what discount rate(s) to use to determine the present value. Relevant cash flow calculations can be confusing because there are many sources and uses of funds. Also, perspective matters. Cash available for a debt holder is most likely different from that of an equity holder. The number of periods of cash flow we count in a forecast is also of major concern. Many company owners would suggest that their company is worth more than just the cash flows that can be spun out of the firm during the forecast period. They would suggest that there is a terminal value to a firm, since after the forecast period the firm could be liquidated, run without capital investment, or operated in perpetuity. Finally, once we understand what cash flow to count and for how long, we then need to figure out the proper rate or rates to discount the cash flows in order to obtain a present value. Figure 9.1 depicts the overall process.

FREE CASH FLOW: A MATTER OF PERSPECTIVE

Imagine a small company that is composed of only one equity holder and no debt. If that company earns just enough money to cover costs and expenses, then there are no earnings to dividend out to the equity holder or to retain to build equity value. If

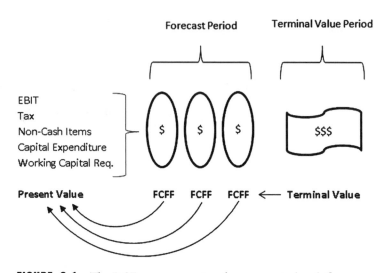

FIGURE 9.1   The DCF process requires forecast period cash flow calculations to be discounted back at appropriate rates.

this is what is expected in perpetuity, the company is worth only the invested amount to the equity holder. It may be worth the salaries the workers are earning, but from the equity holder's point of view, aside from the liquidation value of the assets, the company is worthless.

So, what is value? For the firm as a whole, meaning from the perspective of both debt and equity holders, it is any cash that is left over after meeting operating expenses, working capital needs, capital reinvestment, and taxes. Formally, this is known as *free cash flow to the firm* (FCFF). While there are a number of methods to derive FCFF, the easiest is to use the following formula, which is also represented in Figure 9.2:

$$\text{FCFF} = \text{EBIT} * (1 - \text{Tax Rate}) + \text{Non-Cash Items} - \text{Capital Expenditures} - \text{Working Capital Needs}$$

The FCFF formula often causes confusion as to what each term means, so we should go through the terminology. We start the formula with *earnings before interest and taxes* (EBIT). Some prefer to start with net income, but since FCFF also includes the perspective of debt holders it is easier to begin with EBIT. The reason it is easier is because interest payments are value to debt holders. If we start with net income, we would have to calculate and add back the after-tax interest. Instead, we could just start with EBIT and remove tax, since tax is an actual cash flow out.

The next part of the formula, *non-cash items*, is actually an addition to FCFF. This is because non-cash items are just as their name implies: not actual cash.

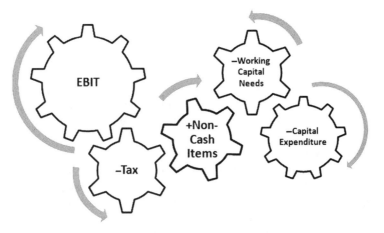

FIGURE 9.2   Free cash flow to the firm is any cash left after funding the absolute necessary cash outlays to keep the firm running.

Amounts from concepts such as *depreciation*, *amortization*, *deferred taxes*, and so on have been removed from EBIT and therefore should be added back. We have to go through this add-back process because these items have tax effects that need to be included in the EBIT calculation in order to determine the proper tax amount. Once tax is calculated, we then add back the non-cash items since they are not real cash flow.

After adding back non-cash items, we can move on to capital expenditure, which is clearly a real cash outlay. Capital expenditures are typically a necessity to keep the business generating income and therefore must be removed from any "free" cash. Similarly, if a company's business is oriented around intangibles, such as a film company, then intangible investment would be included here.

Finally, we have *working capital needs*, which is one of the most confused parts of the FCFF formula. In Chapter 8, we defined *working capital* as *current assets less current liabilities*. Working capital is critical to a business because the current assets and liabilities keep operations running on a day-to-day basis. Therefore, there should always be enough funding from current liabilities to cover the assets that are created; otherwise, we need to fund working capital from another source. The idea is similar to our balancing problem from Chapter 7. When assets were greater than liabilities, we plugged liabilities with short-term debt. When liabilities were greater than assets, we plugged assets with excess cash. If current assets are greater than current liabilities, we will have a positive working capital figure. We need to compare this to the next period's working capital in order to understand the working capital needs. If in the next period working capital increases, it means there is a need to fund it through other sources. This need therefore draws cash from our free cash flow.

Let's take a look at a simple example involving the following current asset and liability accounts over two periods:

2009	2010
Current Assets: 200	Current Assets: 500
Current Liabilities: 100	Current Liabilities: 200
Working Capital: 100	Working Capital: 300

In this data, we have a difference in working capital of 200 (2010 working capital of 300 less 2009 working capital of 100). This means that our working capital needs have increased from 2009 to 2010 and, assuming we funded 2009's working capital, we will require an additional 200 in working capital to maintain the current asset figures.

The other way to think about it is from a cash change perspective. In Chapter 8, we implemented the cash change method by examining the difference between current asset and current liability accounts each period. In the previous example, we see that current assets have increased between 2009 and 2010. An increase in assets costs cash. Think about current assets comprising solely inventory. In order to go from 200 in inventories to 500 in inventories we need to pay for 300 in raw materials, work in process, or finished goods. That's a −300 effect on cash. The opposite is true for liabilities. As they increase, we are essentially taking in cash. Think about current liabilities comprising solely short-term debt. If it went from 100 to 200, it would mean we added 100 of funding. That's a 100 effect on cash. If we sum up the cash change, we get −200.

We now have two amounts, 200 and −200, for use as the working capital component of the FCFF formula. This is exactly where the confusion lies. Either one is correct, as long as we apply it correctly. The positive 200 can be thought of as our working capital needs and should be subtracted from FCFF. Alternatively, the −200 can be thought of as the working capital cash change and should be added. Either method we choose will get us to the same FCFF answer.

While FCFF is a good indicator of cash flow to the firm, it is not representative of cash flow to an equity investor. The reason for this is that debt has priority over equity, and cash flow to debt reduces the available cash flow to equity. If we are looking at free cash flow from an equity perspective, we should instead use the following formula to derive the *free cash flow to equity* (FCFE):

$$\text{FCFE} = \text{FCFF} - \text{Interest Expense} * (1 - \text{Tax Rate}) - (\text{Principal Repayments} - \text{New Debt Issue}) - \text{Preferred Dividends}.$$

Notice in this formula the post-tax interest expense is taken away from cash available. We use post-tax figures for the interest because from an equity holder's point of view the interest is a tax shield to the company and reduces the tax liability. In addition, any principal repayments made to debt holders should be removed

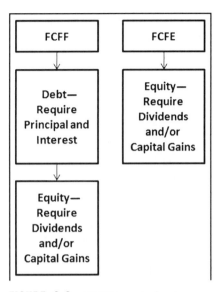

FIGURE 9.3 FCFF is cash that is spun out of the firm that can be paid to debt and equity holders, whereas FCFE is cash that can be paid to equity holders.

from the cash available to equity holders. However, if new debt is being issued, this could be available to the equity holder depending on the covenants attached to the issue. Finally, while not technically debt, preferred stock pays dividends that have a priority over common stockholders. Keep in mind that preferred dividends are often cumulative issues, and if their payment is missed one period it will have to be made up in future periods, prior to paying common shareholders. Figure 9.3 shows the difference between FCFF and FCFE.

MODEL BUILDER 9.1: IMPLEMENTING FREE CASH FLOW

1. Insert a new worksheet after the Cash Flow Statement sheet and name it **DCF**. In cell A1, enter the text **Discounted Cash Flow Valuation**.
2. Set up the dates and timing by entering the following formulas in the corresponding cells:

   E2: =Vectors!E9
   E3: =Vectors!E10

   Copy and paste these formulas over their respective rows to column Z.

3. We are going to implement FCFF in the example model and should therefore label the rows we anticipate needing for the calculation. Enter the following text in the corresponding cells:

C5: **EBIT**
C6: **Tax**
C7: **EBI**
C8: **Depreciation**
C9: **Amortization of Intangibles**
C10: **Change in Net Working Capital**
C11: **Capital Expenditures**
C12: **Free Cash Flow to the Firm**

4. EBIT is easy to find since it is directly calculated on the income statement. Enter the following formula in cell E5 on the DCF sheet:

=**'Income Statement'!E17**

Copy and paste this value over the range E5:J5.

5. Taxes need to be removed since they are real cash being paid out. To determine this amount we should reference the tax rate from the Vectors sheet. In cell E6 on the DCF sheet, enter the following formula:

=**Vectors!E31**

Copy and paste this value over the range E6:J6.

6. Just as the FCFF formula suggests, remove tax from EBIT to get the earnings before interest. Do this by entering the following formula in cell E7:

=**E5*(1-E6)**

Make sure to copy and paste this value over the range E7:J7.

7. Non-cash items are removed next. In our example model we have two non-cash items: depreciation and amortization. Enter the following formulas in the corresponding cells:

E8: =**'Income Statement'!E15**
E9: =**'Income Statement'!E16**

Copy and paste these formulas over to column J in their respective rows. Keep in mind that we will modify the depreciation formula later in this chapter to show an optional terminal value enhancement.

8. The next row takes into account any working capital needs. Enter the following formula in cell E10:

=**'Working Capital'!E10**

Copy and paste this formula over the range E9:J9. If you are referencing the completed model, you will notice that the formula is different. This is similar to step 7 since we will come back to this formula and modify it after learning about terminal value in this chapter.

9. Capital expenditures need to be removed from the free cash flow available. Enter the following formula in cell E11:

   =-Capex!E10

   Notice that since we calculated capital expenditures as positive values on the Capex sheet we need to put a negative sign in front of the reference. Identical to the previous step, capital expenditures will have a special treatment after we learn about terminal value, which will require a modification to this formula. For now, copy and paste this formula over the range E11:J11.

10. Enter the following formula in cell E12 to sum up all of the components to free cash flow:

    =SUM(E7:E11)

    The figure returned is the FCFF for the first projection period. Copy and paste the formula over the range E12:J12. Refer to Figure 9.4 for detail on what this section of the model should look like.

TERMINAL VALUE: BEYOND THE FORECAST PERIOD

One of the first numbers I turn to when auditing someone else's model is the *terminal value*. This value, which represents an estimation of the firm's value at the end of or beyond the forecast period, can have a significant impact on overall value. It is also a calculation that can be heavily distorted by poorly thought-out assumptions.

A B	C		E	F	G	H	I	J
2			Projected ---->					TV Year
3			12/31/2008	12/31/2009	12/31/2010	12/31/2011	12/31/2012	12/31/2013
4								
5	EBIT		113.40	110.54	121.02	132.15	153.59	173.73
6	Tax Rate		30%	30%	30%	30%	30%	30%
7	EBI		79.38	77.38	84.71	92.50	107.51	121.61
8	Depreciation		—	19.00	19.00	20.60	20.60	6.78
9	Amortization of Intangibles		—	3.33	5.83	7.33	1.50	—
10	Change in Net Working Capital		28.69	(20.80)	(0.09)	(0.08)	(0.07)	(0.77)
11	Capital Expenditures		(110.00)	—	(10.00)	—	—	(7.46)
12	**Free Cash Flow to Firm**		(1.93)	78.91	99.46	120.36	129.54	120.17

FIGURE 9.4 The DCF sheet first calculates the FCFF for each forecast period and for a terminal value column.

FIGURE 9.5 There are many ways to calculate a terminal value. Three of the most popular include a cash flow multiple, asset liquidation, and stable growth.

The terminal value can be calculated in a number of ways. Figure 9.5 shows an overview of the ways to calculate terminal value. The simplest ways are the ones often tossed around conference calls when people estimate the value of a firm by multiplying its last year's cash flow by an industry or market multiple. "That firm is trading at eight times EBITDA and this one is valued at ten times" is a statement akin to what you might hear. While rudimentary, this method can be applied to a terminal-year cash flow to estimate terminal value.

A more detailed method for assessing terminal value is examining the assets of the firm to see what they are worth after the forecast period. Some debt bankers might do a worst-case analysis and assume that if the company that they lent money to could not pay back or refinance debts at maturity, then as bondholders they would push for liquidation. Assessing the value of the assets versus the debt exposure is their exit strategy. Therefore, another view of terminal value in this situation is a liquidation of assets. In this case, the assets would have to be valued as if they were being sold off after the forecast period, taking into account any appreciation, depreciation, or inflation.

If a market value that far out is difficult to assess, then estimations of return value on the assets can be made. Estimating the periodic worth of the assets over the average life of the assets and discounting that stream of values to the time period at the end of the forecast period can help establish such a value.

Finally, many corporate founders and owners would shudder at the thought of breaking up their company or running it into the ground after a forecast period. Perhaps they have legitimate reasons to believe their company will continue operating and even grow beyond the forecast period. For this reason, valuation analysts began to use a *stable-growth model*. The stable-growth model assumes that a company will continue to operate and possibly grow in perpetuity. The idea is that the firm as a going concern has value. Just as the forecast period value is based on free cash flow, the stable-growth model is based on cash flow expected in perpetuity.

Formally, the stable-growth model examines a long-term cash flow expectation and takes that cash flow into perpetuity with or without a growth rate. We can formalize the stable-growth model with the following formula:

Free Cash Flow $(t + 1)$/(Discount Rate − Long-Term Growth Rate)

Quick Method	Detailed Method

FCF(final forecast period grown by LT growth)	Rebuild FCF and Possibly Adjust:
	    Working Capital (maintenance level)
	    Capital Expenditure (maintenance level)
	    Depreciation (use % relationship to Capex)

Regardless of method, the stable-growth method requires the long-term assumptions for WACC and growth.	

FIGURE 9.6 A simplified approach to estimating the FCF for the terminal value can miss key differences in expectations between the short and long term. The alternative is a more detailed method that builds in long-term expectations.

In this formula, the Free Cash Flow $(t + 1)$ is a free cash flow (FCF) one period after the forecast period that can be created in two ways: by growing the final forecast period's free cash flow by a long-term growth rate or by recalculating all of the components of free cash flow so they reflect the long term, in the period after the last forecast period. The first method is very easy. Simply take the last forecast free cash flow and grow it by the assumed long-term growth rate. The difference between short-term and long-term growth is one reason we have a forecast period versus a terminal value in the first place. Often, though, near-term assumptions are expected to change in the distant future. A major disadvantage of simply growing the last forecast period's free cash flow is that that free cash flow might not be representative of the expected long-term cash flows of the firm. See Figure 9.6 for more detail.

The alternative method, which addresses the flaws of the first method, is to recalculate all of the components of free cash flow to make sure they are reflective of long-term assumptions. In our example model, think about the long-term attributes of each of the items that we identified for FCFF:

- *EBIT:* In the long term, earnings are expected to grow at a long-term, stable growth rate.
- *Tax:* If the firm is expected to have a different tax regime than the one that has been assumed for the forecast period, this should be changed for the long term.
- *Non-cash items:* Non-cash items such as depreciation and amortization may have an assumption that is aggressive if there is excessive depreciation in the final forecast period due to perhaps a large capital expenditure. Conversely, if the forecast period is unusually light on capital expenditures, then the lack of depreciation taken out in perpetuity could be conservative. Overall, we need to keep in mind that the final forecast period may have an assumption that is unusual and something that will not be witnessed in perpetuity. In such a

case, with depreciation we can always turn to the industry or market to apply a comparable ratio instead of using the final forecast period's value. In the case of depreciation, it is tightly linked to capital expenditure and we should therefore use a capital-expenditure-to-depreciation ratio.

- *Capital expenditures:* Depending on the capital expenditure schedule assumed during the forecast period, the final forecast period's capital expenditure assumption could be aggressive or conservative. If capital expenditure is unusually high in the final period and we used that period's FCFF, we would be deducting a large amount from free cash flow in perpetuity. The opposite is true if there are no capital expenditures assumed for that period and we used that period's FCFF. In such a case, the free cash flow used for the terminal value would be excessively high since no capital expenditures are being removed from it. Since a company most likely needs to invest cash into capital expenditures in order to maintain or grow operational cash flow, an industry or market ratio should be used, as mentioned in the non-cash items point.
- *Working capital needs:* Similar to capital expenditures there is a base level of working capital needs as a company grows. In the forecast period we may have seen unusually high or low levels of working capital needs and should recalibrate the working capital needs expectation to an industry or market standard. Industry percentages of revenue that are tied up in working capital is a good metric to make an assumption.

Once we determine the correct numerator in the stable-growth formula, there are two very important rates required to calculate the rest of the formula. The first rate is the *discount rate*. If we are looking at a firm that is comprised of debt and equity, this rate is the *weighted average cost of capital* (WACC). If we are looking at an equity-only firm, then this rate is the *long-term cost of equity*. Keep in mind that these are long-term rates, which can be different from the forecast period rates. We will cover discount rates later in this chapter, where we will discuss the components of WACC and what needs to be taken into consideration for a long-term rate.

The final rate and assumption that is needed is the *expected long-term growth rate*. Whatever the rate by which we grew our EBIT or prior period's free cash flow, that is the rate that we should use for this part of the formula. You will quickly notice that the long-term growth rate of the firm cannot exceed the cost of capital; otherwise, a nonsensical answer will be returned.

MODEL BUILDER 9.2: CALCULATING AND INTEGRATING A STABLE-GROWTH TERMINAL VALUE

1. In our example model, we will take the more detailed route of recalculating the components of FCFF for the terminal value. While it will appear as if we were calculating another period in the forecast, this is actually just the terminal value calculation. The first part of the FCFF formula that we see is EBIT. We have taken care of this assumption by entering a long-term growth rate in the

	A	B	C	D	E	F	G	H	I	J
9		Live Scenario			Projected ---->					TV Year
10				12/31/2007	12/31/2008	12/31/2009	12/31/2010	12/31/2011	12/31/2012	12/31/2013
11		Income Statement Items								
12		Sales Unit Growth			5.00%	5.00%	5.00%	5.00%	5.00%	2.00%
13		Sales Price Growth			5.00%	5.00%	5.00%	5.00%	5.00%	2.00%

FIGURE 9.7 In the terminal value column (J), the long-term growth figure is used rather than the short-term growth assumption.

terminal-year assumptions. Verify that this is true by going to the Vectors sheet. The Base Case sales unit and price growth should both be set to **2.00%** as compared to 5.00% for the forecast period. Figure 9.7 shows the change from forecast period to terminal value column.

2. We will assume that the long-term tax rate does not change. The first row we encounter where there could be a change between the forecast period and the long-term outlook is depreciation. *Depreciation* is a difficult item to project in the long term on its own since it is dependent on the capital expenditure assumption, which takes into consideration the capital expenditures' lives and salvage values. We can examine history or the industry to understand this relationship and derive a common ratio known as the *capital-expenditure-to-depreciation* ratio. We will set this up in the example model and use this ratio for long-term projections. To do this, we should first assume that we have done our historical/industry analysis and established the capital-expenditure-to-depreciation ratio. Go the Assumptions sheet and enter the text **Capex to Dep.** in cell F27. Enter the value **110%** in cell G27. Name cell G27 **inputs_CapextoDep**. Refer to Figure 9.8 for detail.

3. Go back to the DCF sheet and modify the existing formula in cell J8 so that it is the following:

=IF(J2="TV Year",-J11/inputs_CapexToDep,'Income Statement'!J15)

Notice that this formula checks the field above the dates. In this field we created text that identifies the terminal value column ("TV Year") when the forecast period has ended. If we are in the terminal value column, then we will take the

	F	G	H	I	J	K
22	**DCF Valuation Assumptions**					
23	Forecast Beta	1.90		Unsec. Rating		A
24	LT Beta	1.00		Terminal Value Type	Stable Growth	
25	Market Risk Prem.	6.50%		Final EBITDA Multiple		5.00
26	Net PPE to Net Sale:	3%		Global Growth Adjustor		0.00%
27	Capex to Dep.	110%		Long-Term Debt Ratio		30%
28	LT WC % of Revenue	30%		Long-Term Cost of Debt		5%

FIGURE 9.8 There are many specific assumptions involved in determining the final DCF value.

terminal value capital expenditure amount (determined in step 8 of this Model Builder) and divide it by the capital-expenditure-to-depreciation ratio. If we are in any other time period, the depreciation will be taken from the corresponding time period on the income statement. Make sure to copy and paste the formula in cell J8 over the range E8:J8.

4. The other non-cash item that we have been working with is *intangible amortization*. If intangibles are a core component of the company's operations and require periodic investment, then an assumption should be made in the long term. We are going to assume that the intangibles acquired or purchased in the forecast period were special to the forecast period, and that, in the long term, intangibles will play a minimal role. For this reason we will leave the intangible amortization row formula untouched.

5. Another item that we mentioned might change in the long term is working capital. The working capital needs may not be reflected properly in the forecast period and in our example model we are going to revert to a ratio based on net sales. To implement this, we should go back to the Assumptions sheet and enter the text **LT WC % of Revenue** in cell F28. Next, enter the value 30% in cell G28 and name that cell **inputs_WCPctofRev**.

6. Modify the following formula on the DCF sheet in cell J10:

=IF(J2="TV Year",-((inputs_WCPctofRev*'Income Statement'!J7)-(inputs_
  WCPctofRev*'Income Statement'!I7)),'Working Capital'!J10)

Copy and paste this formula over the range E10:J10. Notice that this formula checks to see whether the current column is the terminal value year. If it is, then the working capital expected as a percentage of the current period is subtracted from the working capital expected from the prior period, using the working capital percentage of revenue assumption. Otherwise, the working capital is expected as calculated on the Working Capital sheet.

7. The next part of the terminal value FCFF is capital expenditures. As with depreciation, we may have a different expectation regarding the long-term capital expenditure assumption. Since we used the capital-expenditure-to-depreciation ratio to calculate depreciation, it would be circular to use the same ratio on depreciation to calculate capital expenditures. Aside from intimate knowledge of management plans, another method of estimating capital expenditures is by looking at a historical or industry *net PPE–to–net sales* ratio. We should create this ratio on the Assumptions sheet. Go to the Assumptions sheet and enter the text **Net PPE to Net Sales** in cell F26. Enter the value **3%** in cell G26 and name that cell **inputs_NetPPEtoNetSales**.

8. With this new ratio we should modify the formula in cell J11 to be:

=IF(J2="TV Year",(-inputs_NetPPEtoNetSales*'Income Statement'!J7)+((-
  inputs_NetPPEtoNetSales*'Income Statement'!J7)/inputs_CapexToDep),-
  Capex!J10)

This formula checks to see whether the current column is the terminal value column. If it is, then the net PPE–to–net Sales ratio is multiplied by the current column's expected income. The result of this product is the expected net PPE. Since we are focusing on the capital expenditure for that period we should add back the expected depreciation off of that amount. We do this by adding the net PPE divided by the capital-expenditures-to-depreciation ratio, which is essentially the depreciation. This figure would actually get us to gross PPE, but since we are not assuming any historical gross PPE, we can interpret the figure as the capital expenditures. Copy and paste this formula over the range E11:J11. Figure 9.9 emphasizes the TV year section.

9. The terminal value FCFF should be automatically calculated by the existing formula in cell J12 on the DCF sheet. Notice that this value, in the example model, is significantly lower than the last forecast period's FCFF. This is due to the use of ratios to help determine the proper maintenance capital expenditures, depreciation, and working capital needs. If we had used the last forecast period's FCFF and grown it by the expected long-term growth rate, we might have created an aggressive assumption for the terminal value FCFF. This error would be compounded into perpetuity.

10. We are now prepared to calculate the terminal value. However, we may want an option on how to calculate the terminal value since there can be multiple methods. The two that we employ in the example model are a stable-growth and an EBITDA-multiple method. In order to build this functionality in we need to create a couple of options on the Assumptions sheet. On the Assumptions sheet, enter the following text in the corresponding cells:

I24: **Terminal Value Type**
I25: **Final EBITDA Multiple**

A	B	C	D	J
2				TV Year
3				**12/31/2013**
4				
5		EBIT		173.73
6		Tax Rate		30%
7		EBI		121.61
8		Depreciation		17.65
9		Amortization of Intangibles		-
10		Change in Net Working Capital		(3.95)
11		Capital Expenditures		(19.41)
12		**Free Cash Flow to Firm**		115.90
13		**Terminal Value**		1,467.09

FIGURE 9.9 The terminal value year often requires careful thought since it is a shift from the short-term to the long-term perspective.

11. Since there can be multiple terminal value methodologies we will create a data validation list for the model user to select a method. Go to the Hidden sheet and enter the following text in the corresponding cells:

    D16: **lst_TVType**
    D17: **EBITDA Multiple**
    D18: **Stable Growth**

    Name range D17:D18 **lst_TVType**.

12. Back on the Assumptions sheet, create a data validation list in cell K24 using the named range lst_TVType as the source. Also, enter **5** as a proxy value for the EBITDA multiple in cell K25. Name cell K24 **inputs_TVType** and cell K25 **inputs_EBITDAMult**.

13. On the DCF sheet, enter the following formula in cell J13:

    =IF(J2<>"TV Year",0,IF(inputs_TVType="Stable Growth",J12/(J18-Vectors!J12),DCF!J12*inputs_EBITDAMult))

    This formula uses a conditional test that we have not yet seen. The symbols <> are synonymous with *not equal to*. Thus, if the current column is not equal to the terminal value column, then there is no terminal value calculation. Otherwise, we should have a terminal value calculation. This calculation can be based on one of the two methods we entered on the Assumptions sheet: the stable-growth method, which we have explained, or a simple EBITDA multiple that is often mentioned in conference calls.

    If a model user selects Stable Growth, then the FCFF from the terminal value column (cell J12) is divided by the long-term weighted average cost of capital (cell J17) minus the long-term growth rate from the Vectors sheet. Note that since we have not calculated the weighted average cost of capital yet, this formula will return an error if Stable Growth is selected. For now, let's assume a stable-growth method, which will be changed from an error after we cover discount rates in the next section of this chapter. Copy and paste cell J13 over the range E13:J13.

14. The final calculation we should implement is to total the FCFF and terminal value for discounting. An important concept to remember is that the terminal value is not an additional year in the timeline. Once we calculate it, we should assume it is part of the final year's forecast cash flow. Enter the following formula in cell J14:

    =IF(J2="TV Year",0,J12+K13)

    Copy and paste this formula over the range E14:J14. The first part of the formula is an IF function that tests whether the current column is the terminal value column. If this is the case, then the cash flow estimation should be done.

B	C	D	E	F	G	H	I	J
12	Free Cash Flow to Firm		(1.93)	78.91	99.46	120.36	129.54	115.90
13	Terminal Value		-	-	-	-	-	1,467.09
14	Combined Periodic Value		(1.93)	78.91	99.46	120.36	1,596.63	-

FIGURE 9.10   The terminal value is added to the final forecast period's free cash flow. The combined values are discounted back to the present value.

Otherwise, we should add the current period's FCFF, plus the terminal value from the next period. This effectively brings the terminal value back to the final forecast period. These combined cash flows are what we now want to discount and are shown in Figure 9.10.

DISCOUNT RATES AND METHODS

Our final requirement to determine a valuation is the rate at which we discount the FCFF and terminal value. What appears to be such a simple, singular requirement rapidly multiplies into branches of corporate finance concepts and mathematical techniques. In our example, we have focused on FCFF, which is representative of the free cash flow to the entire firm. Therefore, the rate at which we discount the cash flows should also represent the firm. To truly represent the firm's costs, such a rate must be composed of both an equity and debt cost. The costs should then be weighted by the firm's expected capital structure each period or by the capital structure that management expects. The rate that ensues from such a process is known as the *weighted average cost of capital* (WACC), as shown in Figure 9.11. To really understand the WACC, we should first delve into its major components: the cost of equity and the cost of debt.

Cost of Equity

The cost of equity is the return an equity holder would demand for offering equity funds. The theory behind this rate is derived from the *capital asset pricing model* (CAPM). Basically, an equity investor should get paid for the risk he or she takes on through investment. The return should at minimum be slightly higher than the risk-free rate in the market; otherwise, the equity investor should simply invest in risk-free securities. So, the starting place for the cost of equity is the *risk-free rate*. This is the absolute floor on the expected returns. It would be highly unlikely, though, that equity investors would accept the risk-free rate, since the firms or projects that they are investing in will have elements of risk.

CAPM suggests that investors should get paid an investment rate that is above the risk-free rate, accounts for market returns, and incorporates compensation for nondiversifiable risk. The first two are returns based on a default-free investment and

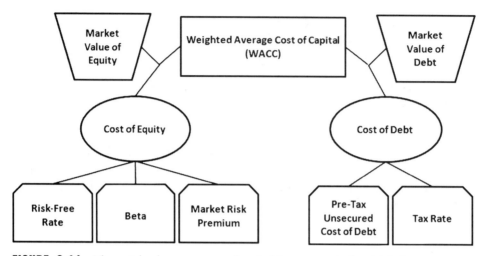

FIGURE 9.11 The weighted average cost of capital is composed of multiple factors.

the market as a whole, respectively. We will discuss them later in the chapter. To capture nondiversifiable risk we need to understand how the firm under consideration performs versus the market. Specifically, beta has been established as the metric to capture this risk and is formally defined as:

$$\text{Beta} = \text{Covariance of the Firm's Returns with the Market's Returns} / \text{Variance of the Market's Returns}$$

Beta is a metric of the firm's expected returns given the market's returns. Typically, the market is an index relevant to the firm. For many U.S. stocks, the S&P 500 is used as the benchmark.

Market risk is measured by calculating the actual returns of stocks compared to the actual returns of default-free securities (typically government securities). Be sure that the risk-free rate used to calculate the market risk premium is the same risk-free rate that is used for the risk-free rate part of the cost-of-equity calculation. Once the returns of the market and the risk-free rate are known, the difference between these two is the *market risk premium*. Both risks are shown in Figure 9.12.

We can piece together all of this information to get the formal cost-of-equity equation:

$$\text{Cost of Equity} = \text{Risk Free Rate} + \text{Beta} * \text{Market Risk Premium}$$

The only part we have not talked about is the risk-free rate. Typically, a long-dated Treasury rate, such as the 10-year Treasury, is used. In projections, this figure

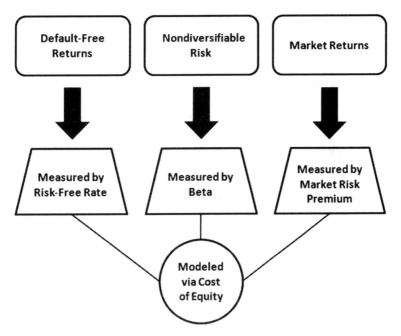

FIGURE 9.12 Beta and the market risk premium contribute to the cost of equity.

can be adjusted for inflation. We use the risk-free rate as the basis and then add the product of the firm's beta and the market risk premium.

Aside from inflation there are other considerations when forecasting these items. For beta, we should be worried about the capital structure of the firm. When a firm's capital structure changes, beta also changes. History has shown that as a firm's leverage increases, so does the volatility of a firm's returns. This means that the beta we use in one period may not be the correct beta to use in other periods. We may also assume that if a firm is in business in perpetuity, as in the stable-growth terminal value, beta stabilizes. Frequently, assumptions between 1.0 and 1.2 are used for a stable beta.

Cost of Debt

The cost of debt is simpler in calculation than the cost of equity, but equally challenging to construct properly. The cost of debt is formalized by the following equation:

$$\text{Cost of Debt} = \text{Pre-Tax Debt Interest Rate} * (1 - \text{Tax Rate})$$

Since debt interest is tax deductible, the tax-shielded portion reduces the overall cost of the debt, which is why we multiply the pre-tax debt interest rate by (1 − Tax

Rate). Note that in extreme cases the tax shield may be affected by other items, such as net loss for the year. If this is the case, the effective tax rate could be lowered and the benefit from an interest tax shield diminished.

Determining the pre-tax debt interest rate is more challenging. For a publicly rated company this rate is usually tied to the creditworthiness of the firm. Rating agencies such as Moody's, Standard & Poor's, and Fitch provide ratings of companies based on credit analysis. This credit analysis often involves assessing the company's expected cash flow vis-à-vis its capital structure. Submetrics can include interest and debt service coverage ratios, quick ratios, liquidity ratios, and so on. Industry and market analyses and the company's ability to respond to them under various stress scenarios are also factored into the ratings decision.

Once a company is rated, its debt tends to price close to other similarly rated entities. For instance, using Standard & Poor's scale we could say that two A-rated firms would pay similar spreads over LIBOR. As a financial modeler, one can use the existing debt market prices to help price our example company's debt. A challenge we may encounter is that our financial model is a projection over time, particularly the forecast period. Over time, a company's ratings can change either up or down. To account for this, advanced work can be done to estimate rating changes. This is done by creating transition matrices, which are sets of probabilities of possible ratings upgrades or downgrades from a preexisting state. These transition matrices allow an analyst to simulate credit risk fluctuations of a firm. As the expected rating of the firm changes, so does the pre-tax debt interest rate.

For private companies this analysis can be difficult, but not impossible. The default risk of a private company can be estimated by examining the historical assets versus the liabilities of the firm. We can create probabilities of the asset/liability ratio changing based on history and simulate that ratio going forward. If that ratio drops below one, or in some cases below a certain threshold below one, we can assume that the company is defaulted. If we simulated this many, many times we could get a default probability for the firm and try to link that to a historical rating of companies in the same or related industry. We can then use the market spreads for the determined rating.

Capital Structure Effects on WACC

Calculating the cost of equity and cost of debt is only half of the work. By name alone, the WACC implies that we weight each of these rates by certain amounts. Theory suggests that the proper weights are the market values of equity and debt. The market value of equity is easy as it is the current stock price multiplied by the shares outstanding. The market value of debt is more challenging since we would need to discount the debt at the appropriate yield. Further complicating matters is that in a projection model we would need to project these yields in the future. For these reasons, many assume the book value of debt instead.

MODEL BUILDER 9.3: CALCULATING AND IMPLEMENTING THE WEIGHTED AVERAGE COST OF CAPITAL

1. In order to calculate the WACC for any period, we should have the necessary assumptions for the cost of equity and debt. Starting with the cost of equity, we require the risk-free rate, beta, and the market risk premium. We will assume the risk-free rate each period is from our 10Y U.S. Treasury rate assumption on the Vectors sheet. Beta and the market risk premium are necessary inputs that we have yet to enter. Go to the Assumptions sheet and enter the following text and values in the corresponding cells:

   F23: **Forecast Beta**
   F24: **LT Beta**
   F25: **Market Risk Prem.**
   G23: **1.9**
   G24: **1.0**
   G25: **6.5%**

   Name cell G23 **inputs_Beta**, cell G24 **inputs_LTBeta**, and cell G25 **inputs_RiskPrem**. Notice that we have a forecast period beta and a separate, more stable long-term assumption for beta.

2. Go to the DCF sheet and enter the text **Cost of Equity** in cell C17. In cell E16, enter the following formula:

   =IF(E2="TV Year",Vectors!E34+(inputs_LTBeta*inputs_RiskPrem),Vectors! E34+(inputs_Beta*inputs_RiskPrem))

   This formula checks to see whether the current column is the terminal value column. If it is, then the risk-free rate from the Vectors sheet is added to the long-term beta multiplied by the market risk premium. Otherwise, we are in a forecast period and the risk-free rate from the Vectors sheet is added to the forecast period beta multiplied by the market risk premium. We could get more specific and create beta assumptions for each forecast period if we believe the risk profile or the capital structure of the company is going to change over that time span. Remember to copy and paste the formula over the range E17:J17.

3. Next we will complete the cost of debt. We should note the current rating of the firm on the Assumptions sheet, even though the example model does not have a table of ratings and spreads. On the Assumptions sheet, enter the text **Unsec. Rating** in cell L23. Enter the text **A** in cell K23. This means that we are assuming the firm is an A-rated entity according to Standard & Poor's. We assume that this is the unsecured risk rating of the firm. Be very careful when looking up ratings on companies since secured ratings can be higher because they are backed by assets and do not represent the true credit risk of the firm.

4. If we simplify our assumption and compute the book cost of debt, we need to know each debt's rate and the balance each period. Remember that in theory we should be using market value instead of book value, but in the example model we will use book value. Most of the values for debt are already prepared for us, except short-term debt. Earlier we referenced the Vectors sheet to calculate interest amounts, but never explicitly calculated the short-term debt rate in a different cell. We should do this to assist in the cost-of-debt calculation. On the DCF sheet, enter the text **Cost of ST Debt** in cell C15. Then enter the following formula in cell E15:

=IF(AVERAGE('Balance Sheet'!D31:E31)<inputs_Precision,0,'Income Statement'!E28/AVERAGE('Balance Sheet'!D31:E31))

This formula backs out the implied interest rate, based on the interest from short-term interest divided by the average balance. Copy and paste this formula over the range E15:J15.

5. Prior to calculating the cost of debt we have to consider the terminal value period. Since we will be using the book value of debt as a proxy and using the rates estimated from that debt for the cost of debt, the long-term debt rate is unknown. We can research this figure and estimate it. Let's assume that the long-term debt rate is 5.00% by entering that value on the Assumptions sheet in cell K28. Name that cell **inputs_LTCostofD**. Also, create a label in cell I28 by entering the text **Long-Term Cost of Debt**.

6. We are now ready to compute the cost of debt. First create a label on the DCF sheet by entering the text **Cost of Debt** in cell C16. Next enter the following formula in cell E16:

=IF(E2="TV Year",inputs_LTCostofD,IF(SUM('Balance Sheet'!D31,'Balance Sheet'!E35)<=inputs_Precision,0,((E15*AVERAGE('Balance Sheet'!D31:E31)+(Debt!E16*Debt!D53)+(Debt!E26*Debt!D54)+(Debt!D36*Debt!D55))/(SUM(Debt!D53:D55)+AVERAGE('Balance Sheet'!D31:E31)))*(1-E6)))

What appears to be a complex formula is really just calculating a weighted average. The first check is to see whether the current period is the terminal value period. If this is the case, we may have to have an assumption for the cost of debt in the long term. This assumption was created on the Assumptions sheet. The next check is to see whether there is any debt on the balance sheet. If there is not, then there is no need to calculate any further and the cost of debt is 0. If there is debt, though, the first influence could be short-term debt, which uses a multiperiod balance since we are unclear as to exactly when the debt came on the books. Otherwise, the long-term debt is taken at the end-of-period balance for the prior period, multiplied by each issuance's respective rate. Dividing all of these products by the balances produces the *weighted average pre-tax cost of debt*. We then remove the tax rate to get to the *after-tax* cost of debt. Copy and paste this formula over the range E16:J16.

7. We are almost ready to calculate the WACC, but as in step 5 we have to consider another change of assumptions for debt in the terminal value period. An issue that we might have with a projection is that the capital structure changes as the planned debt amortizes. In the long term, management may have an expected capital structure that they plan to adhere to. If this is the case, we may need to reweight the capital structure in the terminal value period to reflect this expectation. On the Assumptions sheet, enter the text **Long-Term Debt Ratio** in cell I27. In cell K27, enter the value **30%**. Name cell I27 **inputs_LTDebtRatio**.

8. The final step is to get the WACC by weighting the cost of debt and the cost of equity by the debt and equity values each period. Enter the text **WACC** in cell C18 and in cell E18 enter the following formula:

=IF(E2="TV Year",(E16*inputs_LTDebtRatio)+(E17*(1-inputs_LTDebt Ratio)),((E16*('Balance Sheet'!D35+AVERAGE('Balance Sheet'! D31:E31)))+(E17*'Balance Sheet'!D43))/SUM(AVERAGE('Balance Sheet'! D31:E31),'Balance Sheet'!D35,'Balance Sheet'!D43))

This formula first tests to see whether the current period is the terminal value period. If this is the case. then the long-term debt ratio is used as the weight plus the cost of equity multiplied by one minus the long-term debt ratio. Otherwise, the cost of debt is multiplied by the total debt outstanding at the time period and added to the cost of equity multiplied by the outstanding equity. A consideration with this formula is that the debt and equity amounts are taken from the prior period, which assumes that their increase comes toward the end of the period. This is consistent with the issue date of the debt and an assumption for the equity values. If the balances are assumed to come in at different periods, this formula should be adjusted accordingly. The sum of these products is then divided by the sum of the debt and equity balances to produce the WACC. Copy and paste this formula over the range E18:J18. Figure 9.13 shows how the DCF sheet should develop.

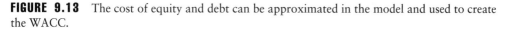

	B / C	D / E	F	G	H	I	J
15	Cost of ST Debt	5.35%	5.35%	0.00%	0.00%	0.00%	0.00%
16	Cost of Debt	0.00%	4.49%	4.71%	4.71%	4.73%	5.00%
17	Cost of Equity	15.35%	15.85%	16.35%	16.85%	17.35%	12.00%
18	WACC	14.17%	13.69%	15.26%	16.21%	17.04%	9.90%
19	**Cumulative Discount Value**	979.39	1,120.13	1,194.60	1,277.47	1,364.16	

FIGURE 9.13 The cost of equity and debt can be approximated in the model and used to create the WACC.

B	C	D	E	F	G	H	I
19	Cumulative Discount Value		979.39	1,120.13	1,194.60	1,277.47	1,364.16
20							
21		Firm Value (Present Value)	$ 979.39				

FIGURE 9.14 When discounting with multiple rates, we cannot just use the present value function and reference the rate and future value. This will blend the discount rates over time. We must bring the values back one period at a time until we reach the current period.

Time Value of Money and Discounting

Most corporate finance professionals are familiar with the core tenet of *time value of money*, where money in the present is worth more than money in the future. Any cash flow in the future needs to be discounted to the present value in order to make valid comparisons or decisions today. The mathematics behind discounting is relatively easy and made even easier with Excel. These calculations and functions are discussed at the end of this chapter in the Toolbox. The challenge for a financial modeler is determining the correct cash flow and discount rate(s), which is why we spent the majority of this chapter focusing on the cash flow and discount rates. The only part we need to discuss is the commonly confused method of discounting with multiple discount rates.

An error that permeates many discounted cash flow models with changing discount rates is overusing each discount rate. Let's just use a simple two-period example. Assume the discount rate in period 1 is 5.0% and the cash flow 100, while the discount rate is period 2 is 6.0% and the cash flow 200. In theory, to get a value we should discount these rates to the present value and sum up the discounted amounts. However, some analysts discount the period 2 cash flow (200) at 6.0% for two periods and the period 1 cash flow (100) at 5.0% for one period. This is incorrect since the period 2 cash flow should be discounted only for one period at 6.0% and then at 5.0% for the next cash flow. Figure 9.14 shows the difference in results between the correct and incorrect methods.

MODEL BUILDER 9.4: DISCOUNTING WITH MULTIPLE RATES TO DETERMINE THE CORPORATE VALUE

1. Go the DCF sheet and enter the text **Cumulative Discount Value** in cell C19. This row will contain the cumulative discount value, one period back for each period. This will allow us to use multiple discount rates correctly. In cell E19, enter the following formula:

=(E14+F19)/(1+E18)^1

H19		f_x	=(H14+I19)/(1+H18)^1				
B	C	D	E	F	G	H	I	J
15	Cost of ST Debt		5.35%	5.35%	0.00%	0.00%	0.00%	0.00%
16	Cost of Debt		0.00%	4.49%	4.71%	4.71%	4.73%	5.00%
17	Cost of Equity		15.35%	15.85%	16.35%	16.85%	17.35%	12.00%
18	WACC		14.17%	13.69%	15.26%	16.21%	17.04%	9.90%
19	**Cumulative Discount Value**		979.39	1,120.13	1,194.60	1,277.47	1,364.16	

FIGURE 9.15 Given the changing discount rates, we must use a custom formula to discount the cash flows to derive the firm value.

This formula takes the current period's cash flow, plus the next period's cash flow, and discounts the combined value back one period. Ultimately, the value in cell E19 is today's present value of the corporation. If the formula for discounting with multiple discount rates is unclear, refer to the Toolbox at the end of this chapter.

2. To make the firm value clear, enter the text **Firm Value (Present Value)** in cell E21 on the DCF sheet. Next, enter the following formula in cell G21:

=E19

Name cell G21 **outputs_FirmValue**. The new section to the DCF sheet is shown in Figure 9.15.

AFTER THE CORPORATE VALUATION

Although we have achieved our goal of determining a corporate value given a multitude of assumptions, we should realize there is a bit more to accomplish. Just as we stated in Chapter 1, a good financial modeler does not stop simply at the result, but puts time into explaining the result and understanding risk. To assist in this process, we need to create outputs that are intelligible, easy to understand, and quick to work with in Excel. Similarly, we may want to access the power of Visual Basic Applications (VBA) to eliminate circular references, automate scenario generation, and print sheets in bulk. Chapter 10 focuses on output reporting, and Chapter 11 provides a primer to VBA, useful code for discounted cash flow models, and a thorough explanation of each line of code.

TOOLBOX

Weighted Averages Using SUMPRODUCT and SUM

In the Model Builders in this chapter, we had to calculate weighted averages multiple times. While our example model has a number of items that are spread out over

Cost of Debt	0.08
Cost of Equity	0.14
Market Value of Debt	6540
Market Value of Equity	3200

FIGURE 9.16 In this example, we will create the WACC quickly from the cost of debt, cost of equity, market value of debt, and market value of equity.

separate sections, making the weighted average calculation challenging, a standard weighted average where the elements of the average are aligned is very easy to calculate in Excel. Imagine having the cost of debt, cost of equity, market value of debt, and market value of equity as seen in Figure 9.16.

With this data set, the values to which we want to apply a weighted average are the cost rates, weighted by the market values. You will not find a prebuilt weighted average function in Excel, but the closest we can get without creating our own user-defined function is using SUMPRODUCT and SUM in combination.

SUMPRODUCT is a mathematical function that takes the following entry parameters:

SUMPRODUCT(array 1, array 2. . .)

Multiple, equal-size arrays can be referenced as array 1, array 2, and so on. The function multiplies each respective value in each array, meaning that in a two-array example the first value in array 1 would be multiplied by the first value in array 2, the second value in array 1 would be multiplied by the second value in array 2, and so on. All of the products are then summed up to produce the final result.

Most understand the SUM function, so all that is left is how we use these two functions in combination. A simplified formula that can help us remember how to calculate the weighted average is to take the SUMPRODUCT of the values and weights and divide by the sum of the weights. Going back to our example earlier, with the cost of debt, cost of equity, market value of debt, and market value of equity, we can calculate the WACC by using the SUMPRODUCT function on the rate array and the market value array. In the same formula, we use the SUM function on the market value array. Figure 9.17 shows the complete calculation.

Present Value Functions: PV, NPV, XNPV

PV Excel has multiple time-value-of-money functions built in; however, there are nuances to each one that require the user to put some thought into them to get

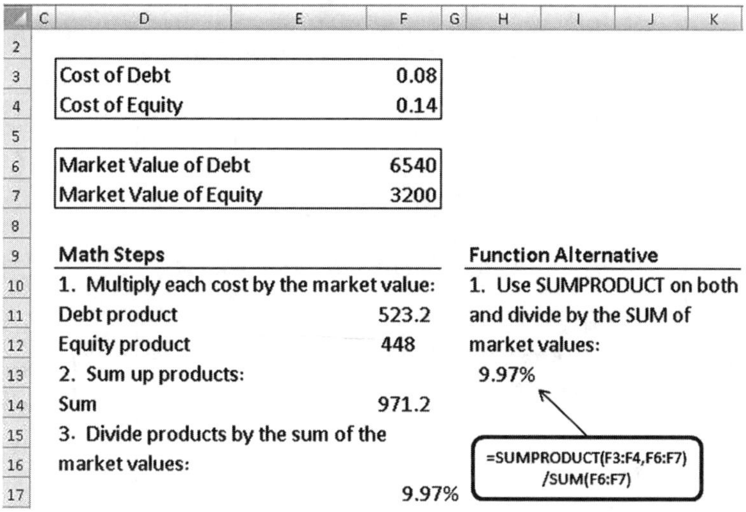

FIGURE 9.17 Although we could calculate the WACC using mathematical formulas, SUMPRODUCT and SUM work well together to calculate a weighted average quickly.

the correct return value. The first function that we will examine in detail is the PV function. The PV function calculates the present value of a future cash flow or a fixed series of cash flows. The entry parameters for the PV function include:

PV(Discount Rate, Number of Periods, Payment, Future Value, Cash Flow at End of Period or Beginning)

The discount rate is the first entry that is absolute necessary. This rate should correspond to the periodicity of the discount periods (e.g., if the discount periods are annual, then the rate should be per annum). Before we explain the next few parameters, we should understand that the PV function can be used in two ways: to derive the present value of a cash flow at a point in time or to derive the present value of a series of cash flows. Given the flexibility of this function to do either calculation, the second entry parameter is either the number of periods in the future the single cash flow is generated or the number of periods in the future series of cash flows. The third entry parameter is only in the case of using the PV function with a series of cash flows. This entry parameter is the cash flow that is assumed to be generated each period for the number of periods assumed in the second entry parameter. If the PV function is being used to calculate a present value based only on a single future value, the payment should be left blank and a comma inserted to move on to the fourth entry parameter. The fourth entry parameter is if the PV function is being used with a single future value. This entry parameter is the future value that is being

	C	D	E	F	G	H	I	J	K
4		*Using the PV function for a single future value*							
5									
6		Period	0	1	2	3			
7		Cash Flow		0	0	100.00		=-PV(H8,H6,,H7)	
8		Discount Rate		5.00%	5.00%	5.00%			
9		PV	86.38						
10									
11		*Using the PV function for a series of values*							
12									
13		Cash Flow	100						
14		Discount Rate	0.0500					=-PV(E14,E15,E13)	
15		# of Payments	3						
16		PV	272.32						
17									
18		*The above is equivalent to:*							
19		Period	0	1	2	3			
20		Cash Flow		100.00	100.00	100.00			
21		Discount Rate		5.00%	5.00%	5.00%			
22		PV	272.32	95.24	90.70	86.38			

FIGURE 9.18 Care should be taken when using the PV function since it can be used in multiple ways.

discounted. Finally, regardless of whether the PV function is being used with a series of cash flows or a single future value, the last entry parameter sets whether the cash flow is assumed to come at the end of the period or at the beginning of the period. Most likely this is omitted, which sets the function to end-of-period calculation.

Figure 9.18 shows an example of how the PV function is used in different ways. The first way shown is a single future value of 100, discounted over three periods at 5.0%. The second way is a payment of 100 for three periods, discounted at 5.0%.

NPV The next function that we will examine is NPV, which stands for *net present value*. The name itself implies that a net value will be determined from a gross value, which is one way to use the function. Unfortunately, due to preprogrammed timing, this function is often used incorrectly. Let's first examine how financial modelers tend to use the function correctly.

Many financial modelers take advantage of the NPV function's ability to accept multiple cash flows. The entry parameters for NPV are:

NPV(Discount Rate, Array of Cash Flows to Be Discounted)

An easy example is shown in Figure 9.19, where a bond's cash flows are being discounted at 6.0%. Instead of calculating each period's present value and summing

	A	B	C	D	E	F
1	**NPV**					
2						
3						
4		**Period**	0	1	2	3
5		Interest		50	50	50
6		Principal				1000
7		Combined CFs	0	50	50	1050
8						
9		Market Rate	0.05			
10		Present Value	=npv(C9,D7:F7)			

FIGURE 9.19 The NPV function is quick to use for single discount rate, equal-interval problems.

them up, the NPV function provides this for us. In such an example, the NPV function is being used to calculate the gross present value since no cost assumption was entered. It's when we begin to use the NPV function to determine that net present value that we run into errors. To help this, we should identify the two most common errors created when using NPV, the second of which involves periodicity:

1. The first cash flow referenced is assumed to be one period from today. While this is fine with the previous bond example, the error that could occur is when we try using the cost of the bond in the calculation. Many people would put a −1000 for time period 0 and then use the NPV function, referencing the cost as the first cell in the entry array. The problem with this is that the first entry is assumed to be one period from today, even if it is negative. This means that the negative value will be discounted one period. In most cases we are assuming that the cost takes place today, not one period from today.

2. Since we didn't provide Excel with any information regarding the time between each period, Excel must assume that these time periods are equal. In cases where the periods between cash flows are uneven the NPV function will return the incorrect value. This is often the case when a project or funding closes on a specific date and the next period is an uneven amount of time from the closing date.

XNPV To overcome the limitations of the NPV function in regard to periodicity, Excel's designers created the XNPV function. This function is similar to the NPV function; however, it uses exact dates rather than assuming equal amounts of time between periods. The entry parameters for the XNPV function include:

XNPV(Discount Rate, Array of Cash Flows to Be Discounted, Dates Corresponding to Each Cash Flow)

The XNPV function is very similar to NPV in that it references multiple cash flows and calculates a present value with a single discount rate. The added functionality is that we can assign dates to each cash flow by referencing a corresponding set of dates. While this may seem to be a minor difference, there are actually a couple of considerations that we need to make regarding this function:

1. The first cash flow entry in the XNPV function is assumed to be the present value, regardless of the date that corresponds to it. This is very different from the NPV function where the first value is assumed to take place one period from the present.
2. The XNPV function is not standard on Excel 2003 or earlier and is activated only once the Analysis Tool Pak is added in. Even after this Tool Pak is added in, the function does not provide automatic parameter entry prompts like many other functions.

Discounting Process with Multiple Rates

Even with all of the present value functions that Excel has built in, there is still a lack of a function to discount multiple cash flows at different rates. Currently, the best way to accomplish this is mathematically, by building our own formula. Let us assume we have a series of three cash flows in three future periods with three different discount rates. The best way to learn how this process works is by thinking in terms of being transported in time to the second discount period and trying to determine the present value of the cash flows in that period. That calculation would discount the third period's cash flow back one period at the third period's discount rate. We would also add the second period's cash flow, giving us the total present value as of period 2.

Now imagine going back in time one period to period 1. To calculate the present value as of that period, we would take the present value we calculated in period 2 and discount it one period at the period 2 discount rate to get the present value as of period 1. We have to remember to add the cash flow from period 1 to derive the period 1 present value. If we were to repeat this process one more time we would have today's present value. Figure 9.20 shows this process and the formula that consolidates the calculations.

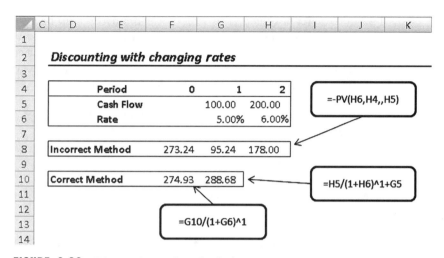

FIGURE 9.20 Discounting with multiple discount rates requires special consideration and a formula that is not part of a preprogrammed function.

COVAR, VAR, and VARP for Beta Calculation

In this chapter, we discussed the concept of beta, but did not go into its calculation. *Beta* is an attempt to capture non-diversifiable risk. It is done by historically analyzing the returns of a company versus a market index. In the case of U.S. companies, the S&P 500 is frequently used. The comparison that is actually done is examining the covariance of the company's returns and the market index's returns, while controlling for the variance of the market index's returns. This is formalized in the following equation:

$$\text{Beta} = \text{Covariance of Company Returns and Market Index Returns} / \text{Variance of the Market Index Returns}$$

We can quickly calculate this formula in Excel using prebuilt functions. The first function to learn is COVAR, which stands for *covariance*. The entry parameters for COVAR are:

COVAR(first range of data, second range of data)

For our beta example, the first range of data is the company's returns and the second range of data is the market index returns. Note that the order of range entry does not matter. Calculating the covariance is not like a regression, where we are concerned with dependency. Covariance is just quantifying how two data sets move together.

Two other functions can help us with the denominator in the beta equation: VAR and VARP. Both VAR and VARP calculate the variance of a data set. The entry parameters are any set of data in Excel. The key difference between the two functions is that VAR calculates a sample variance, while VARP calculates a population variance. Variance of a sample is calculated by the following formula:

SUM((each individual data point − mean of all data points)^2)/(number of data points − 1)

Variance of a population is calculated by:

SUM((each individual data point − mean of all data points)^2)/number of data points

In the case of calculating beta, we are assuming the market index represents a population and should therefore use the following Excel-based formula:

COVAR(stock returns, market index returns)/VARP(market index returns)

CHAPTER 10

Output Reporting

Disappointing situations to witness with financial modelers is when they have built an elegant, mathematically correct model, but fail to set up a system for explaining results. These situations cause confusion among analysts who must interpret model results. Even worse are ensuing perceptions of skepticism toward a model that is difficult to understand, often rendering the model useless. To mitigate against such a circumstance, we implement a strong output reporting system to explain our results.

A good reporting system organizes core assumptions, analytical results, and financial metrics in an easy-to-read format. While our financial model may have created formulas to optimize calculation, the output reporting optimizes understanding. An example of this difference is decimal places. Throughout our example model we used numbers without regard to the place value. Although the calculations work well, the readability is impaired because it is difficult to understand the actual values of the results. The output reporting system should make this clear.

Further, we might want graphical representations of results. These are easily created in Excel by using the Chart functionality. We can then enhance these charts with tools that allow us to quickly change the data in a graphical way. Also, to ease the updating of pertinent information, we might also want to tap into Excel's ability to connect to other data sources, such as the Internet.

OUTPUT SUMMARY

In order to explain results, it is useful to create a separate section in the model, known as the Output Summary, that organizes and formats key information. The primary sections of an Output Summary for a corporate entity should include:

- *Descriptive characteristics:* stock ticker, stock price information, important dates and timing, capital structure parameters, industry/market ratios, and cash flow priority settings.
- *Financial statements:* income statement, balance sheet, and cash flow statement
- *Key rates and ratios:* growth rate(s), interest rates, and important ratios such as interest and debt service coverage

An important concept to keep in mind is that the Output Summary should not contain *any* hard-coded values. The entire Output Summary should be automated and controlled by the other sheets in the model. This will prevent any error between scenarios, where assumptions are changing.

MODEL BUILDER 10.1: PREPARING FOR THE OUTPUT SUMMARY SHEET

1. Prior to actually creating the Output Summary sheet, there are a number of preparations in the example model that are necessary. The first is to set the units. Currently, we do not know the units in the model. For all we know, the values could be in terms of billions. To make this clear, we will create a data validation list that allows the user to select the units for all of the figures. Go to the Hidden sheet, and enter the following text in the corresponding cells:

   D6: lst_Units
   D7: Hundreds
   D8: Thousands
   D9: Millions
   D10: Billions

   Name the range D7:D10 lst_Units.

2. For each unit description, we want to create a multiplier for entered values so that on the Output Summary the numbers are clear. Still on the Hidden sheet, enter the following values in the corresponding cells:

   E7: 100
   E8: 1000
   E9: 1000000
   E10: 1000000000

   On the Assumptions sheet, enter the text **Units** in cell B13. Then, create a data validation list in cell D13 using the named range lst_Units as the source. When we create the Output Summary in Model Builder 10.3, the model user will be able to select the units, which will cause the Output Summary values to be multiplied by the associated unit value on the Hidden sheet. Thus far, the new section on the Hidden sheet should look like Figure 10.1.

WEB DOWNLOADS

Obtaining information is often a time-consuming process. If the information that we are obtaining is organized in a consistent manner from a reputable source, we

From the Assumptions Sheet **From the Hidden Sheet**

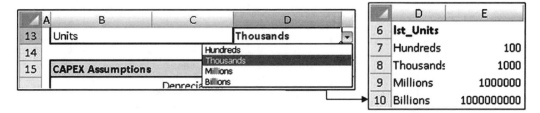

FIGURE 10.1 Assumptions regarding units will control the look of the Output Summary via the Hidden sheet.

can hook up Excel into that source so the information is automatically downloaded. Excel can connect to multiple external data sources:

- Microsoft access databases
- Text files, primarily converting .txt or .csv
- The Web
- SQL servers
- XML files
- Custom in-house databases, often using additional programs such as Hyperion EssBase
- Custom external databases, such as Bloomberg (common to finance)

While many of the database connections are useful for finance applications, most financial analysts will get the most use out of connecting to the Web. Stock information, interest rates, and currency exchange rates can be automatically downloaded from web sources and used in financial models.

Beyond understanding the external data features Excel provides, it is important to learn how to optimally implement these connections. Often, information downloaded from external sources is imported in a raw, unrefined format. In order to control for the possible mess that external data connections can cause within a model, the information should be downloaded to a separate sheet, which can be later hidden, and cleaned up with a number of useful Excel functions.

MODEL BUILDER 10.2: CONNECTING THE EXAMPLE MODEL TO THE WEB

1. Useful data for the Output Summary can come straight from the Web. To manage the information from the Web, we will create a separate sheet. Insert a

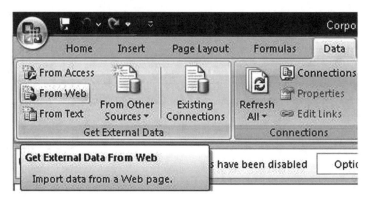

FIGURE 10.2   External data such as that from the Web is downloadable via the Data tab.

worksheet after the Hidden sheet and name it **Web Downloads**. Enter the text **Web Downloads** in cell A1 of the new sheet.

2. In cell B3, enter the text **Stock Information**. This is where we will create a web query in order to automatically download information from the Web. Accessing Excel's external data depends on which version of Excel is being used:
   - *For Excel 2007*: Go to the **Data** tab on the ribbon. On the far left there should be a button called "Get External Data." Select **From the Web**. This will open what looks like a web browser. Go to step 3 of this Model Builder to continue with the web download process. This selection is shown in Figure 10.2.
   - *For Excel 2003 and earlier*: Go to the **Data** menu, select **Import External Data**, and then select **New Web Query**. This will open the same web browser window as in Excel 2007.

3. Note that you must be connected to the Internet for this function to work, regardless of whether you are in Excel 2007 or Excel 2003 or earlier; otherwise, the web browser–looking box will have an error in it. If you are connected to the Internet, the web browser–looking box should automatically navigate to your home page. When this box is open you can navigate to any page that you like.

   You will notice there are little arrows throughout each web page. These arrows mark information that is organized in a table format that can be down-loaded to Excel. By clicking once on these labels you should see the arrow turn blue, along with a blue border around the table. The data within the blue border will be imported into Excel. While the color will not show, the dialogue box is shown in Figure 10.3.

   For this example we will navigate to www.finance.yahoo.com. On that web page, enter the stock ticker **SMP** in the appropriate field, purely as an example (the example model is not set up to represent SMP's valuation). Left-click on the little arrow next to the stock information that includes last price, 52-week-high, 52-week-low, and so on. Select two tables. Next, click on the

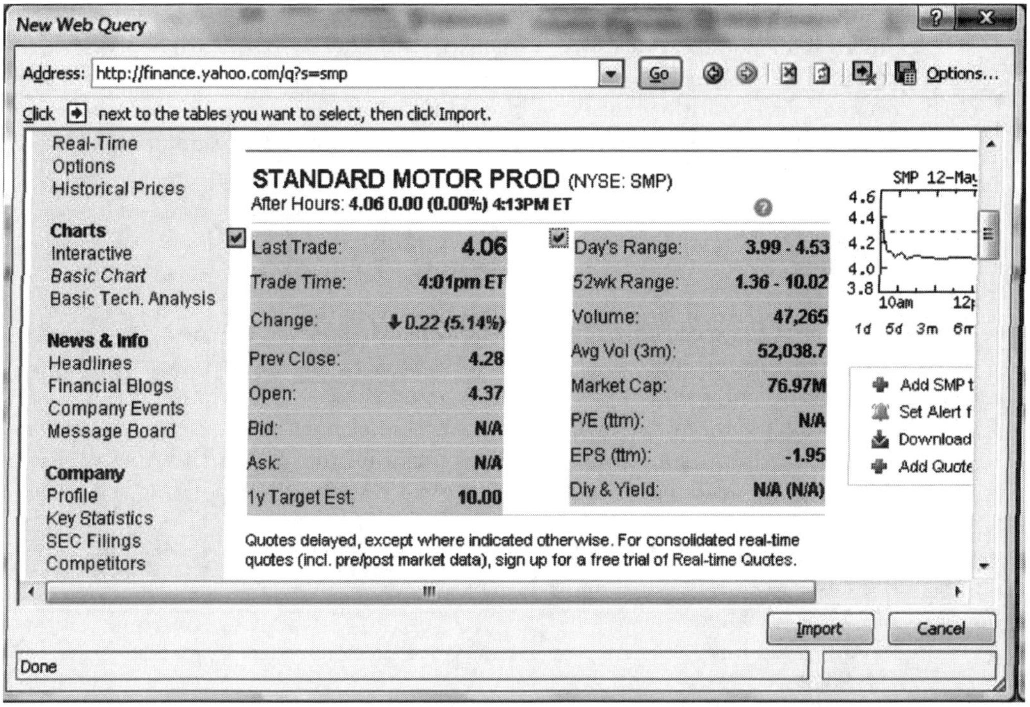

FIGURE 10.3 The Web query dialogue box allows you to quickly import data from the Web.

Import button on the bottom-right of the web browser–looking box. Excel will then prompt you with another dialogue box, asking where you would like to import the information. Select **Existing Worksheet**, and enter cell **B4** as the cell where the information should be stored.

4. Once the data is stored, it may require cleanup. In the example model, we want the 52-week high and low in separate cells, but the web download puts them in one single cell (cell C14 on the Web Download sheet). Parsing functions that help clean up text are described in further detail in the Toolbox later in this chapter; however, we will go through how to extract the information needed. On the Web Download sheet, enter the following text in the corresponding cells:

E3: **Clean Up**
E4: **52wk High**
E5: **52wk Low**

5. We will parse out text from cell C14 in order to get the numerical stock prices that represent the 52-week high and low. Two of Excel's parsing functions, RIGHT and LEFT, are well suited for this task. We could use the LEFT function

on cell C14, with a 4 as the second parameter, to get the value 1.36; however, this formula could break down. If the stock price trended upward over the next year and the 52-week low was over 10.00, our function would pick up only one decimal place. For this reason we should use an IF function to prepare for such price movements. Enter the following formulas in their corresponding cells on the Web Download sheet:

F4: =IF(RIGHT(C14,7)="-",RIGHT(C14,4),RIGHT(C14,5))
F5: =IF(LEFT(C14,2)=".",LEFT(C14,4),LEFT(C14,5))

Notice that these cells use tests to determine whether the low or high is one or two digits. Depending on the text that is included in your web download, you may need to enter similar conditional statements to ensure data integrity.

6. Once we have the web download information cleaned up, we can reference it directly on the Assumptions sheet for quick viewing. Go to the Assumptions sheet and enter the following text and formulas in the corresponding cells:

B4: **Ticker Symbol**
B5: **Last Price**
B6: **52-Week High**
B7: **52-Week Low**
D4: **SMP**
D5: **='Web Downloads'!C4**
D6: **='Web Downloads'!F4**
D7: **='Web Downloads'!F5**

The final outcome of the web download functionality is displayed on the Assumptions sheet, as seen in Figure 10.4.

	A	B	C	D
1		*Project Basic Cash Flow*		
2				
3		**Dates, Timing, & Global Assumptions**		
4		Ticker Symbol		**SMP**
5		Last Price		2.66
6		52-Week High		10.02
7		52-Week Low		1.36

FIGURE 10.4 The Assumptions sheet references the Web Downloads sheet, where a web query is set up to download stock information from the Web.

MODEL BUILDER 10.3: CREATING THE OUTPUT SUMMARY SHEET

1. Insert a worksheet after the DCF sheet and name it **Output Summary**. This Model Builder is a bit different from many of the earlier ones in that readers will have to rely on the complete example model on the CD-ROM for many of the cell references. This is because the Output Summary contains many repetitive references that are best seen directly in the example model. However, there are a few cells and formulas that should be explained. For now, go to the example model and copy over the text, references, and formulas noting the following:

2. The first notable formula on the Output Summary sheet is in cell K9:

=IF(COUNTIF(Assumptions!O4:O8,"OK")=COUNTA (Assumptions!O4:O8),"Pass","Fail")

The purpose of this formula is to return a "Pass" if all of the internal validations from the Assumptions sheet have passed. Otherwise, a "Fail" is returned. This functionality is accomplished by using the COUNTIF function to count the number of internal validations that are set to "OK." If the COUNTIF function is new to you or unclear, refer to the Toolbox at the end of this chapter. The COUNTIF function will return a number from 0 to 5 depending on the number of internal validations that have "OK." The number returned is compared to a count of the total internal validation tests. Counting the total internal validation tests is done using the COUNTA formula, which counts the total nonblank cells in a reference range. This function is also explained in this chapter's Toolbox. An IF function tests whether the number of tests with an "OK" is equal to the total number of tests. If so, a "Pass" is returned; if not, a "Fail" is returned. The top of the Output Summary is depicted in Figure 10.5.

	A	B	C	D	E	F
1	*Project Basic Cash Flow*					
2						
3	Case Description					
4	Stock Ticker:	SMP		Unsecured Rating:	A	
5	Last Price:	2.66		Forecast Beta:		1.90
6	52-Week High:	10.02		Long Term Beta:		1.00
7	52-Week Low:	1.36		Risk Premium:		6.50%
8	Last Historical FY	12/31/2007		Capex to Dep:		110.00%
9	Current FY	12/31/2008		WC% of Revenue:		30.00%
10						
11	Scenario:	Base Case				

FIGURE 10.5 The top of the Output Summary contains basic information that describes the firm and the scenario under analysis. Note that this is a partial screen shot of the top part of the Output Summary and that there are more columns in the example model.

3. We should go to cell B17 in the Output Summary sheet. The following formula should be already entered in the example model:

='Income Statement'!D5*OFFSET(Hidden!$E$6,
   MATCH(inputs_Units,lst_Units,0),0)

A standard OFFSET MATCH combination is used to multiply the values from the income statement by the units that the user selected. This will put the values from the financial statements in terms of units that the user desires. Notice that this is done for the income statement, balance sheet, and cash flow statement.

4. The final section of the Output Summary sheet that should be customized is a section covering key rates and ratios. If you implemented the Output Summary sheet from the example model, you will have four key rates and ratios. The text that should be entered in corresponding cells is as follows:

A118: **Interest Coverage Ratio (EBITDA)**
A119: **Debt Service Coverage Ratio (EBITDA)**
A120: **10Y Treasury**
A121: **1M Libor**

Be mindful that this section should be determined by the needs of the specific transaction you are working on. In this example we have been focusing on debt quite a bit, so the two ratios in cells A118 and A119 are debt related. They are actually quite common to corporations since the ability of the firm to service debt is paramount to financial viability. The first of the two ratios, the *interest coverage ratio* (ICR), examines the interest expense compared to EBITDA each period. The second ratio, the *debt service coverage ratio* (DSCR), examines both interest and principal expense compared to EBITDA each period. Typically ICRs and DSCRs are calculated with either EBITDA or EBIT as the numerator. Be careful here as it can be done differently depending on who is doing the analysis. As for the denominator, you should also be careful to see what interest expense or principal due is being calculated. Concepts such as *payment in kind* (PIK) interest and nonscheduled principal are frequently excluded from these ratios. Also, these ratios are sometimes calculated using four-quarter averages in order to reduce volatility.

5. Implement the key rates and ratios in the example model by entering the following formulas in the corresponding cells:

C118: =IF('Income Statement'!E32<inputs_Precision,0,'Income Statement'
        !E13/'Income Statement'!E32)
C119: =IF(('Income Statement'!E32+Debt!E21+Debt!E31+Debt!E41)
        <inputs_Precision,0,'Income Statement'!E13/('Income Statement'!
        E32+Debt!E21+Debt!E31+Debt!E41))
C120: =Vectors!E34
C121: =Vectors!E37

	A	B	C	D	E	F	G	H
116	Key Rates and Ratios		Projected ---->					TV Year
117		12/31/2007	12/31/2008	12/31/2009	12/31/2010	12/31/2011	12/31/2012	12/31/2013
118	Interest Coverage Ratio (EBITDA)		212.82	46.05	80.81	127.33	247.62	661.74
119	Debt Service Coverage Ratio (EBITDA)		212.82	12.02	14.63	16.99	24.37	41.99
120	10Y Treasury		3.00%	3.50%	4.00%	4.50%	5.00%	5.50%
121	1M Libor		4.20%	4.20%	4.20%	4.20%	4.20%	4.20%

FIGURE 10.6   The Output Summary should also provide summary calculations such as key ratios.

Copy and paste these formulas over to column H in their respective rows. Figure 10.6 shows the bottom part of the Output Summary where key rates and ratios are stored.

CHARTS

Important data should stand out to users to be understood quickly. Charts are an excellent way to visualize data. Excel makes it easy to create multiple types of charts, but what are often not known are the tricks to make them appear dynamic. The effect can go a long way in the field of finance, where data is often seen as a dry set of black-and-white figures. Figure 10.7 shows a chart with dynamic capabilities.

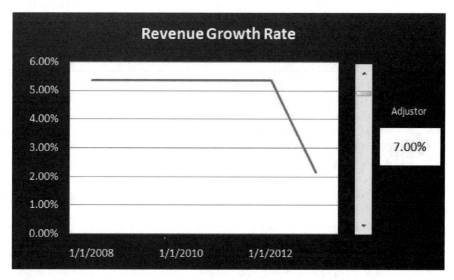

FIGURE 10.7   This chart on revenue growth allows the user to move a scroll bar to visualize the effects of incrementally changing the growth rate.

MODEL BUILDER 10.4: CREATING DYNAMIC CHARTS

1. In this Model Builder, we will create the Chart sheet, which contains a number of charts to visualize data. One of these charts will contain functionality known as a *scroll bar*, which, when hooked up correctly, makes the chart seem dynamic. Insert a worksheet after the Output Summary and name it **Charts**.

2. Prep the Charts sheet by entering the following formulas and text:

   A1: =inputs_ProjName
   A2: ="Units in"&inputs_Units
   L1: "Analysis Date:"
   N1: =TODAY()

   Notice that in cell A2 we used the "&" symbol for concatenating. If this is not clear, refer to the Toolbox later in this chapter.

3. Create four charts. Refer to the example model for chart ideas. In order to continue with this Model Builder you should at least make one of those charts based on the revenue unit and sales growth rate. The other three examine the debt amortization of each issuance, the firm's capital expenditure plan, and periodic working capital expectations. In all versions of Excel, the process of creating a chart is simplified by using the Excel chart wizard. From this step on, you should either create at least the first revenue growth rate chart or refer to the complete example model for reference.

4. While creating charts is straightforward, making them appear dynamic is not as easy. To do this, we will use a combination of Form tools and Text boxes. On the Charts sheet, go to the revenue growth rate chart. Make sure that there is room on the right side of the chart. On that side we will insert a scroll bar. To do this, we must access the Form tools, which differs depending on your version of Excel:

   - *For Excel 2007:* In this version of Excel, we have to view the Developer tab first. However, when Excel 2007 is first installed, the default setting does not make the Developer tab visible. Go to the **Office** button, **Excel Options**, and under the **Popular** selection check the checkbox to **Show the Developer tab in the Ribbon**. The Developer tab should then be visible. On the Developer tab there is a section named "Controls" and a button named "Insert." Left-click on **Insert** to view the Form and ActiveX tools. We will be using only the Form tools since ActiveX controls require code to run. Figure 10.8 shows this selection.

   - *For Excel 2003 or earlier:* To view the Form tools, go to the **View** menu, select **Tool Bars**, and further select **Forms**.

     Regardless of the version of Excel you are using, select a **scroll bar** from the Form tools. Drag the cursor over the right side of the revenue growth rate chart so that a vertical rectangle–shaped scroll bar is created.

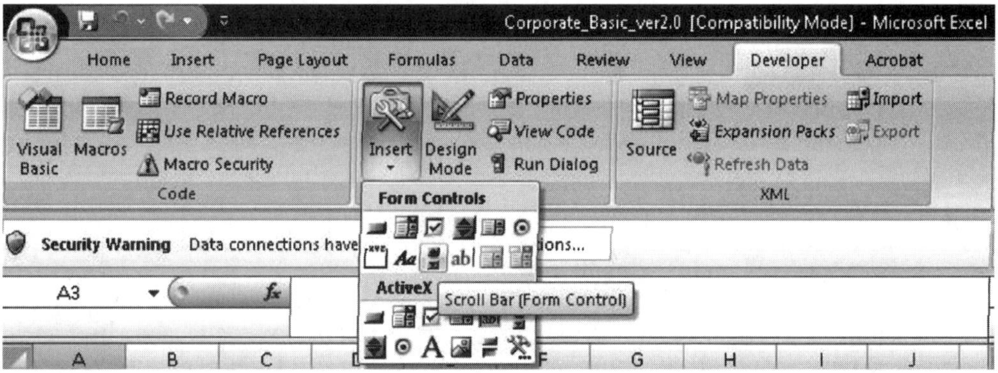

FIGURE 10.8 Form tools can be selected from the Developer tab and are useful for creating dynamic charts.

5. In order to make any of the Form tools work, we have to create a cell link. The *cell link* is a cell-based response to the user's actions on the Form tool. Right-click on the scroll bar on the Charts sheet and select **Format Control**. Under the **Control** tab, select the **Cell link** field. Navigate to the Hidden sheet and select **D21**. Press **OK**.

6. We can immediately test how the scroll bar works by going to the Charts sheet and moving the bar in the scroll bar up or down. Go to the Hidden sheet and notice that the value in cell D21 changes. The change is dependent on the settings under the Format Control selection of the scroll bar. Go back to the Charts sheet and right-click on the scroll bar again. Under the **Control** tab you will notice the following options (functional descriptions are provided, but not part of the Excel dialogue box) to control how the cell link changes when the user moves the scroll bar:

   ▪ *Current value:* The value the cell link is currently set to. Enter a value of **0**.
   ▪ *Minimum value:* The lowest value the cell link can be. It must be an integer. Enter a value of **0**.
   ▪ *Maximum value:* The highest value the cell link can be. It must be an integer. Enter a value of **100**.
   ▪ *Incremental change:* The unit of increase or decrease the value in the cell link changes when the user selects and moves the bar in the scroll bar. Enter a value of **1**.
   ▪ *Page change:* The unit of increase or decrease the value in the cell link changes when the user selects in between the bar and the upper or lower bound of the scroll bar. Enter a value of **10**.

7. Since we can use only integers with the scroll bar and in our example we want to change rates, we need to create an additional calculation on the Hidden sheet. Go to the Hidden sheet and enter the following formula in cell D22:

=D21/100

Name cell D22 **ctrl_GlobalGrowth** and label the area by entering the text **Growth Chart Link** in cell D20. Name cell D22 **ctrl_GlobalGrowth**.

8. A user making scenario changes might want to adjust the global growth setting. We will create this reference on the Assumptions sheet. Go to the Assumptions sheet and enter the following formula in cell K26:

=ctrl_GlobalGrowth

Name this cell **inputs_GlobalGrowth.**

9. In Chapter 3, we implemented inputs_GlobalGrowth in the growth rate formula on the Vectors sheet. We can now move the scroll bar on the Charts sheet and see the growth rate assumption change. We might want to see the growth rate adjustor value directly on the chart. This can be done by going to the Charts sheet and inserting a rectangle shape. To insert shapes in Excel:

- *For Excel 2007:* Go to the **Insert** tab, select **Shapes**, and select a rectangle.
- *For Excel 2003 or earlier:* Go to the **View** menu, select **Tool Bars**, select **Drawing**, click on **Autoshapes**, and select a rectangle.

  Draw a rectangle to the right of the scroll bar. Left-click and select the newly drawn rectangle. Many users do not realize it, but a shape can contain a

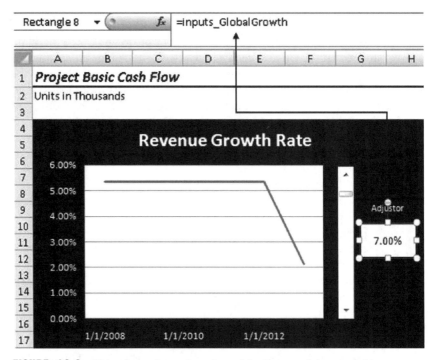

FIGURE 10.9 Using forms in conjunction with charts and drawing objects produces a powerful, dynamic effect.

value. It's as simple as going to the formula bar, once the shape is selected, and entering a reference. With the rectangle selected, go to the formula bar and enter the following reference:

=inputs_GlobalGrowth

10. We can label the rectangle by inserting a text box above the rectangle with the text **Adjustor** inside. To create a text box:
    - *For Excel 2007:* Go to the **Insert** tab, select **Text Box** under **Basic Shapes**.
    - *For Excel 2003 or earlier:* Go to the **View** menu, select **Tool Bars**, select **Drawing**, click on **Autoshapes**, and select a text box.

    Figure 10.9 shows the completed text box, the rectangle, and how the rectangle is connected using a function in the formula bar.

TOOLBOX

Parsing Functions: LEFT, RIGHT, MID (and the DATE Function as a Bonus)

Financial analysts frequently want the ability to parse text if they use Excel with other electronic sources such as web downloads or copying and pasting financial data from .pdf documents. To do this, users can access Excel's prebuilt parsing functions. Each of these functions takes user-defined "pieces" of text in a cell. To examine each parsing function, we will run through an example using a date that was cut from a .pdf report. When the date is pasted into Excel, it comes out in this format:

20090501

Assume that the user knows that the intended date was May 1, 2009; however, the numbers shown above have been exported instead. In this situation, Excel does not recognize the date format and will assume it is text (or possibly a number, depending on the source of data). We can start cleaning up this information by first parsing out the year.

To get the year from the text string above, we can use the LEFT function. The LEFT function takes the following parameters:

LEFT(text or cell reference containing text, number of characters to return starting from the left side)

The parameters explain the function well. If we used the LEFT function on the cell that contains 20090501 and used 4 as the second parameter, the value 2009 would be returned.

We can then take a similar approach to get the day, but this time using the RIGHT function. The RIGHT function takes the exact same parameters as the LEFT function, but instead of starting from the left side of the text, it starts from the right. To get the day from the text string we would use the RIGHT function with a 2 as the second parameter. This would return 01.

The final piece of information required is the month, which is stuck in the middle of the text string. While we could use the LEFT and RIGHT function in combination, an easier approach is to use the MID function. The MID function takes the following parameters:

MID(text or cell reference containing text, number of characters to start taking text from, number of characters to return starting from the second parameter value)

In our example, we would use the MID function on the text, a 5 for the second parameter, and a 2 as the third parameter. A common mistake in using this function is not realizing that the second parameter is where the third parameter will start parsing. Some initially think that the second parameter should be the number of characters prior to the parsing location. Test this out in Excel and you will quickly see the difference.

The final step would be to use the DATE function to create a date value. The DATE function accepts the following parameters:

DATE(Year, Month, Day)

We can quickly see that if we were to use the year, month, and day returned from the parsing functions, within the DATE function, we would have a serial-formatted date value. All of these functions can be quickly copied down rows or across columns to adjust improperly formatted text. They can also be used with the web downloads in order to remove excess information. The process is reviewed in Figure 10.10.

CONCATENATE and &

Just as we can parse text using functions, we can join text together using functions. The first of two methods is the CONCATENATE function. This function accepts the following parameters:

CONCATENATE(text to be joined, text to be joined . . .)

Essentially, multiple text entries or cell references containing text can be entered using this formula. The results are then joined together in the cell where the function resides. Remember that when text is entered directly in functions the text string requires double quotes at the beginning and the end. Even if you would like to create a space, you must bound it by double quotes. If you fail to use double quotes correctly,

```
┌─────────────────────────────────────────────────────────────┐
│ PDF Downloaded Date                                          │
│ 20090501                                                     │
│                                                              │
│ 1. Parse the year using the LEFT function:                   │
│ =LEFT(C3,4)                                                  │
│                                                              │
│ 2. Parse the day using the RIGHT function:                   │
│ =RIGHT(C3,2)                                                 │
│                                                              │
│ 3. Parse the month using the MID function:                   │
│ =MID(C3,5,2)                                                 │
│                                                              │
│ 4. Use the DATE function to get a serial-formatted date:     │
│ =DATE(C6,C12,C9)                                            │
└─────────────────────────────────────────────────────────────┘
```

FIGURE 10.10 Parsing functions allow us to clean up downloaded data so that it can be used for financial modeling purposes.

Excel will think you are referencing a function or a named range, which it will most likely not find (unless there is coincidental duplicity), and return a #NAME? error.

The shortcut to using the CONCATENATE function is using the "&" symbol. For instance, if cell A1 contained my first name, Keith, and cell B1 contained my last name, Allman, I could join the two together in cell C1 by the following formula:

=A1&" "&B1

Notice that double quotes were used with a space in order to separate the first and last names. Otherwise, if **A1&B1** were entered, the name would appear as KeithAllman.

LEN

Occasionally, we might need to know the number of characters in a text string. This information can be useful for working with external data that has variable returns in the same cell. For instance, in the example model we reference the stock price from the Web Downloads sheet. Since the stock price has text attached to it we used the LEFT function to parse out the numerical information. This is fine if the stock stays under $10, but if the stock goes into double digits we will lose a decimal place's worth of data. We could use the LEN function on the web download to count the number of characters. We could then test the LEN return to see whether it is a value that corresponds to a single-digit stock price or a double-digit stock price. If the return corresponds to a double-digit stock price, then our LEFT function's second parameter would be one value higher than the initial LEFT function.

COUNTIF, COUNTA

Cell-counting functions are important for conditional tests as we have seen in this chapter. Two valuable counting functions are *COUNTIF* and *COUNTA*. COUNTIF accepts a range of cells and counts them if the contents meet a certain criteria. The entry parameters for the COUNTIF function include:

COUNTIF(range of cells to be counted, criteria of cell contents to test whether the cell should be included in the count)

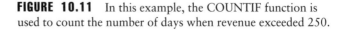

| | E4 | ▼ | | f_x | =COUNTIF(D4:D23,">250") |

	A	B	C	D	E
3			Date	Revenue	
4			5/12/2009	127.47	15
5			5/13/2009	294.57	
6			5/14/2009	47.58	
7			5/15/2009	498.08	
8			5/16/2009	733.61	
9			5/17/2009	807.67	
10			5/18/2009	594.02	
11			5/19/2009	666.35	
12			5/20/2009	756.10	
13			5/21/2009	672.23	
14			5/22/2009	534.00	
15			5/23/2009	465.66	
16			5/24/2009	151.18	
17			5/25/2009	536.50	
18			5/26/2009	855.64	
19			5/27/2009	19.05	
20			5/28/2009	726.60	
21			5/29/2009	970.72	
22			5/30/2009	770.97	
23			5/31/2009	161.57	

FIGURE 10.11 In this example, the COUNTIF function is used to count the number of days when revenue exceeded 250.

In the example model, we used the COUNTIF function to quantify the number of internal validations that passed. This was done by referencing the internal validation cells as the range of cells to be counted and the criteria of the cell contents being an "OK." Cells in the range that had a value of "OK" are counted. An alternative example is shown in Figure 10.11.

The value returned from the COUNTIF function is compared against the number of internal validation tests. Rather than hard-coding the number of tests into the formula, we use another counting function called COUNTA. This function counts the number of nonblank cells in a range. It accepts the following parameters:

COUNTA(range of cells to possibly count)

COUNTA returns a numerical count of nonblank cells, which means that even a zero that is entered into a cell will be counted.

Hyperlinks

Hyperlinks are a useful tool to quickly move through areas of the workbook. In the case of the Output Summary and Vectors sheets, we used them to navigate to specific section of the same sheets. On the Output Summary sheet created in this chapter, we inserted text into cells in row 11 that jumped to respective sections of the sheet. This is done by right-clicking on a cell with text and selecting **Hyperlink**. This action will bring up the Hyperlink dialogue box, where a user can select to link the cell text to an existing file or web page, to a location within the workbook, in a new document, or to an e-mail address that will initiate the default mail application. Select **Place in This Document**. From this selection the user has the option of selecting a sheet and a cell reference or a named range. This selection is where users will be brought to when they left-click on the original cell's text. In the case of the example model, we selected cells from the Output Summary sheet that correspond to where the Output Summary income statement, balance sheet, cash flow statement, and key ratios and rates reside.

Automation Using Visual Basic Applications (VBA)

A powerful capability of all Microsoft Office applications is the ability to program actions using the *Visual Basic Applications* (VBA) programming language. For Microsoft Excel, VBA is especially useful for frequently used commands that require multiple procedures and repetitive actions, and in more advanced situations for calculations that exceed the spreadsheet's processing ability. Examples relevant to corporate valuation modeling include creating a system to run various sensitivity scenarios, implementing iterative processes in code that overcome the circular references left in DCF models due to financial plugs, and installing buttons and checkboxes to control sheet printing and report distribution. Implementing such functionality requires a basic understanding of the VBA language and how the language interacts with Excel.

Most users have unknowingly used VBA by recording a macro to complete simple repetitive tasks. However, few take the step to learn how to write and edit VBA code by hand. The problem most users have with unlocking the full potential of VBA is learning how an *object-oriented programming* (OOP) language works. While entire books can and have been written on using VBA, this chapter introduces the model operator to the basics of using VBA through additions to the example model. Beginners might find additional texts helpful for further explanation, while intermediate-to-advanced users might want to skip to the specific code examples.

THE OBJECT-ORIENTED PROGRAMMING LANGUAGE (OOP)

Programming in VBA requires a shift in thought. We have to move from thinking about financial modeling in terms of Excel worksheet, cells, functions, and formulas to *text-based* instructions. This means we have the difficult task of taking visual tools that manipulate concepts and replacing those tools with text. To complicate matters, the text is written in English, but not in a manner we are accustomed to.

To help us make sense of this new language, we should learn about its structure. If one pictures the first soon-to-be computer programmers sitting in a room and deciding how they would recreate the world in code, one could imagine grandiose

Examples			
	Tangible	Financial	Excel
Object	Car	Loan	Cell Range
Property	Car Color	Loan Term	Cell Fill
Method	Drive Car	Amortize Loan	Copy Cell

FIGURE 11.1   There are a multitude of examples for objects, methods, and properties.

thoughts about virtual reality, artificial intelligence, and genetic algorithms. Although that's the cutting edge today, the foundations are much simpler. If we were to isolate three basic elements of OOP, we would see this recreation is based on items around us, descriptions of those items, and instructions to put the items into action. These elements are otherwise known as *objects*, *properties*, and *methods*. Examples of each are shown in Figure 11.1.

Objects

As part of the name, it's clear that objects are important to OOP. Objects can be thought of as the nouns of OOP. They are not as granular as something like atoms or molecules, but more of a representation of items around us, such as people, cars, or houses. To make the transition to finance, we can think of an object like a financial instrument, such as a loan. To make the transition to Excel we must visualize each cell, worksheet, and workbook as objects.

Properties

If objects are the nouns of OOP, properties are the adjectives. Properties describe objects to differentiate each object from similar objects. If we use a car as an example, we can have a green car, a red car, a Honda, a Toyota, and so on. In terms of our financial example, where a loan is an object, that loan can have its own unique balance, rate, and term. Continuing with our Excel example, a cell could have a characteristic such as its fill color.

Methods

Finally we get to action. Methods put objects into action just as verbs bring nouns to life. Cars are brought into action through driving and can move forward, left, right, and backward. A loan can be amortized over time in order to pay the balance down. In Excel we can do many different actions; some of the easiest are copying and pasting the contents of one cell to the next.

FOLLOW THE RULES

With the least amount of reference to the movie *The Matrix* possible, I should state that in computer programming we must follow the rules. Objects can be described only by properties and put into action only by methods that have been created for the object. For instance, so far, cars cannot fly; therefore, if we tried to use a "fly" method on a car object that we created in the standard sense of a car, the code would crash. Unless we specifically program in the fly method, the code will not work.

On an even simpler note, we will not be creating our own objects in this chapter. This means that we must use the objects that have been created for us in the default VBA libraries and can use only the properties and methods that the Excel designers have associated with those objects. If we try to use existing properties or methods with objects that are not associated with those properties or methods, we will also encounter errors.

Similarly, there will be commands that are part of the VBA language that must be used in specific ways. We cannot deviate from the preprogrammed applications of these commands. Any disordering or misspelling will cause the code to break down. Following such a specific rule set and learning what is virtually an entirely new language is part of the reason why many people become so frustrated learning VBA. In this chapter, we will limit the objects, properties, methods, and commands to those that are absolutely critical to financial modeling. Also, while there may be more efficient VBA coding that can run faster than what we are implementing, the subject matter and techniques that we will learn will be limited to as few new concepts as necessary and the fastest ones to pick up as a new programmer.

THE VISUAL BASIC EDITOR

To help us organize and work with the VBA language, the designers of Microsoft Office included an *integrated development environment* (IDE) called the *Visual Basic Editor* (VBE). VBA code can be written, stored, run, and debugged from the VBE. This makes our life easier as new programmers since we do not need to compile in a separate program or create executable files to run our programs. To access the VBE:

- *For Excel 2007:* Visual Basic options are contained on the Developer tab of the ribbon. Chapter 10 explains how to get the Developer tab to show up on the ribbon if it is not visible. An alternative to this process is pressing **ALT-F11**; however, the Developer tab should be kept visible to easily access other tools.
- *For Excel 2003 or earlier:* Go to **Tools, Macro, Visual Basic Editor** or use the **ALT-F11** keyboard shortcut.

The VBE will open in a separate window and should appear as in Figure 11.2.

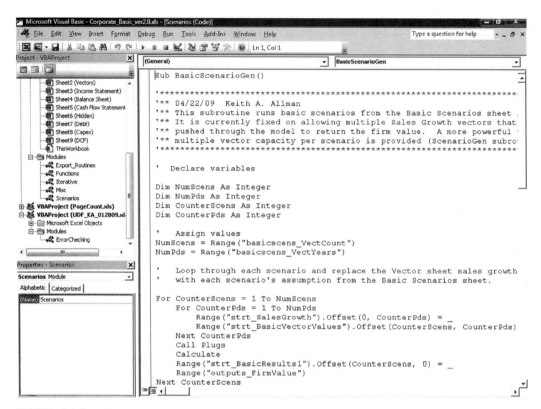

FIGURE 11.2 The Visual Basic Editor (VBE) is Visual Basic Applications' (VBA) integrated development environment.

The Menu Bar

The general menu bar features recognizable commands such as File and Edit; however, most of the options within each command will seem strange to a new user. View and Insert are the two key menus that we will use. In addition to menus, there are many buttons that will appear new. Look at the Standard Toolbar that should appear as a default setting.

The Standard Toolbar has a few buttons that will be useful for the basic operation of the VBE. Keep in mind the following:

- *View Microsoft Excel* jumps back to the Excel workbook.
- *Run Sub/UserForm* runs the code currently selected.
- *Break* breaks the code currently being run.
- *Reset* resets the code after a break has occurred.
- *Object Browser* opens the library of VBA objects.

The menu bar is shown in Figure 11.3.

FIGURE 11.3   The menu bar assists in the code-writing process.

The Project Explorer and the Properties Window

To the left side of the VBE, there are two important windows: the Project Explorer and the Properties Window. The Project Explorer looks a little like Windows Explorer in the way it organizes information. It is set up as a directory tree where more detailed information within a general concept can be expanded or compressed by clicking on + and − symbols.

The most general category in VBA is a Project, which is essentially the Excel workbook. The workbook that you are in is distinguished by its name, which is in brackets. A common mistake is to have multiple workbooks open and to start typing code in the wrong workbook. Make sure that the workbook that you want the code stored in is selected. Keep in mind that even if you have just one workbook open there may be multiple VBAProjects listed. The other projects are most likely add-ins, particularly since you may be using Excel after installing the VBA Analysis Tool Pak, as recommended in Chapter 1. Other add-ins that are installed are identified as .xla for .xlam files.

The first subfolder contains the Excel objects, which are the individual sheets in the workbook. Code can be stored under a sheet or for the workbook in general, but code stored in these areas is for very special purposes and should not be done until a user understands more about the VBA language. Just as we will be careful which workbook is selected, we should be careful if a sheet or **ThisWorkbook** is selected.

The area in which we will be entering our code is in a module. *Module* is a fancy term for a separate area to enter code. Code is often organized by purpose and functionality into separate modules. Within modules we can write code in two styles: subroutines and functions. A *subroutine* is like writing a list of commands. The computer reads this list in the order that it is entered and, in Excel's case, causes calculation or affects the workbook. Basic macros use one subroutine to accomplish a task, whereas more advanced macros often use multiple subroutines. Related subroutines are stored in the same module. For instance, a module might be named **Print_Routines** and contain three subroutines that format and print different sections of the Excel workbook. Figure 11.4 shows the project explorer.

The area that typically opens below the project explorer is the *properties* window. The properties window allows a user to graphically view and alter the properties of any object in Excel, simply by clicking on the object and going to the properties window. The properties window is shown in Figure 11.5.

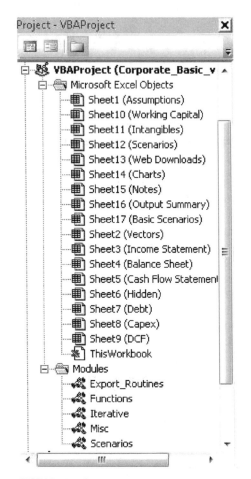

FIGURE 11.4 The VBE project explorer is similar to a Windows directory. It helps us organize and locate our code.

WRITING CODE: SUBROUTINES AND FUNCTIONS

Although there are two ways of writing code, all of the code that we will write in this section is structured as subroutines. A subroutine is a way of writing code that is like a list of commands. When the commands are run, they are completed in order from beginning to end.

A *function* is code that returns a value when parameters are entered into it. Whereas a subroutine can return a value as a result of the commands entered, a function explicitly takes in parameters and returns a value from those parameters. Functions in VBA can be created not only to calculate in the computer's memory, but also for use on the sheet just as with any preprogrammed function we use.

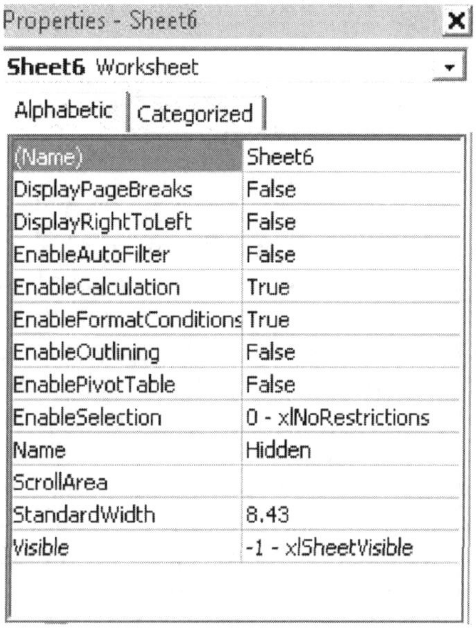

FIGURE 11.5 Objects in the workbook and on the worksheet can be viewed and altered using the properties window. In this example, a worksheet object is selected and its properties displayed.

UNDERSTANDING VBA CODE AND PRACTICING CODING TECHNIQUES

Before we jump right into a financial example using code, we will complete two separate examples to get a foundation in coding. The examples will be quite easy and seem unrelated to finance, but they introduce the core concepts involved in many of the underlying subroutines in the example model. Overall, we will seek to understand the following concepts and techniques:

- Moving data between Excel and VBA
- For Next loops
- Variables
- Offset property

To get practice with these concepts and techniques, the next two Model Builder exercises will not contribute to the actual example model, but are intended to develop the reader's skill prior to actually implementing the techniques in a financial modeling context.

MODEL BUILDER 11.1: MOVING DATA USING VBA

1. For this Model Builder, you should open a new workbook and save it as **VBATestCode.xls**. In this workbook we will set up the functionality to enter a name in one range, press a button, and have that button run code that replicates the name in a different cell.

2. The first step we usually take in any VBA project is prepping the workbook with as much Excel functionality as possible. By drawing on VBA only when we absolutely have to, we simplify our code and make it much easier for users to interpret. Obviously, this easy example can be entirely accomplished on the sheet, but let's learn about VBA by going through the steps.

3. Enter the text **Name** as a label in cell A1 of the first sheet. Then name cell A2 **MyName**. Also name cell C5 **Destination**. Naming ranges in Excel allows us to refer to them in a much easier and more reliable format than referring to them using the R1C1 (row-and-column) notation.

4. Press **Alt-F11** to get to the VBE. If you have multiple workbooks open, make sure to navigate to the correct VBAProject (VBAProject(VBATestCode_Book.xls)). In this project, insert a module by going to the **Insert** menu and selecting **module**. Click on the newly inserted module (Module1) to ensure that the correct code window is visible to the right.

5. Thinking about the basic structure of OOP and VBA that we learned earlier, we should recognize that the cells in the workbook are objects. In fact, we have applied names, which are properties, to two of the objects so we can refer to them in an easy fashion. We need to understand that we will be writing a list of commands to move the name from the MyRange cell to the Destination cell. This will be done using a subroutine. Click on the code window and enter the code `Sub NameMover()` and press **Enter**. An `End Sub` should automatically appear underneath. This process is how we initiate a subroutine and is done every time we want to create a new subroutine.

6. After we have initiated the subroutine, we should think about our task at hand. We probably want to refer to the MyName cell in some way. In VBA we can refer to a cell or a range of cells as "Range objects." This is done using the following convention:

```
Range(``NamedRange'') or Range(``R1C1 reference'')
```

   In our example, we should enter the following code underneath `Sub NameMover()`:

```
Range(``MyName'')
```

7. We should notice what happens if we type a period (.) after the line of code above. You will see that a drop-down box appears with different named items. This is actually a list of the possible properties and methods that can be used with

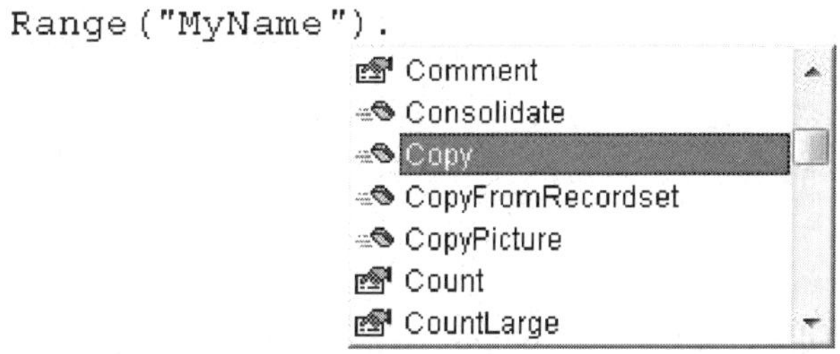

```
Range("MyName").
```

FIGURE 11.6 Properties and methods work with objects by entering a period or dot after the object.

a Range object. The VBE assists us in using properties and methods correctly in this way. Some may think we should try to use the Copy property (you can check and see that it is there in the drop-down list as shown in Figure 11.6). However, we will learn the most efficient method of doing this procedure.

8. We can directly move or assign values in VBA by using the equal sign (=). Modify the code that was just entered in step 6 so that it reads:

```
Range(''Destination'') = Range(''MyName'')
```

Notice here that something seems backwards. We started by focusing on MyName, but now are first referencing the Destination range and setting it equal to the MyName range. This ordering with the equal sign is how VBA works. An easy way to remember this is by thinking of the phrase: "The left side of the equal sign accepts what the right side provides."

One thought on why this concept causes difficulty for many people is that in Western languages we often refer to objects or nouns later. In English, the noun often comes at the end of the sentence, such as "How are you?" In many non-Western languages, the noun comes first. For instance, in Hindi you would say, "Tum kaise ho?," which is translated literally into English as "You how are?" Computer code is more similar to the latter style, where the object we want to affect starts the line of code.

9. This single line of code is all that is required to compose the subroutine. Some experienced VBA programmers may suggest using the Value property after each range object so that the code looks as follows:

```
Range(''Destination'').Value = Range(''MyName'').Value
```

But this is not necessary, unless we are concerned with cell formats or formulas. If we are concerned with those, we might need to use additional properties, such as the Formula property, if we want a formula to be replicated.

10. To run this subroutine, we could use the Run button on the VBE tool bar that we discussed earlier, but everyone gets satisfaction out of creating buttons and

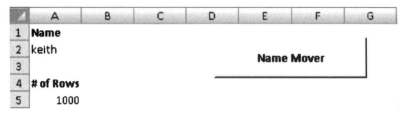

FIGURE 11.7 The subroutine for the NameMover macro is controlled by a Forms button.

pushing them to do things, so we should learn about buttons. Go back to the Excel sheet where we named the ranges and entered our name. To insert a button, go to the **Forms** tools. If getting to these tools is unclear, refer to Chapter 10 for a review of the process. Select the **button** tool. Left-click and drag a button directly on the sheet that we were working in. The minute the left-click is released, a dialogue box will come up prompting the user to select a macro to assign to this button. Select the **NameMover** macro.

11. Once the macro is assigned, we can change the name from Button1 to any custom name that we desire. Name the button **Name Mover**. Select outside of the button so that we are no longer editing the button itself. When the pointer is scrolled over the button, it should change from the default arrow to a hand. Push the button and the NameMover macros should run successfully. The final view of the sheet is shown in Figure 11.7.

12. The final code should read:

```
Sub NameMover()
Range("Destination") = Range("MyName")
End Sub
```

Loops

The real power of VBA is brought out when we work with loops. Looping is a programming technique that repeats a section of code for a certain number of iterations or until a condition is met. This is important for financial modeling for a number of reasons:

- Loops allow systematic movement throughout a model so multiple cells can be referenced and manipulated quickly and repetitively.
- Memory-intensive calculations can be done quickly. For instance, if we were to amortize a pool of 5,000 loans on a monthly basis, an Excel-based implementation would crash. However, a VBA-based implementation would work quickly.
- Loops can exceed Excel's limitations. If we were to run a simulation for 100,000 iterations, we would not be able to do this on the Excel sheet in Excel 2003 or

earlier. Even in Excel 2007 we would still want to use VBA since the previous point about memory and calculation speed problems would occur.

Overall, we will find loops an essential technique to learn in order to have full flexibility with coding.

Variables

In order to learn a basic loop, we must also learn about variables. *Variables* are just as we remember from algebra: symbols that represent a value that can vary. In the case of VBA, the symbol is most likely text and the value can be a number, text, date, or TRUE or FALSE value. Variables are important to use in coding for two main reasons:

1. *Code management:* We should structure code so that we assign values to variables early in the code and then use the variables throughout the code. The reasoning behind this is that if we need to change the value reference, we will have to do it only once in the beginning of the code. Then the variable used throughout the code will be fine. However, if we did not use a variable and directly referenced the Excel sheet every time we needed a value, we would have to change all of the references throughout the code if the Excel sheet reference changed.
2. *Memory management:* Using variables allows us to reduce memory use and make our programs run faster. This is done in two separate ways. The first is a byproduct of proper code management above. If we use variables throughout our code, we limit the in-and-out processes between VBA and Excel. These processes are much more memory demanding than basic calculation with variables. Limiting our code to as few in-and-out processes as possible will create fast, robust code.

   The second way is that variables can be defined to hold certain types of data. Some types of data use less memory than others. For example, a Boolean or TRUE/FALSE variable in VBA requires 2 bytes of memory as compared to a Variant, which can require up to 24 bytes of memory. By defining variables we constrain their memory usage, which can greatly speed up our programs.

Offset Property

A useful property to help with movement through Excel worksheets is the *offset* property. In Chapter 2 we learned the OFFSET function, which starts at a reference point and references another cell depending on the row and column inputs entered. VBA can do a similar process with the offset property. This property works with a Range object. The Range object is the starting reference point. Then two entries are needed: a number for the number of rows to move up or down and a number for the number of columns to move right or left. Here is how this would look in code:

```
Range(''Test'').Offset(1, 5)
```

	A	B	C	D	E	F
	Test		f_x	Starting Cell		
1	Starting Cell					
2						Return Value

FIGURE 11.8 In the example code, Range("Test").Offset(1, 5), A1, which is named "Test," would be referenced and offset by 1 row and 5 columns. The example code would then equal the value in cell F2.

In this example, the Range object Test would be offset by 1 row and 5 columns. Whatever value is in the cell that is referenced through the offset property will be returned by this section of code. The Excel sheet example is shown in Figure 11.8. We could then load that value into a variable by writing:

```
Variable = Range(''Test'').Offset(1, 5)
```

MODEL BUILDER 11.2: A FIRST LOOK AT LOOPS AND VARIABLES IN VBA

1. To learn about loops and variables in an easy manner, we are going to extend our first code example. In this Model Builder example, we will write code that repeats our name as many times as we like. Go back to the Excel sheet in VBATestCode.xls where the name information was entered. Add the text **# of Rows** in cell A4. Enter the value **1000** in cell A5 and name cell A5 **TotalRows**.
2. Press **Alt-F11** to get to the VBE. In the VBATestCode project, select **Module1**. We will create new code in the same module as in the previous Model Builder, directly underneath the last code created. Enter the code `Sub NameRepeater()` on the line after the previous code's `End Sub`.
3. The first task we should always do when we get more proficient with VBA coding is to declare variables. Declaring variables makes the system aware of the variable name and what type of data can be entered into it. The term for declaring a variable is more technical in VBA. The proper command to use is known as *dimensioning a variable*, which is done with the term *Dim*. Enter the following code on the next line:

```
Dim Name As String
Dim TotalRows As Integer
Dim RowCounter As Integer
```

In this step, we declared three different variables. The first one is called "Name," and it can contain only text, or, in programming terminology, a *string*. The second variable is called "TotalRows," and will contain a number that is indicative of the total number of rows the name will be repeated. The third variable is called "RowCounter," which will be used in the VBA code itself. The idea that a variable can be created just for use in a program causes confusion for some. Variables can be representations of items from the Excel sheet or they can be created only for use in VBA.

4. The second major task of our program is assigning values to the variables. Recall the statement above: "The left side of the equal sign accepts what the right side provides."

   We can apply this same logic to variables. Enter the following code starting on the next empty line in the NameRepeater subroutine:

```
Name = Range("MyName")
TotalRows = Range("TotalRows")
```

   This section of code assigns values from the Excel sheet to the variables. Now the variable Name has the text value from whatever name is entered in cell A2 of the Excel sheet and TotalRows as the numerical value from cell A5.

5. The next line of code that should be entered is:

```
For RowCounter = 1 To TotalRows
```

   The wording of this code is something entirely new. This is the initiation of a *For Next* loop. These types of loops are initialized by setting a variable (RowCounter) equal to a value (1) and then performing code that follows this line until a Next statement is reached. After the next statement is reached, the variable increases by an integer of 1. This process continues until the first variable is equal to the second variable after the To statement (TotalRows).

   Informally, I refer to the RowCounter variable as a *counter* variable since it essentially keeps the count of the loop. It is not only convenient that the counter variable keeps the count, but it can be also used for calculation and reference throughout the loop, as we will see.

6. Once we initiate the loop, the next line of code is what gets repeated. Enter the following line of code after the previous one:

```
Range("Destination").Offset(RowCounter, 0) = Name
```

   In this line, we use the offset property mentioned earlier. However, there are key differences between this line of code and the example shown earlier. First, the code is reversed from the example. This is because we want a range to equal a variable value, not a variable equaling a range value. The second difference is that we use a variable for the value of the offset, rather than a hard-coded value. This is how we draw upon the power of a loop to "move" through a worksheet.

   Walking through what would happen, the first loop would be initiated and RowCounter would equal 1. The range object Destination would then be offset

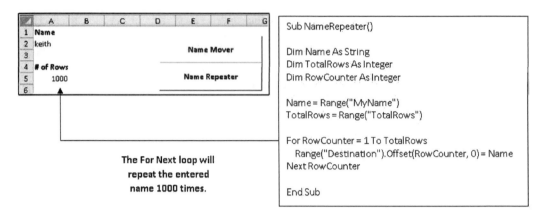

The For Next loop will repeat the entered name 1000 times.

```
Sub NameRepeater()

Dim Name As String
Dim TotalRows As Integer
Dim RowCounter As Integer

Name = Range("MyName")
TotalRows = Range("TotalRows")

For RowCounter = 1 To TotalRows
    Range("Destination").Offset(RowCounter, 0) = Name
Next RowCounter

End Sub
```

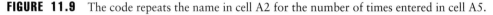

FIGURE 11.9   The code repeats the name in cell A2 for the number of times entered in cell A5.

by 1 row and 0 columns. When the loop gets repeated, RowCounter would increase to 2 and the range object Destination would then be offset by 2 rows and 0 columns.

7. The final key part of the For Next loop is the Next. We could just write Next, but we should identify the counter variable in case we start using multiple For Next loops. Enter the following code in the next line after the previous line of code:

```
Next RowCounter
```

This line of code instructs the program to go back up to the start of the For Next loop and begin the process again, unless the counter variable is equal to the value after the To statement. Figure 11.9 provides an overview of the code supporting the Excel sheet.

8. Make sure to end the program with a line stating End Sub. The final code for this subroutine should read:

```
Sub NameRepeater()
Dim Name As String
Dim TotalRows As Integer
Dim RowCounter As Integer

Name = Range("MyName")
TotalRows = Range("TotalRows")

For RowCounter = 1 To TotalRows
  Range("Destination").Offset(RowCounter, 0) = Name
Next RowCounter

End Sub
```

COMMON ERRORS FOR FIRST-TIME VBA PROGRAMMERS

If your macro did not work in Model Builder 11.1 or 11.2, we need to debug the problem. We can save a lot of time by understanding the most common errors for new programmers. The primary errors include:

- Spelling or inconsistent names
- Going beyond scope
- Forgetting part of a multistep process

Spelling

The number-one error is spelling. You will most likely get the run-time error: '1004:' Method 'Range' of object '_Global' failed. This common error means that you tried to refer to a range object that does not exist. It usually does not exist because the programmer spelled the range object name differently than the name on the Excel sheet. Check the Name Manager names versus the names used in VBA for inconsistencies.

There can also be simple typo problems with spelling. For example, if you misspell `Offset`, such as `Ofset`, the code will break down instantly.

Scope

Another common error is trying to use a value with a variable that is beyond the variable's scope. This means that we could have declared a variable as text and tried to pass a numerical value into it. This generates an error. Also, if we declared a value as an integer and tried to pass the number 1,000,000 through it, we would generate an error since 1,000,000 exceeds the maximum numerical value for an integer (32,767).

Missing Steps

Some VBA techniques are multistep processes and quickly break down if one of those steps is missing. For example, we learned how a basic For Next loop works. If we start a For Next loop with the For section, but forget to insert the Next code, the entire subroutine will break down. There are other similar issues as you learn more about VBA, such as If statements requiring an End If.

VBA WITHIN A FINANCIAL MODELING CONTEXT

The next section of this chapter marks a switch from the introduction of VBA to application. We will focus on three main problems that VBA allows us to overcome:

1. Eliminating circular references
2. Generating multiple scenarios
3. Performing repetitive administrative functions

Each problem will be solved by a Model Builder section that will add functionality to the example model. The circular reference created to balance the balance sheet will be converted to a looping solution, a new scenario generator sheet will be built and run by code, and finally, an Excel/VBA printer solution will be installed to rapidly export results.

MODEL BUILDER 11.3: ELIMINATING CIRCULAR REFERENCES

1. We will take a simple approach to our first macro for use in the example model. To eliminate the need for the circular reference we need to mimic the iterative process that is taking place. Essentially, the circular reference is loading up initial values, calculating, and then loading up the results of the calculation into the same formula. This goes on for a number of iterations. At the most basic level, this could be solved by a person copying and pasting the asset and liability plugs into the plug areas on the balance sheet. Done repetitively, the balance sheet should balance. Prior to actually writing code, we should set up our sheet for the process. The Excel sheet needs are minimal for this subroutine. All we need to do is name the following ranges with the corresponding names:

   'Debt'!E14:J14 = rng_SurplusOutDS
   'Balance Sheet'!E31:J31 = rng_STOut
   'Balance Sheet'!E48:J48 = rng_SurplusIn
   'Balance Sheet'!E49:J49 = rng_STIn

2. Press **Alt-F11** to get to the VBE. Insert a module and name it **Iterative**. Modules can be named by left-clicking on the newly inserted module and then going to the Properties Window. There you can enter a name for the module under Name.

3. Start a new subroutine by entering the following code in the Iterative module:

```
Sub Plugs()
```

4. Something you may notice in the example model is green text all over the place. The green text is known as *comments*; these are useful to explain what a subroutine is doing or what specific lines of code intend to accomplish. Comments are not read when the code is run and are purely for the user's knowledge. Comments are entered by starting a line of code with an apostrophe ('). Every new line of code will require its own apostrophe to start the commenting process.

5. The next lines of code will be variable declarations:

```
Dim i As Integer
Dim iteration As Integer
```

These two lines of code create two variables: *i* and iteration. Many programmers tend to use single-letter variables, such as *i*. These are frequently used as counter variables for loops.

6. After the previous line of code, enter:

```
Application.ScreenUpdating = False
```

This is a special command that turns off Excel's screen updating, meaning that as the subroutine runs, nothing will change on the screen even if the code is moving items around in our model. If we did not turn it off, we would see the screen move around as the code ran. Although screen updating does add an impressive "automation" element, it is a waste of memory and slows our programs down.

7. The next two lines of code after turning off screen updating should be:

```
iteration = 100
Calculate
```

Here we assign our iteration variable a value of 100, which will be the total number of times to loop or iterate. We also use a special command called "Calculate," which calculates the entire workbook in case the workbook was last saved with the manual calculation setting turned on.

8. Enter the following line of code:

```
For i = 1 To iteration
```

This line of code initiates a For Next loop. We use the variable *i* as a counter variable and loop through to the number of iterations that are loaded into the iteration variable. In more advanced sheets, we could create a sheet value for the number of iterations and load that value into the iteration variable. For the purposes of this subroutine, 100 iterations is plenty and probably not necessary to adjust.

9. The heart of the code is next:

```
Range("rng_SurplusIn").Copy
Range("rng_SurplusOutDS").PasteSpecial xlPasteValues
Range("rng_STIn").Copy
Range("rng_STOut").PasteSpecial xlPasteValues
```

Every loop copies the surplus cash calculated in the rng_SurplusIn range and pastes only those values into the rng_SurplusOutDS range. Notice that we used the Copy and PasteSpecial methods and that the PasteSpecial method has a qualifier for us to tell VBA the type of special paste that we are looking for. The same process is done for the short-term debt. Refer to Figure 11.10 for additional reference.

	A	B	C	D	E	F	G	H	I	J
48	Surplus Cash				0.00	71.09	144.85	244.88	357.00	474.92
49	Required Short-Term Debt				19.92	0.00	0.00	0.00	0.00	0.00

**The plugs are put back in the
model via VBA code.**

	A	B	C	D	E	F	G	H	I	J
31	ST borrowings			0.00	19.92	0.00	0.00	0.00	0.00	0.00

	A	B	C	D	E	F	G	H	I	J
14	Surplus Funds for Prin				-	71.09	144.85	244.88	357.00	474.92

FIGURE 11.10   The plugs' values are copied and pasted using code to avoid having a circular reference in the model.

10. Prior to finalizing the loop, we should make sure the sheet is calculated. Enter the following code to calculate again:

```
Calculate
```

11. One problem with running code, particularly with the screen updating turned off, is that we do not know the progress. This can be accomplished by inserting the following code:

```
Application.StatusBar = "Solving Assets and Liabilities,
Iteration " _ & i & " of " & iteration
```

   As with the screen updating code, we are interested in affecting the Excel application itself. However, in this case we want to change the status bar (the bar on the bottom of Excel that normally states "Ready"). We will have it say our custom text, plus the two variables. The reason we use the two variables is that they will change with each loop and show the model user which loop the code is processing out of the total number of loops. The text and variables are joined together with the & symbol, which works identically to the Excel sheet version.

12. We are finally done with the loop and close it off with the following line of code:

```
Next i
```

   Remember that if we forget this simple line of code, the entire subroutine will break down and generate an error.

13. Since we adjusted some of the Excel application's settings we should switch them back to what they were before. Enter the following code:

```
Application.ScreenUpdating = True
Application.StatusBar = False
```

This turns screen updating back on and changes the status bar back to "Ready." Be careful of using a True for the status bar. The default setting is False. If a True is entered in this part of the code, the status bar on the Excel sheet will read "True."

14. Finalize the code with an `End Sub`.

15. The final code should read (note that comments are inserted):

```
Sub Plugs()

' Declare variables
Dim i As Integer
Dim iteration As Integer

Application.ScreenUpdating = False
iteration = 100
Calculate

' Loop through each iteration, replacing the Surplus and ST
        Debt values in with their
' corresponding out areas.
For i = 1 To iteration
        Range("rng_SurplusIn").Copy
        Range("rng_SurplusOutDS").PasteSpecial xlPasteValues
        Range("rng_STIn").Copy
        Range("rng_STOut").PasteSpecial xlPasteValues
        Calculate
        Application.StatusBar = "Solving Assets and Liabili-
            ties, Iteration " _
        & i & " of " & iteration
Next i

Application.ScreenUpdating = True
Application.StatusBar = False

End Sub
```

16. To make it easier to run, create a button on the Assumptions sheet and assign the Plugs subroutine to it. You may want to locate it near cell J3 and name it **Balance Model**.

MODEL BUILDER 11.4: CREATING A SCENARIO GENERATOR

1. The next functionality to implement is the ability to generate multiple results by altering assumptions. Although we could run scenarios by hand, it would take a long time to run a number of variations. In the complete example model there are two sheets dedicated to scenario analysis: Basic Scenarios and Scenarios.

   In this Model Builder we will learn how to create the Basic Scenarios sheet functionality. This sheet and the code behind it accepts multiple sales growth vectors, runs each vector through the model, balances the model, and captures the resulting change on the firm value prior to running the next scenario. The Scenarios sheet in the complete example model will not be covered since it is an advanced version that requires search code.

   The first step in creating the Basic Scenarios functionality is to insert a worksheet after the DCF sheet and name it **Basic Scenarios**.

2. The purpose of the Basic Scenarios sheet is to create an area where we can enter sensitivity vectors. We also need to create formulas that provide data about the scenarios that we anticipate running. Enter the following text in the corresponding cells on the Basic Scenarios sheet:

   A1: **Basic Scenarios**
   B5: **Scenario Data**
   B6: **Scenario #**
   C3: **Number of Periods**
   C6: **Vector**
   F3: **Number of Scenarios**
   K5: **Scenario Results Summary**
   K6: **Scenario #**
   L6: **Firm Value**

3. Carry over the dates from the Vectors sheet to the Basic Scenarios sheet. Start with a reference to the Vectors sheet cell E10 in cell D6 on the Basic Scenarios sheet. Copy and paste that reference over the Basic Scenarios sheet range D6:I6.

4. We will focus on Sales Growth for now. To give us data to work with for each scenario, let's try out 10 scenarios. Copy the scenario data from range B7:I16 on the Basic Scenarios sheet in the complete example model and paste it into the same sheet and range in your model. Do the same for the scenario numbers in range K7:K16. Thus far, the Basic Scenarios sheet should look like Figure 11.11.

5. Two formulas are needed to summarize the number of periods and the number of scenarios in the scenario analysis. Enter the following formulas in the corresponding cells on the Basic Scenarios sheet:

   D3: =COUNT(D6:I6)
   H3: =COUNT(B7:B65536)
        Name cell D3 **basicscens_VectYears** and cell H3 **basicscens_VectCount**.

	B	C	D	E	F	G	H	I	J	K	L
1	**Basic Scenarios**										
2											
3		Number of Periods		6		Number of Scenarios		10			
4											
5	Scenario Data									Scenario Results Summary	
6	Scenario #	Vector	12/31/2008	12/31/2009	12/31/2010	12/31/2011	12/31/2012	12/31/2013		Scenario #	Firm Value
7	1	Sales Unit Growth	0.00%	0.00%	0.00%	0.00%	0.00%	0.00%		1	
8	2	Sales Unit Growth	1.00%	1.00%	1.00%	1.00%	1.00%	0.25%		2	
9	3	Sales Unit Growth	2.00%	2.00%	2.00%	2.00%	2.00%	0.50%		3	
10	4	Sales Unit Growth	3.00%	3.00%	3.00%	3.00%	3.00%	0.75%		4	
11	5	Sales Unit Growth	4.00%	4.00%	4.00%	4.00%	4.00%	1.00%		5	
12	6	Sales Unit Growth	5.00%	5.00%	5.00%	5.00%	5.00%	1.25%		6	
13	7	Sales Unit Growth	6.00%	6.00%	6.00%	6.00%	6.00%	1.50%		7	
14	8	Sales Unit Growth	7.00%	7.00%	7.00%	7.00%	7.00%	1.75%		8	
15	9	Sales Unit Growth	8.00%	8.00%	8.00%	8.00%	8.00%	2.00%		9	
16	10	Sales Unit Growth	9.00%	9.00%	9.00%	9.00%	9.00%	2.25%		10	

FIGURE 11.11 The first step in creating a powerful VBA scenario generator is creating the control sheet for it in Excel.

6. There are a number of ranges we need to name as reference points throughout the model. This will allow us to navigate the model very easily in VBA. On the Basic Scenarios sheet, name the following cells with the corresponding names:

C6: strt_BasicVectorValues
L6: strt_BasicResults1

7. If we take a moment to remove ourselves from the minutiae and look at our overall plan, we will see that we have a number of possible sales growth vectors that will be run through the model. They will have to be moved to the Vectors sheet using code, but the question arises: Where do we move them—Base Case area? Downside Case area? Instead of using existing areas, which could confuse users, we should make a separate area on the Vector sheet for VBA-generated cases. Go to the Vectors sheet and copy all of the labels and references from the complete example model so that there is a *VBA-generated case* section. This new section should look like Figure 11.12.

	B	C	D	E	F	G	H	I	J
132									
133	**VBA Generator Case**			Projected ---->					TV Year
134			12/31/2007	12/31/2008	12/31/2009	12/31/2010	12/31/2011	12/31/2012	12/31/2013
135	**Income Statement Items**								
136	Sales Unit Growth			10.0%	10.0%	10.0%	10.0%	10.0%	4.0%
137	Sales Price Growth			10.0%	10.0%	10.0%	10.0%	10.0%	4.0%
138	Cost Unit Growth			5.0%	5.0%	5.0%	5.0%	5.0%	5.0%
139	SGA (% of revenue)			14.0%	14.0%	14.0%	14.0%	14.0%	14.0%
140	Op Ex (% of revenue)			6.0%	6.0%	6.0%	6.0%	6.0%	6.0%
141	Non-Op Ex (% of revenue)			1.8%	1.8%	1.8%	1.8%	1.8%	1.8%

FIGURE 11.12 A new section on the Vectors sheet accepts the scenario data from the Basic Scenarios sheet. Note that this is a partial screen shot and that there are more rows of data.

8. In order to use the VBA-generator case section on the Vectors sheet, we need to modify lists and formulas. On the top of the Vectors sheet in cell B7, enter the text **VBA Generator Case**. Modify the named range lst_Scenario so that cell B7 is included in that named range. Next go to each CHOOSE formula in the Vectors sheet range E12:J36 and insert a reference for the possibility of the VBA Generator Case. The functionality that is being built in is to have the user select the VBA Generator Case from the Assumptions sheet, which will populate the values from the VBA-generator case section on the Vectors sheet to the live scenario section. The values that are inserted in the VBA-generator case section are modified by the values from the Basic Scenarios sheet. By implementing such a system we allow for both Excel scenario generation and VBA scenario generation, depending on what the user desires. An overview of the process is provided in Figure 11.13.

9. For our Basic Scenarios functionality we will name one cell on the Vectors sheet to make our VBA code easier to write. On the Vectors sheet, name cell D32 **strt_SalesGrowth**. We are now ready to write the necessary code.

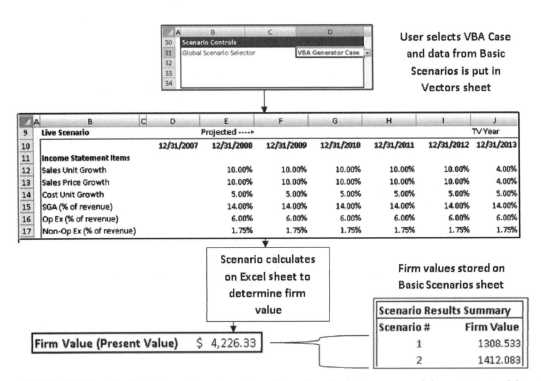

FIGURE 11.13 The Basic Scenarios subroutine utilizes the calculation power of the existing model to quickly return multiple firm values.

10. Press **Alt-F11** to get to the VBE. Insert a new module in your model and name that module **Scenarios**. In that module start a subroutine by entering the following code:

```
Sub BasicScenarioGen()
```

11. Just as in the last subroutine, our first step is to declare variables. Enter the following code after the last line of code:

```
Dim NumScens As Integer
Dim NumPds As Integer
Dim CounterScens As Integer
Dim CounterPds As Integer
```

   Notice that we create four variables: one that will represent the total number of scenarios, one that will represent the total number of periods, one that will count the scenarios as we loop through them, and one that will count the periods as we loop through them.

12. Also similar to the last subroutine, we will assign values to certain variables. Enter the following code in the subroutine:

```
NumScens = Range("basicscens_VectCount")
NumPds = Range("basicscens_VectYears")
```

   This code takes the values from the Basic Scenarios sheet and loads them into the variables that we created.

13. We will initiate two loops, which is something we have yet to do. This is done because we want to loop through each scenario, but for each scenario we want to loop through each period. Because we will first loop through the scenario, this is known as the *outer* loop; the second loop, the periods, is referred to as the *inner* loop. To start this process enter the following code:

```
For CounterScens = 1 To NumScens
 For CounterPds = 1 To NumPds
```

14. The key to each loop is that for each period within a scenario we want to replicate the value that is on the Basic Scenarios sheet and put it into the VBA generator case section of the Vectors sheet. We will use the same offset property as before to accomplish this. Enter the following code:

```
Range("strt_SalesGrowth").Offset(0, CounterPds) = _
Range("strt_BasicVectorValues").Offset(CounterScens,
CounterPds)
```

   One thing that may confuse new programmers is the use of the underscore. Underscores are used to continue a line of code to another line for readability. The functionality is such that this appears to be one line of code to the computer, but since it would be tedious to scroll right to read long lines of code we can continue the same line of code on the next line by inserting a space and an underscore. Do not forget the space prior to the underscore; otherwise, an error will be generated.

Overall, this section of code does what we want. It offsets from a location on the Basic Scenarios sheet and puts the value in the cell that it is referencing into the corresponding period location on the Vectors sheet.

15. The next few steps should be done carefully since it is extremely important what is put prior to the Next statements in our code. We are fine right now to enter the following code after the last two lines of code:

```
Next CounterPds
```

16. However, before entering another Next statement for the scenarios, there are a few things we need to do in between the scenario loop. At this point, we have entered new values in our model, which means that the balance sheet is most likely unbalanced. Instead of relying on the circular reference or rewriting the Plugs subroutine, we can just run the Plugs subroutine from the BasicScenarioGen subroutine. Do this by entering the following line of code:

```
Call Plugs
```

The Call statement calls a subroutine and is followed by the subroutine's name.

17. After we balance the model, we should make sure that everything is calculated and force another calculation of the workbook just in case. While this may be redundant, our processing time is relatively low, so we can enter the following line of code:

```
Calculate
```

18. Now, if we were to loop to the next scenario, we would essentially lose any result from the previous scenario! Although we could pull any number of results from our model, we will keep it simple and focus on the firm value, which is already a named range (outputs_FirmValue). Enter the following code to copy the firm value onto the results section of the Basic Scenarios sheet:

```
Range("strt_BasicResults1").Offset(CounterScens, 0) = _
Range("outputs_FirmValue")
```

19. We can loop to the next scenario to repeat the process for each scenario on the Basic Scenarios sheet. Also remember to make sure that the End Sub statement is there. The last lines of code should be:

```
Next CounterScens
End Sub
```

20. The final code should be:

```
Sub BasicScenarioGen()

' Declare variables

Dim NumScens As Integer
Dim NumPds As Integer
Dim CounterScens As Integer
Dim CounterPds As Integer

' Assign values
NumScens = Range("basicscens_VectCount")
NumPds = Range("basicscens_VectYears")

' Loop through each scenario and replace the Vector sheet
     sales growth vector
' with each scenario's assumption from the Basic Scenarios
     sheet.

For CounterScens = 1 To NumScens
 For CounterPds = 1 To NumPds
 Range("strt_SalesGrowth").Offset(0, CounterPds) = _
 Range("strt_BasicVectorValues").Offset(CounterScens,
     CounterPds)
 Next CounterPds
 Call Plugs
 Calculate
 Range("strt_BasicResults1").Offset(CounterScens, 0) = _
 Range("outputs_FirmValue")
 Next CounterScens

End Sub
```

21. For the user to use this code, we should create a button on the Assumptions sheet, beneath the previous button, and assign the BasicScenarioGen subroutine to it. We should name that button **Generate Scenarios**. Also, the user should know that for this functionality to work the VBA Generator Case needs to be selected on the Assumptions sheet in cell D31 (inputs_ScenSelector).

MODEL BUILDER 11.5: AUTOMATIC SHEET PRINTING

1. The final code that will be explained is the *printing* subroutine. The overall goal of this functionality is to have the user select checkboxes on the Assumptions sheet for the sheets in the model that are to be sent to the default printer. Most of this macro is actually controlled by items on the Excel sheets. Figure 11.14

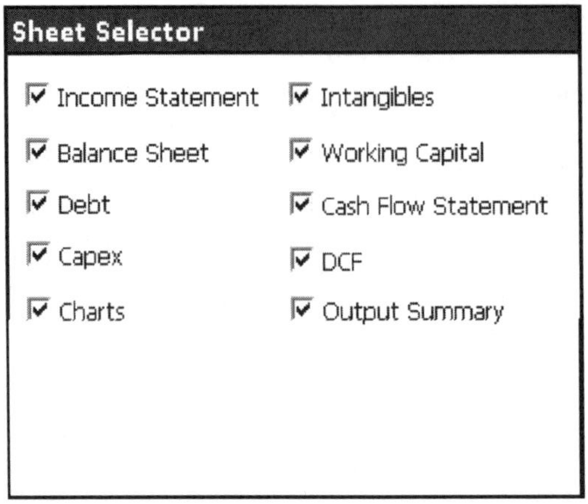

FIGURE 11.14 The automatic sheet printer is primarily controlled by form functionality on the Assumptions sheet.

depicts this section of the Excel sheet. Go to the Assumptions sheet, and enter the text **Sheet Selector** in cell F3.

2. Create a checkbox for each sheet that you anticipate printing in the area beneath cell F3 on the Assumptions sheet. Name each checkbox the same as the sheet name that you are referring to. Go to the Format Control of the first checkbox and make the cell link to cell N4 on the Hidden sheet. Go to the Hidden sheet and notice the pattern of implementation that will emerge. When the checkbox is checked, a TRUE should show up in cell N4; when the same checkbox is unchecked, a FALSE should show up. In cell M4, enter the name of the sheet that corresponds to the name of the sheet that the checkbox is referring to (and that should also be the title of the checkbox). Repeat this process for every sheet that should possibly be printed, continuing down the rows. For instance, the next checkbox should be linked to cell N5 with the name of the sheet in cell M5. This section is shown in Figure 11.15. Once this is done, name the range of sheet names on the Hidden sheet **ctrl_SheetSelector** and cell N3 **strt_SheetNameTFs**. For labeling purposes, enter the text **ctrl_SheetSelector** in cell M3.

3. We should also count the number of possible sheets to print. Still on the Hidden sheet, enter the following formula in cell L15:

=COUNTA(ctrl_SheetSelector)

   Name L15 ctrl_SheetCt.

4. Notice the functionality that we have built in. For each sheet that could possibly be printed we have a checkbox on the Assumptions sheet. When the user checks

	L	M	N
1			
2			
3	**ctrl_SheetSelector**		
4	Income Statement		TRUE
5	Balance Sheet		TRUE
6	Debt		TRUE
7	Capex		TRUE
8	Intangibles		TRUE
9	Working Capital		TRUE
10	Cash Flow Statement		TRUE
11	DCF		TRUE
12	Charts		TRUE
13	Output Summary		TRUE
14			
15	10		

FIGURE 11.15 The checkboxes are linked to the Hidden sheet, where a list of TRUE or FALSE values will be stored to control the printing subroutine.

one of those boxes, it changes the value of cells on the Hidden sheet to either TRUE or FALSE. We can probably guess that we are going to loop through each of the sheet references on the Hidden sheet to see whether there is a TRUE or FALSE value and print only the sheets that have a TRUE value next to them. Since our code will look at the actual sheet names in the model as it loops through and use the sheet names listed on the Hidden sheet for referencing purposes, it is extremely important that the sheet names listed in ctrl_SheetSelector are identical to the names on the tab of each worksheet.

5. We are now ready to create the code for the printer functionality. Press **Alt-F11** to go to the VBE. Insert a new subroutine and call it **Export_Routines**. Start the subroutine with the following line of code:

```
Sub Printer()
```

6. As we have been doing in the past two Model Builders, the next step is to declare variables. Enter the following code:

```
Dim iSheetCt As Integer, TotalSheets As Integer
Dim SheetNameTemp As String
```

7. Our next step is to assign values to certain variables. In this case, we need only know the total number of sheets to possibly print. To accomplish this task, enter the following code:

```
TotalSheets = Range("ctrl_SheetCt")
```

8. We will initiate a loop for each sheet. Thinking about the process we want to loop through each sheet to possibly print. Start the loop by entering the following code:

```
For iSheetCt = 1 To TotalSheets
```

9. The block of code that is within the loop is the most important. Enter the following code:

```
If Range("strt_SheetNameTFs").Offset(iSheetCt, 0) = True Then
  SheetNameTemp = Range("strt_SheetNames").Offset(iSheetCt, 0)
  Worksheets(SheetNameTemp).PrintOut
    End If
```

This code uses an IF THEN statement, a VBA technique that we have not mentioned yet; however, this is relatively easy to understand given our understanding of the IF function in Excel. An IF THEN statement works very similarly, by testing a conditional test and returning one value if the condition is TRUE and possibly a separate value if it is FALSE (note that this would require also using an ELSE statement, but this is not necessary for this example).

In our subroutine we want to test whether each worksheet name on the Hidden sheet has a TRUE value next to it. If this is TRUE, then we store the name of the worksheet into the SheetNameTemp variable. We then take that name and use it within a Worksheet object. A Worksheet object is similar to a Range object in that it references an object within the Excel application. Rather than referencing just a cell, it is referencing an entire sheet. Once we have referenced the sheet we then use the PrintOut method, which sends the sheet to the default printer. If there is no TRUE next to a sheet name on the Hidden sheet, then nothing gets printed. Finally, this block of code is finished off with an End If statement, which is a required parameter for an IF THEN statement to signify the end of the statement.

10. We finish off the code with a Next statement to repeat the loop so every worksheet name on the Hidden sheet is tested and printed if the conditional test is met. An `End Sub` is also included at the end of the subroutine. The last part of the code should read:

```
Next iSheetCt
End Sub
```

11. The final code for the Printer subroutine should be:

```
Sub Printer()

Dim iSheetCt As Integer, TotalSheets As Integer
Dim SheetNameTemp As String

TotalSheets = Range("ctrl_SheetCt")

For iSheetCt = 1 To TotalSheets
  If Range("strt_SheetNameTFs").Offset(iSheetCt, 0) = True Then
  SheetNameTemp = Range("strt_SheetNames").Offset(iSheetCt, 0)
  Worksheets(SheetNameTemp).PrintOut
  End If
Next iSheetCt
End Sub
```

12. Automate the running of this macro by creating a button on the Assumptions sheet underneath the previous subroutine's button. Name this button **Print Selected Sheets**.

CONTINUING WITH VBA

Learning a new language is a constantly evolving process that takes years to perfect. Computer-based languages are included in this category. Much as new learners of foreign languages limit their usage to certain words and phrases at first, we have limited our VBA language to a core set of statements, objects, properties, and methods that are best suited for financial modeling. Although perhaps not the most efficient or robust techniques, they are easy to learn and powerful when implemented.

There are specific techniques that I would suggest financial modelers learn next. These include:

- More practice with multiple For Next loops
- Learning Do While and Do Until loops
- More practice with IF THEN ELSE statements
- Learning how to create and work with arrays
- Learning how to create and use functions both in VBA and for use in Excel

The list could go on and on, but the techniques above and those discussed in this chapter are very useful for financial modeling application. Be careful as your skill develops not to overuse VBA. The general idea is to use it when you absolutely need it. Otherwise, you risk overcomplicating models and making them difficult for yourself and others to troubleshoot.

CONCLUSION

We have dedicated quite a bit of time to constructing a powerful discounted cash flow model for corporate valuation. Do not stop here. The model captures only as much as we tell it to. This thought was reinforced when I was on a consulting engagement in Dubai. A senior member of a prominent investment bank was giving a speech to his junior staff. One thing he said has stayed with me on every analysis I undertake: "Be thoughtful about the deal."

I took this to mean we should think through each aspect of the deal in detail. This is paramount to corporate transactions since every industry in every region can have a unique set of circumstances requiring thought. Thinking through the deal structure and identifying transaction parties, risks, mitigating factors, market forces, economic situations and so on should be done day-in and day-out until the transaction closes. The financial model will provide an excellent medium for organizing these items and quantifying certain aspects, but by no measure is it an absolute solution.

Financial modeling is about creating a target for business decisions. Occasionally, we will hit a perfect bull's-eye with little effort, but we must focus our energy on nudging the deal process toward the bull's-eye. This requires the ability to think through the intricacies of a transaction and deal with the needs of parties involved to get a deal done. The combination of a thoughtful process with a powerful corporate valuation model will produce transactions where risk and reward are properly structured.

About the CD-ROM

This appendix provides you with information on the contents of the CD that accompanies this book. For the latest-and-greatest information, please refer to the ReadMe file located at the root of the CD.

SYSTEM REQUIREMENTS

- A computer with a processor running at 120 MHz or faster
- At least 32 MB of total RAM installed on your computer; for best performance, at least 64 MB
- A CD-ROM drive

NOTE: Many popular word processing programs are capable of reading Microsoft Word files. However, users should be aware that a slight amount of formatting might be lost when using a program other than Microsoft Word.

Using the CD with Windows

To install the items from the CD to your hard drive, follow these steps:

1. Insert the CD into your computer's CD-ROM drive.
2. The CD-ROM interface will appear. The interface provides a simple point-and-click way to explore the contents of the CD.

If the opening screen of the CD-ROM does not appear automatically, follow these steps to access the CD:

1. Click the **Start** button on the left end of the taskbar and then choose **Run** from the menu that pops up.
2. In the dialog box that appears, type *d:\\start.exe.* (If your CD-ROM drive is not drive D, fill in the appropriate letter in place of *d.*) This brings up the CD interface described in the preceding set of steps.

Using the CD with Macintosh

To install the items from the CD to your hard drive, follow these steps:

1. Insert the CD into your computer's CD-ROM drive.
2. The CD icon will appear on your desktop; double-click to open.
3. Double-click the **Start** button.
4. Read the license agreement and click the **Accept** button to use the CD.
5. The CD interface will appear. Here you can install the programs and run the demos.

NOTE: Please be aware that Excel 2008 for Mac does not support VBA. Files containing VBA will have reduced functionality when run using Excel 2008.

WHAT'S ON THE CD

The following sections provide a summary of the software and other materials you'll find on the CD.

Content

The included CD-ROM contains the following files that support the text:

- *Corporate_Basic_Model.xls:* This is a complete discounted cash flow model that the user will construct through the Model Builder exercises. It requires a version of Excel 2000 or later and the following add-ins (installation instructions are included in the text):
  - Analysis Tool-Pak
  - Analysis Tool-Pak VBA

  In addition, there are a number of modules containing VBA code stored in Corporate_Basic_Model.xls. This code should be referenced for Chapter 11.
- *GrowthRates.xls* and *GrowthRates_Complete.xls:* These two Excel files are for use in Chapter 3. They provide exercises relating to determining growth rates for analysis. GrowthRates.xls can be opened and directly worked in as it is incomplete and intended for the user to work through. GrowthRates_Complete.xls is the completed version of what the user should complete.
- *VBA_TestCode_Book.xls:* This Excel file is for Chapter 11. It provides a completed version of what Model Builder 11.1 and 11.2 should look like. If any of the text in those sections of Chapter 11 is unclear, readers should refer to this file for the complete versions.

Finally, there is a workbook that corresponds to the Toolbox at the end of Chapter 3:

- *Tool Box Ch.3.xls:* Due to the number of complicated Excel functions in Chapter 3's Toolbox, this Excel file provides examples. Scroll through the tabs for examples dedicated to each function.

Applications

The application *Excel Viewer* is used on the CD. Excel Viewer is a freeware viewer that allows you to view, but not edit, most Microsoft Excel spreadsheets. Certain features of Microsoft Excel documents may not work as expected from within Excel Viewer.

Shareware programs are fully functional, trial versions of copyrighted programs. If you like particular programs, register with their authors for a nominal fee and receive licenses, enhanced versions, and technical support.

Freeware programs are copyrighted games, applications, and utilities that are free for personal use. Unlike shareware, these programs do not require a fee or provide technical support.

GNU software is governed by its own license, which is included inside the folder of the GNU product. See the GNU license for more details.

Trial, demo, or evaluation versions are usually limited either by time or by functionality (such as being unable to save projects). Some trial versions are very sensitive to system date changes. If you alter your computer's date, the programs will time out and no longer be functional.

CUSTOMER CARE

If you have trouble with the CD-ROM, please call the Wiley Product Technical Support phone number at (800) 762–2974. Outside the United States, call 1(317) 572–3994. You can also contact Wiley Product Technical Support at http://support.wiley.com. John Wiley & Sons will provide technical support only for installation and other general quality-control items. For technical support on the applications themselves, consult the program's vendor or author.

To place additional orders or to request information about other Wiley products, please call (877) 762–2974.

About the Author

Keith **Allman** is the Manager of Analytics and Modeling at Pearl Street Capital Group, where he focuses on private equity fund of funds and venture debt funds. He has been involved in quantitative analytics for nearly 10 years. His first position was with MBIA in their quantitative analytics group, where he modeled corporate securitizations and infrastructure projects. After four years in that role, he moved to Citigroup to model structured products for their conduits and eventually emerging market transactions for their Principal Finance group.

During his tenure in the Principal Finance group, Allman was responsible for valuing large-scale infrastructure projects and whole businesses in order to determine the optimal investment structure. Besides being able to apply standard corporate finance modeling, his background in structured finance allowed him to create unique analyses for companies and projects that exhibited qualities from both sectors. In addition, this framework was developed for specialized work with development banks.

After nearly three years at Citigroup, and upon the publication of his book, *Modeling Structured Finance Cash Flows in Excel: A Step-by-Step Guide* (February 2007, John Wiley & Sons), he formed his own consulting and training firm, named Enstruct. Enstruct has serviced clients worldwide in capital markets and equity valuation, distressed valuation, and quantitative-based training. Enstruct continues to operate worldwide and has a strong client base in emerging markets. Concurrently with consulting and training, Allman produced a second text, *Reverse Engineering Deals on Wall Street: A Step-by-Step Guide* (December 2008, John Wiley & Sons).

Aside from for-profit work, Allman volunteers with Relief International, providing pro bono credit-risk training to microfinance initiatives in the Middle East and assisting in structuring microfinance fund transactions.

Allman received bachelor degrees from UCLA and a master's degree from Columbia University.

For more information regarding the CD-ROM, see the
About the CD-ROM section on page 263.

CUSTOMER NOTE: IF THIS BOOK IS ACCOMPANIED BY SOFTWARE, PLEASE READ THE FOLLOWING BEFORE OPENING THE PACKAGE.

This software contains files to help you utilize the models described in the accompanying book. By opening the package, you are agreeing to be bound by the following agreement:

This software product is protected by copyright and all rights are reserved by the author, John Wiley & Sons, Inc., or their licensors. You are licensed to use this software on a single computer. Copying the software to another medium or format for use on a single computer does not violate the U.S. Copyright Law. Copying the software for any other purpose is a violation of the U.S. Copyright Law.

This software product is sold as is without warranty of any kind, either express or implied, including but not limited to the implied warranty of merchantability and fitness for a particular purpose. Neither Wiley nor its dealers or distributors assumes any liability for any alleged or actual damages arising from the use of or the inability to use this software. (Some states do not allow the exclusion of implied warranties, so the exclusion may not apply to you.)

WILEY

John Wiley & Sons, Inc.